The AA Best Drives Italy

www.theAA.com/bookshop

Written by Paul Duncan

Published by AA Publishing, a trading name of Automobile Association Developments Limited, whose registered office is Southwood East, Apollo Rise, Farnborough, Hampshire, GU14 0JW. Registered number 1878835.

ISBN-10: 0 7495 4369 8
ISBN-13: 978 0 7495 4369 3

The contents of this publication are believed correct at the time of printing. Nevertheless, AA Publishing accept no responsibility for errors, omissions or changes in the details given, or for the consequences of readers' reliance on this information. This does not affect your statutory rights. Assessments of the attractions, hotels and restaurants are based upon the author's own experience, and contain subjective opinions that may not reflect the publisher's opinion or a reader's experience. We have tried to ensure accuracy, but things do change, so please let us know if you have any comments or corrections.

A CIP catalogue record for this book is available from the British Library.

Colour separation: Daylight Colour Art, Singapore
Printed and bound by G. Canale & C. S.P.A., Torino, Italy

Find out more about AA Publishing and the wide range of travel publications and services the AA provides by visiting our website at www.theAA.com

First published January 1991
Revised second edition 1995, published in this format 1997
Reprinted December 1997
Reprinted and updated 2000
Revised third edition 2003
Reprinted December 2003
Revised fourth edition 2005

Cover credits: AA WORLD TRAVEL LIBRARY/K Paterson f/cover, b/cover (centre bottom); AA WORLD TRAVEL LIBRARY/T Souter b/cover (top); AA WORLD TRAVEL LIBRARY/A Kouprianoff b/cover (centre bottom); AA WORLD TRAVEL LIBRARY/M Jourdan b/cover (bottom)

Opposite: *Vatican guard, Rome*

A02026

CONTENTS

ABOUT THIS BOOK

This book is not only a practical touring guide for the independent traveller, but is also invaluable for those who would like to know more about Italy.

It is divided into 5 regions, each containing between 3 and 6 tours that start and finish in major towns and cities which we consider to be the best centres for exploration.

Each tour has details of the most interesting places to visit en route. Panels catering for special interests follow some of the main entries – for those whose interest is in history, wildlife or walking, and those who have children. There are also panels which highlight scenic stretches of road and which give details of local events, crafts and customs.

The simple route directions are accompanied by an easy-to-use map at the beginning of each tour, along with a chart showing how far it is from one town to the next in kilometres and miles. This can help you to decide where to take a break and stop overnight, for example. (All distances quoted are approximate.)

Before setting off it is advisable to check with the information centre at the start of the tour for recommendations on where to break your journey and for additional information on what to see and do, and when best to visit.

Tour Information
See pages 164–73 for addresses, telephone numbers and opening times of the attractions mentioned in the tours, including the telephone numbers of tourist offices.

Accommodation and Restaurants
See pages 159–63 for a list of recommended hotels for each tour. Also listed are restaurants where you may like to stop for a meal. There are, of course, other possibilities to be found along the way.

Motoring
For information on motoring in Italy see pages 158–9.

Banks
Usual banking hours are 8 or 8.30am to 1.30pm and 2.30 or 3pm to 4pm Mon–Fri. Check locally as times can vary in the afternoons. All banks are closed at weekends and on national holidays. On weekdays, evenings and holidays, money can be changed at main railway stations and airports.

View over Firenze (Florence), showing the Duomo and the Campanile di Giotto

Credit Cards
All principal credit cards are accepted by most establishments, but not petrol stations. Check before buying.

Currency
The unit of currency is the Euro (€). Bank notes come in denominations of 5, 10, 20, 50, 200 and 500 Euros; coins come in denominations of 1, 2, 5, 10, 20 and 50 centimes, and 1 and 2 Euros.

Customs Regulations
Items for personal or professional use may be brought into Italy free of charge, but take receipts for valuable articles to avoid paying duty on them. Travellers' allowances for Italy are the same as other EU countries. Check current guidelines.

Electricity
The current is 220 volts AC, 50 cycles, with two round-pin plugs. British, Australian or New Zealand appliances normally requiring a slightly higher voltage will work. For visitors from North America with appliances requiring 100/120 volts, and not fitted for dual voltage, a voltage transformer is required.

Emergency Telephone Numbers
Police and general emergencies tel: 113
Fire tel: 115.
Medical tel: 118

Entry Regulations
The only document necessary for UK, Irish, Commonwealth and US citizens is a valid passport for any stay of up to three months. Visitors from EU countries need only a visitor's card. Visa regulations can change – check before you travel.

Health
Health insurance is recommended, but visitors from EU countries are entitled to health services as available to Italians. This means obtaining, prior to departure, Form E111 or equivalent from a post office.

The high cost of treatment makes insurance essential if you are a non-EU citizen. For medical treatment and medicines, keep all bills and claim the money back later.

Vaccinations are unnecessary unless you are travelling from a known infected area. However, it is advisable to drink bottled water and to wash all fruit and vegetables.

Maps
The spellings of place-names on the maps include accents to help with pronunciation. These do not occur in the text.

Post Offices
Post offices are generally open 8am–1.30/2pm Mon–Fri and to 11.45pm on Sat. On the last day of the month offices close at noon. Times do vary, however, from place to place.

Public Holidays
1 January – New Year's Day
6 January – Epiphany
Easter Monday
25 April – Liberation Day
1 May – Labour Day
2 June – Proclamation of Republic (celebrated on following Saturday)
15 August – Ferragosto (Assumption)
1 November – All Saints
8 December – Immaculate Conception
25–26 December – Christmas.
In addition, some towns and cities have special saints' days and other holidays when businesses may close.

Route Directions
The following abbreviations are used in the book for Italian roads:
A – Autostrada (motorway)
SS – Strada Statale (state road)
dir, ter, bis, q, qu – suffixes to state roads (SS) relating to links and extensions of major roads.

Shops
Shops are generally open Monday to Saturday 8.30–1.30 and 3.30–7.30. Many close on Monday mornings, and food shops often close Thursday afternoons.

Telephones
Telecom Italia (TI) payphones are usually on streets and in bars, tobacco shops and restaurants. Most take coins or a phone card (*scheda telefonica*). It is much easier to use these prepaid telephone cards which you buy at the same outlets. Tear the corner off the card first. The dialling tone is short and long tones.

Hotels usually add a surcharge to calls from rooms.

To call abroad, dial 00, then the country code, followed by the city code then the number. The prefix for the UK is 0044; for Eire 00353; for the US and Canada 001; and for Australia 0061. If you wish to make a reverse charge or person-to-person call you will need to go through the operator – dial 15 for European countries or 170 for elsewhere. Alternatively, use the 'countrydirect' service: dial 172 1001 for Canada; for the United States dial either 172 1011, 172 1022 or 172 1877.

Time
Local standard time is one hour ahead of Greenwich Mean Time (GMT), except from late Sep–late Oct when it's the same. Italian Summer Time (clocks go forward an hour) operates from the last weekend of March to the last weekend of September.

Tourist Offices
The Italian State Tourist Office (ENIT) is represented in the following:
Australia – Level 26, 44 Market Street, Sydney NSW 2000 (tel: 92 621666, enitour@ihug.au).
Canada – 175 Bloor Street East, Suite 907, South Tower, Toronto, Ontario M4W 3R8 (tel: 416/925-4882, enit.canada@on-aibn.com)
UK – 1 Princes Street, London W1R 9AY (tel: 0207 408 1254)
US – 630 Fifth Avenue, Suite 1565, New York 10111 (tel: 212/ 245-4822, enitny@italiantourism.com).

PIEDMONT, LOMBARDY, EMILIA-ROMAGNA, VENETO

Italy is separated from the rest of the continent by the massive bulk of the Alps. The great range's southernmost peaks and valleys encroach upon Piedmont and Lombardy and on a clear day, from Torino (Turin), Piedmont's capital, and the centre of an arena of mountains, it is possible to look back and admire Mont Blanc. From Torino to Milano (Milan) the landscape descends gently towards the Po, the river that divides Piedmont practically in half. It continues into Lombardy which, with its five magnificent lakes, its rivers and its canals, is endlessly watery and enviably fertile. The Po forms the region's southern border with Emilia-Romagna before it flows out to the Adriatic at the bottom of the Veneto.

Piedmont and Lombardy combined are the cradle of Italy's industry and the source of much of its wealth. It is not by accident that here are the huge Fiat works (Piedmont), some of Europe's best design studios and manufacturers (in Lombardy, especially Milano), the vineyards that produce some of Italy's most excellent wine (eg Barolo from Piedmont) and the vermouth industry (Torino).

The great plain of the River Po, which continues southwards into Emilia-Romagna, was once northern Italy's greatest attraction. Every inch of the plain of Emilia-Romagna, right up to the Apennines in the south, is still under cultivation. So prolific is the area's produce that Bologna, Emilia-Romagna's capital, is known as 'La Grassa', 'The Fat'.

The Veneto is as lush as any of the other regions mentioned. From the flat plain of the Po to the Dolomites of the eastern Alps and the marshy lagoons around Venice, the Veneto is also just as varied. But its reputation has more to do with art and architecture, particularly of the Renaissance. Its hills and southern plain are filled with towns and villages whose past affinities with Venice are acknowledged usually by an ancient stone-carved lion of St Mark – the Venetian symbol – placed conspicuously in the centre of the town.

Milan's French Gothic-style Duomo

The Duke of Savoy presides over Torino's Piazza San Carlo

Torino
Torino is one of the most intellectually active cities in Italy. This, mixed with a dose of Piedmontese sobriety, has provided Italy with marvellous museums, libraries, theatres, exhibitions and a university. Torino's Egyptian Museum is the second most important in the world (after Cairo's), while its Armería Real (Royal Armoury), the Museo dell'Automobile (Motor Museum) and Museo del Cinema are stacked with varied treasures. A baroque-style centre contributes to an almost courtly atmosphere in this elegant and dignified city.

Milano
Milano, capital of Lombardy, is also the economic capital of Italy, and is unquestionably northwest Italy's major art centre. In the Castello Sforzesco (Sforza Castle), the Pinacoteca di Brera (Brera Gallery), the Museo Poldi-Pezzoli and the Pinacoteca Ambrosiana (Ambrosia Gallery), you will find endless works by the 'greats' of Renaissance painting. The Duomo (cathedral) of Milano is the most striking example of northern Italian Gothic architecture that you will see anywhere.

Bologna
Bologna has a well-deserved reputation as Italy's culinary capital: if you like dishes with cream, butter and cheese, or succulent red meat, this is where you will find them at their best. There is a feast of architecture too, as Bologna's medieval and Renaissance centre is still intact. Its old streets are lined with arcades which come into their own when it rains. Museums, galleries, an ancient university, night-clubs and shops are Bologna's other attractions.

Rimini
Rimini has one really important monument, the 15th-century Tempio Malatestiano (Malatesta Temple), with a famous Renaissance façade designed by Leon Battista Alberti for Sigismundo Malatesta. Otherwise, the town is famous for its entertainments of the not so intellectual sort. Sunbathing, night-clubbing and lazy days contribute to Rimini's reputation as one of the Adriatic's most seductive resorts.

Asolo
Not only does the small hilltown of Asolo preserve the memory of famous inhabitants such as Robert Browning and Eleanora Duse, but its ancient centre is full of well-maintained medieval and Renaissance buildings and villas. It has a good monthly antiques market.

Verona
Verona's many treasures include the 14th-century tombs of the Scaligeri, noble medieval palaces, Roman ruins such as the famous Arena (the best preserved amphitheatre in Italy after the Colosseum) and a clutch of medieval and Renaissance churches.

TOUR
1

The Foot of the Mountains

Piedmont is the most western region of Italy. Here you will find some of the country's best known ski resorts. To the east is the great plain of the Po River, beyond which are the hilly and fertile Langhe and Monferrato districts. More or less in the middle is Torino (Turin), the region's capital, with its baroque architecture, a well preserved city centre, Roman remains and an active street life.

3 DAYS • 411KM • 255 MILES

ITINERARY	
TORINO	▶ **Moncalvo (82km-51m)**
MONCALVO	▶ **Asti (22km-14m)**
ASTI	▶ **Alessandria (36km-22m)**
ALESSANDRIA	▶ **Acqui Terme (34km-21m)**
ACQUI TERME	▶ **Alba (60km-37m)**
ALBA	▶ **Serralunga d'Alba (20km-12m)**
SERRALUNGA D'ALBA	▶ **Barolo (12km-7m)**
BAROLO	▶ **La Morra (6km-4m)**
LA MORRA	▶ **Cherasco (6km-4m)**
CHERASCO	▶ **Cuneo (48km-30m)**
CUNEO	▶ **Torino (85km-53m)**

i Piazza Solferino, Torino

▶ *From Torino, take the **A21** towards Asti, about 60km (37 miles). Leave the autostrada at the Asti Est exit taking the **SS10** towards Asti, then the **SS457** going north to Moncalvo, 22km (14 miles).*

1 Moncalvo, Piedmont

Moncalvo is where you will get a real taste of the Piedmontese countryside. Terraced vineyards and tidy, ordered rows of poplar trees climb the slopes on the edge of town. Situated in the middle of the immensely fertile Monferrato district, it is a gastronome's delight – a good place to try the local truffle crop at the annual auction. Towering over the surrounding countryside is the pretty Gothic Church of San Francesco and the remains of an old moated castle. The old centre of town has some 14th-century houses and a gallery of modern art.

▶ *From Moncalvo, retrace the route to Asti.*

2 Asti, Piedmont

Asti is full of places to see and is awash with festivals. Once the city rivalled Milan, and it is well worth spending some time in its old centre. The Gothic Duomo (cathedral) contains fonts made from Romanesque capitals supported on inverted Roman capitals, and 18th-century inlaid choir stalls. Other churches include San Pietro in Consavia with its 10th-century circular baptistery and little adjacent archaeological museum entered by the cloisters. In Piazza San Secondo is the large Gothic Church of San Secondo in which you can see an altarpiece by Ferrari who was much influenced by Leonardo. The Torre San Secondo, a Romanesque tower on a Roman base, is the bell tower for the Church of San Caterina. In fact there are quite a few towers scattered around Asti – the medieval Torre Troiana, and the octagonal Torre dei De Regibus are just two. The town is the scene of a great wine fair at the end of September.

Wild mushrooms, one of Piedmont's gastronomic delights

i Piazza Alfieri 34

SPECIAL TO...

In Asti, the Palio is held in the Campo del Palio in September. This event dates back to the Middle Ages and consists of a colourful horse race, ridden bareback.
The 'offering of the Palio' takes place in May. The events include flag-tossing and the participants wear medieval costume.

▶ *From Asti, return to and take the **A21** going east to Alessandria, about 36km (22 miles).*

3 Alessandria, Piedmont

Alessandria is the centre for the manufacture of the *borsalino*, the ubiquitous felt hat – in fact the city has the world's best hat museum, Museo del Capello

The Foot of the Mountains

The bold red wine Barolo takes its name from this hilltop town

Borsalino (closed for renovation). Not much of old Alessandria has survived except in the 18th-century Duomo (cathedral) and the older Church of Santa Maria di Castello. Among the city's palaces is the Palazzo della Prefettura, designed by Benedetto Alfieri. The 18th-century Cittadella (citadel) is particularly well preserved. The countryside all around Alessandria is as fertile as anywhere in Piedmont, supporting rice fields, wheat, fruit and acres of poplar woods which are used in the making of furniture.

i *Via Savona 26*

▶ *From Alessandria, take the* ***SS30*** *for about 34km (21 miles) to Acqui Terme.*

4 Acqui Terme, Piedmont
Acqui Terme is noted for its hot sulphuric springs, in particular one which bubbles up out of the ground in a fountain at the centre of town. The hottest spring, La Bollente, is housed in a special pavilion, the Nuove Terme. The Romans were aware of its properties but all that remains from their time here are four arches of an aqueduct. The Romanesque Duomo (cathedral) has a very fine 17th-century loggia (gallery), and a good entrance portal. Next to the cathedral are the remains of the Castello dei Paleologi (Castle of the Paleologi) in which there is now an Archaeological Museum containing the finds from the old baths of Acqui – including mosaics.

▶ *From Acqui Terme, go via Bistagno, Bubbio and Castino (west) across country to Alba, about 60km (37 miles).*

5 Alba, Piedmont
Alba is the capital of the Langhe district, an area famous for its vineyards and its white truffles (*tartufi bianchi*). Set beside the Tanaro River, Alba has buildings of terracotta-coloured brick. The Duomo of San Lorenzo was rebuilt by

FOR HISTORY BUFFS

The Langhe countryside around Alba is dotted with little towns, each one dominated by a castle. They do not necessarily have any particular sites of interest, but the towns themselves are picturesque and are worth visiting if you have enough time. Among the best with interesting and dramatic-looking castles is Grinzane Cavour, whose castle was once occupied by the Marquise of Cavour – of the same family as the prominent 19th-century statesman Camillo Cavour. It lies about 6km (4 miles) west of Alba on the way to Barolo.
Another – Roddi's castle – passed through a variety of noble ownerships, ending in 1836 with King Carlo Alberto. Today it is the property of the Catholic Church.

Bishop Novelli in 1486 and inside is Barnardino Fossati's chancel with its 35 carved and inlaid wooden stalls. Other churches include Santa Maria Maddalena and the baroque Church of San Giovanni. Inside the latter you can see the *Madonna delle Grazie* by Barnarba da Modena, 1377. The Council Chamber of the Town Hall, the Palazzo Comunale, houses the *Virgin Crowned* by Alba's greatest painter, Macrino (dated 1501). Much of Alba is still medieval – there are narrow arcaded streets and old doorways. In the old centre is a Saturday market which has been held on the same spot since 1171.

► *From Alba, follow the signs pointing to Diano d'Alba, about 8km (5 miles). From there proceed via Gallo d'Alba to Serralunga d'Alba.*

SPECIAL TO...

Alba has another Palio, this time a donkey race. Held in October, it is supposed to parody the Asti Palio, and to keep alive the memory of a horse race staged by the soldiers of Asti around the walls of Alba in 1275, when they were laying siege to the town.

6 Serralunga d'Alba,
Piedmont

This picturesque place is dominated by a stately castle built between 1340 and 1357 to support the castle at nearby Barolo (see over). These two buildings, as well as other local castles built for the same family, were aligned so as to allow a system of communication using torchlight at night and coloured drapes during the day. The entire town retains its medieval character. Little houses cluster in circles around the castle and nearly every one has an amazing

FOR CHILDREN

Just to the north of Turin is Parco Regionale La Mandria (La Mandria Regional Park). Part of it is a sanctuary for animals – deer in particular, but there are horses and unusual cattle as well. Also near Turin, just to the west, children might enjoy a visit to the Parco Naturale dei Laghi di Avigliana (Avigliana Lakes Nature Park). Here the specialities are ducks, moorhens, kingfishers and other waterfowl.

A wide selection of fine olive oil and wine for sale

view of the surrounding countryside. San Sebastiano, the parish church, was reconstructed in about 1630, but is far older and still preserves its 14th-century bell tower.

▶ *From Serralunga d'Alba, return in the direction of Gallo d'Alba, turning left before the village to Barolo, about 6km (4 miles) further on.*

7 Barolo, Piedmont
Tiny Barolo is perched on a hill overlooking countryside filled with vineyards. Dominated by a vast castle, the Castello Falletti, it gives its name to one of the most renowned Italian red wines. The castle itself is no longer a private home, but still has its original furniture, and housed in it is a museum, a vintage cellar and an *enoteca*, a place for tasting the local wine. The castle is open to the public and has interesting furnished rooms with perhaps the best views in Barolo.

The town is a picturesque place, predominantly terracotta-coloured. You could walk around it in about half an hour. The local parish church is Romanesque and was most probably once the castle chapel – it is filled with the memorials to the Faletti family who once owned the castle.

RECOMMENDED WALKS

There are special walks from La Morra following designated wine routes which take you through vineyards to wine-tasting points. Each path is identified by a different colour according to its destination. The routes also go past inns and local wine cellars where you can sluice your parched throat with the local brew.

▶ *From Barolo, travel north to La Morra, about 6km (4 miles).*

8 La Morra, Piedmont
La Morra has two churches, the bigger one dedicated to San Martino, the town's patron saint, and the smaller to San Rocco. However, the principal reason for coming to La Morra is not to look at old monuments, but to indulge in wine-tasting. There are plenty of places in which to do this. Apart from the Enoteca Civica, with its exhibition and sales of Barolo wine produced by local vineyards, there are smaller, private cellars all over this small hilltown. Even the most obscure wines can be

Picturesque La Morra is a popular stop-over for wine lovers. It boasts a wine museum and walks following designated wine routes

SCENIC ROUTES

The most scenic parts of this tour are the views from La Morra, which is known as the 'Belvedere of the Langhe' – you can see for miles from the highest point in town, the edge of the open-ended main square in the centre. On a good day you can even see the snow-capped Alps in the distance. The countryside all around Barolo, and especially the approach to the town from Alba, is scenic. Take a picnic. The roads are small and under-used and there are clumps of woodlands and views to distant hilltowns.

found here and the range of prices is huge. Near by is the Museo Ratti (Ratti Wine Museum), housed in the former Abbey of the Annunciation.

▶ *From La Morra, cross the River Tanaro, to Cherasco, about 6km (4 miles) away.*

9 Cherasco, Piedmont
Cherasco is famous as the centre of the National Association of Snail Breeders. Not that you will meet any snails within the precincts but the town is the centre of gastronomic events relating to edible snails. The Torre Civico, a 36m (118-foot) high tower, is the most important monument here. It sports a rare clock (1552) showing the phases of the moon.

Among Cherasco's churches, Sant'Agostino, with its baroque altar, and San Pietro, the oldest church in the town, are the most interesting. In the Palazzo Fracassi you can see treasures dating from when the Holy Shroud was housed in the town in the early 18th century. In fact, in 1706, the Shroud itself was kept in the Palazzo Salmatoris. The 14th-century Castello (Castle of the Visconti) still survives and is in excellent condition.

SPECIAL TO...

Cherasco holds the National Gathering of Snail Breeders on the second weekend in June, with associated gastronomic events.

▶ *It is a short distance to the **SS231** which leads directly to Cuneo, about 48km (30 miles).*

10 Cuneo, Piedmont
Cuneo is an important market town. The huge market, which swamps the town's centre every Tuesday, filling every corner of the porticoed Piazza Galimberti, is best known for its chestnuts and raw silk. There are porticoed streets all over town, Via Mondovi being the most characteristic. In the centre, too, is the 13th-century Church of San Francesco, which also houses the municipal museum. The 19th-century home of resistance hero, Duccio Galimberti, contains a fine art collection, library and memorabilia (closed for restoration.

Many of the Piedmontese towns have festivals, relating to the consumption of food and drink, and Cuneo has the Piedmontese Cheese Exposition held in November.

i *Corso Nizza 17*

BACK TO NATURE

Cuneo is practically on the edge of the Parco delle Alpi Marittime (Maritime Alps Nature Park, a protected mountainous area which is home to various wild alpine animals and birds. Ibex and chamois are among the rare species sometimes seen. Alpine marmots are widespread in the alpine meadows and bird life includes citril finches, alpine accentors, griffon vultures and ptarmigan.

▶ *From Cuneo, take the **SS20** back to Torino, about 85km (53 miles).*

TOUR

2

Of Alps, Lakes & Plain

Lombardy is crossed by the huge River Po and studded with great lakes – Maggiore, Garda, Como, Iseo and Lugano. Since the Middle Ages it has been a prosperous commercial region. Milano (Milan) nowadays is the thriving economic capital of Italy but the traces of its cultural past are everywhere.

4 DAYS • 728KM • 452 MILES

ITINERARY	
MILANO	► **Sacro Monte Varese (65km-40m)**
SACRO MONTE VARESE	► **Lago Maggiore (32km-20m)**
LAGO MAGGIORE	► **Como (76km-47m)**
COMO	► **Lecco – around Lake Como (109km-68m)**
LECCO	► **Bellagio (22km-14m)**
BELLAGIO	► **Bergamo (61km-38m)**
BERGAMO	► **Lago di Garda (78km-48m)**
LAGO DI GARDA	► **Mantova (48km-30m)**
MANTOVA	► **Cremona (66km-41m)**
CREMONA	► **Pavia (136km-84m)**
PAVIA	► **Milano (35km-22m)**

i *Via Marconi 1, Milano*

▶ *From Milano, take the* ***A8*** *going north (via Legnano and Gallarate) – the latter about 38km (24 miles) – to Varese, about another 17km (10 miles). About 10km (6 miles) north of Varese lies Sacro Monte Varese.*

1 Sacro Monte Varese,
Lombardia

The 'Sacred Mountain of Varese', with its narrow passages and ancient covered alleys, is only the backdrop for a pilgrimage route more famous nowadays for its art than for its saintly connections. It is supposed to have been founded by St Ambrose in thanks for Lombardy's deliverance from the Arian heresy (the doctrine put forward by the 4th-century theologian Arius, that Christ is not one body with God).

From the bottom of the Sacro Monte to the top, about 800m (2,625 feet), is a cobbled route with 14 chapels at intervals along the Sacred Way, each one dedicated to the Mystery of the Rosary. The shrines are the work of Bernascone and each is filled with life-size terracotta figures, by Bussola, acting out some religious episode. At the top is the lavishly decorated Church of Santa Maria del Monte. The views from the Sacro Monte are wonderful and, to restore you after the climb, you will find cafés and restaurants in the town.

▶ *From Sacro Monte Varese, go back to Varese, then continue on the* ***SS342*** *to Lago Maggiore, about 22km (14 miles).*

2 Lago Maggiore,
Lombardia

Only the eastern shore of Lago Maggiore (Lake Maggiore) is in Lombardia. Its western shore is in Piedmont and its northern part in Switzerland. It would take days to drive around the lake seeing all that there is to look at. These are the highlights.

At Angera is the Borromeo fortress (open to the public), which contains well-preserved 14th-century frescoes, a doll museum and a museum of children's clothing from the 18th century to the 1950s.

Lago (Lake) Maggiore, with its 'Beautiful Isle', Isola Bella

At Arona is another castle, this time ruined. Visit the Church of Santa Maria with, in the Borromeo Chapel, an altarpiece of 1511 by Ferrari.

Stresa is the largest resort on the lake. Full of Victorian-style hotels, it is also dotted with old-fashioned villas and luxurious gardens running down to the water's edge. Some gardens are open, including the Villa Pallavicino.

But the real gem of Maggiore is the Borromean islands. Isola Bella, perhaps the best known, is a huge private garden surrounding a palace (Palazzo Borromeo) – both open to the public. The gardens were laid out for Count Carlo III Borromeo in the 17th century by Angelo Crivelli. The elaborate complex includes white peacocks, grottoes, fountains and statuary. Isola Madre is another of the islands, famous for its large botanical garden which, with its palace, is well worth a visit. You can get a boat to either of these islands from Stresa.

RECOMMENDED TRIPS

Walking is not the best way to explore this area – take a boat trip instead. That way you will get a much better feel of what the lakes on this tour are about. Steamers run to all corners of Lago Maggiore and Como – there are well organised schedules run much like a bus service. Take a short trip to a destination down either lake, have lunch, then return in the afternoon.

▶ *Make for Varese from Stresa, take the* ***SS33*** *to Sesto Calende at the foot of the lake, about 25km (16 miles), then follow the signs to Varese, about 23km (14 miles). From Varese, take the* ***SS342*** *to Como.*

3 Como, Lombardia

Como was the birthplace of the Roman writer Pliny the Elder. In fact you will see signs dotted around Lago di Como (Lake Como) pointing to the sites of the various villas the Pliny family owned here. One of the most elegant towns on the lake, Como is a centre for the production of fine fabrics, and it has an interesting silk museum. There is a waterfront promenade, busy cafés, palm trees and parks. The Duomo (cathedral) dates mainly from the 15th century. The rose window on the façade is Gothic in style and there is excellent carving by the Rodari brothers of Maroggia, from about 1500.

Other relics of old Como include the churches of San Abbondio, San Fedele, which was once the cathedral, and the Porta Vittoria, the late 12th-century city gate. The Museum of Archaeology contains an enormous collection of pre-Roman and Roman finds. The History Museum shares the same building.

Como also has a good art gallery, with classical, abstractionist and futurist works. See also the Temple of Alessandro Volta, which has equipment used by the man who gave his name to the electric volt.

BACK TO NATURE

There is plenty of bird life to observe on and near Lakes Maggiore and Como. Black kites scavenge along the shoreline and herons and egrets are found in undisturbed spots. Ducks and grebes can be seen on the open water and swallows and alpine swifts hawk for insects over the water's surface.

i *Piazza Cavour 17*

▶ *From Como, drive around the lake, starting on the* ***SS340*** *up its left-hand side.*

4 Lago di Como, Lombardia

All around the lake you will see vast villas and castles overlooking the water. Cernóbbio is a pretty town about 7km (4½ miles) from Como. Here is the grand Hotel Villa D'Este, once the home of the English Queen Caroline.

At Tremezzo is the Villa Carlotta, once lived in by Princess Carlotta of Prussia, who laid out its gardens in the 1850s. You can visit this as well as the Villa Arconati, just a few kilometres outside Tremezzo, at Lenno. Further on around the lake are Menaggio and Gravedona.

At nearby Dongo, Mussolini was captured by the partisans in 1945. On the other side of the lake, at Varenna, visit the Villa Monastero with its formal gardens and the Romanesque Church of San Giorgio. One really good way to see the lake – and admire the towns from a distance – is to take a boat trip around it. It is possible to take one that stops at a number of places, using it like a bus. Begin at Como.

▶ *Lecco lies at the foot of the eastern arm of Lake Como, from Como itself a direct distance of 29km (18 miles).*

5 Lecco, Lombardia
Lecco is in direct contrast to its illustrious neighbour Como. More industrial than prettier Como, Lecco's claim to fame is that it was the birthplace of Alessandro Manzoni, the great 19th-century Italian novelist. The Villa Manzoni, his former home, is now a museum – you will find it in Via Promessi Sposi, named after the writer's most famous novel which, translated, means 'The Betrothed' (the street is also known as Via Amendola). While you are in town, visit the Duomo, with its 14th-century frescos in the style of Giotto, and the Ponte Azzone Visconti, a medieval bridge over the Adda river. Although much altered (it no longer has any towers) and enlarged, it still has much of its early character.

i Via Nazario Sauro 6

▶ *From Lecco, take the* ***SS583*** *up the western edge of Lecco's portion of Lake Como to Bellagio.*

6 Bellagio, Lombardia
Bellagio is one of the most beautiful points on Lake Como. Not only is it an interesting old town, but it is splendidly sited on a promontory overlooking the three arms of the lake. There is plenty to do here apart from just sitting in the sun enjoying the view. The 12th-century Basilica of San Giacomo has good carving in the apse. There is Villa Serbelloni, whose gardens can be visited, and Villa Melzi d'Eril, the gardens of which are open to the public. If time is short, the Villa Sebelloni gardens, supposed to stand on the site of the younger Pliny's villa 'Tragedia', are the more interesting.

▶ *Return to Lecco, then take the* ***SS36*** *going south for about 15km (9 miles) until it cuts the* ***SS342****. Take the latter to Bergamo, about 24km (15 miles).*

Bellagio – sometimes called the prettiest town in Europe

FOR HISTORY BUFFS

Near Bergamo, just off the SS573 south of the city, is Malpaga, in whose castle you can see frescos of Bartolomeo Colleoni hosting a banquet in honour of a visit by the King of Denmark in 1474. This is fascinating if you have already seen Colleoni's grandiose tomb in Bergamo.

7 Bergamo, Lombardia
Bergamo is divided into the Città Alta and the Città Bassa, the Upper City and the Lower City. The former is the more interesting, as well as being the older. Its best monuments are in the Piazza Vecchia. In it is the Biblioteca Civica (Civic Library), a late 16th-century building modelled on Venice's great library building, designed by Sansovino. Across the square, past Contarini's fountain surrounded by stone lions, is the 12th-century Torre Civica with its 15th-century clock that still tolls the curfew hour (10pm). Behind the 12th-century Palazzo della Ragione are the Duomo and the ornate Colleoni Chapel. You can just see the base of the latter through the pointed arched loggia beneath the Palazzo della Ragione. Built in 1476, the façade of the Colleoni Chapel is a mass of sculptured decoration and coloured marble. Inside is the tomb and a statue of Bartolomeo Colleoni, who controlled Venice's armed forces in the 15th century. The ceiling fresco is by Tiepolo.

The Church of Santa Maria Maggiore, in Piazza Duomo, is a

fine Romanesque building. Also in the Upper City is the Cittadella (citadel), which contains the Natural History Museum, and the Museo Donizetti – this great composer was born in Bergamo, and you can visit the Teatro Donizetti in the Lower City. Between the Upper and Lower Cities is the Galleria dell'Accademia Carrara, a first-class collection of art, well worth taking in.

i *Piazzale Marconi 106*

▶ *From Bergamo, take the* **A4** *via Brescia to Lago di Garda, about 78km (48 miles) – at Desenzano del Garda at the foot of the lake.*

8 Lago di Garda, Lombardia
The most interesting ports of call around Lago (Lake) di Garda are Salò, Gardone Riviera, Riva del Garda, Malcesine and Sirmione. All are accessible by the steamer, and rather than drive around the

Bergamo's splendid Piazza Vecchia is the town's historic centre

Castello Scaligero, Sirmione, built by the Della Scala family

lake, you could leave the car at Desenzano del Garda and go by boat. Salò has a fine Gothic Duomo (cathedral) with a noteworthy Renaissance portal. At Gardone Riviera, most things to visit have something to do with Gabriele d'Annunzio (1863–1938), one of the greatest writers and poets of his generation. His villa, Vittoriale degli Italiani was specially built for him and can be visited. The villa and grounds are filled with an extraordinary array of bits and pieces, like the great ornate organs in the music room, among which the writer chose to live. There is also a museum and a mausoleum in the villa's grounds.

At Riva del Garda, right at the northern tip of the lake, about 95 breathtaking kilometres (60 miles) away from Desenzano del Garda up the western edge of the lake, and actually in the Trentino region, is a 13th-century tower, the Torre Apponale, and a clutter of other ancient edifices of which the Palazzo Pretorio and the 12th-century Rocca (fortress) are the most interesting. The town's Museo Civico (Civic Museum) contains an interesting collection of armour and archaeological finds from the area, housed in the Rocca.

Malcesine, halfway down the eastern edge of the lake, is the proud possessor of the magnificent Castello Scaligero (Scaliger Castle) dramatically situated at the water's edge. But the castle at Sirmione is more remarkable. Also from the 13th century and one of the Scaligeri castles, its battlements and its dramatic situation half in the water make it possibly the most memorable sight on the Lago di Garda.

From Desenzano del Garda, take the ***SS567*** *for 11km (7 miles) to Castiglione delle Stiviere, at which branch on to the* ***SS236*** *and continue on to Mantova, about 37km (23 miles).*

9 Mantova, Lombardia

Mantova (Mantua) sits on a swampy, marshy bend in the Mincio River. Its claim to fame is that it was the seat of one of the most intellectually active and refined courts of the Italian Renaissance. The Gonzaga family were the rulers and they embellished the town with a remarkable Palazzo Ducale (Ducal Palace) that still contains some of their art collection. The neo-classical rooms have a set of early 16th-century Flemish tapestries and the duke's apartments have a fine collection of classical statuary. Here you will see Rubens' vast portrait of the Gonzaga family. The Camera degli Sposi in the Castel di San Giorgio is world famous for its brilliant frescos by Mantegna, finished in 1474. Apart from a series of portraits of the family, there are others of their favourite dwarfs. In the Casetta dei Nani, the House of the Dwarfs, you can see the miniature rooms where the latter were once thought to have lived. The Palazzo del Té is another Gonzaga palace built by Giulio Romano in 1527 for Federico II Gonzaga's mistress. The Sala dei Giganti, the Room of the Giants, is its masterpiece:

SPECIAL TO...

An exciting trip for young and old alike would be the trip in a cable car from Malcesine to the summit of Monte Baldo, which has spectacular views over the lake and surrounding mountains.

huge frescoed fighting giants seem to bring down the ceiling. The Basilica of Sant'Andrea, designed by Leon Battista (1472), houses a chalice of Christ's blood, a relic once much venerated by the Gonzaga.

SPECIAL TO...

In Mantova is the Good Friday Procession on 1 April. Sacred vases which, according to tradition, contain earth soaked with the blood of Christ, are carried in a procession around the town.

i Piazza A Mantegna 6

▶ *Take the **SS10** for 66km (41 miles) to Cremona.*

10 Cremona, Lombardia
You cannot come to Cremona and not visit the Museo Stradivariano (Stradivarian Museum). The modern violin was developed in this city in 1566, and one of the great masters of violin-making here – though much later – was Antonio Stradivarius. The Town Hall has a valuable collection of violins, including instruments by Stradivari, Amati and Guarneri. There is also the Museo Civico (Civic Museum) in which much space is devoted to Roman Cremona. The Duomo (cathedral) has five wonderful 17th-century Brussels tapestries as well as a series of frescos by local artists. The tall bell tower of the cathedral can also be visited, and there are fine views from the top. Among the town's most interesting churches is Sant' Agostino with a *Madonna and Saints* by Perugino, who was once Raphael's teacher.

i Piazza del Comune 5

▶ *From Cremona, take the **A21** via Piacenza for 33km (20 miles) as far as the Casteggio turning, 82km (51 miles), for the **SS35** to Pavia, a further 21km (13 miles).*

11 Pavia, Lombardia
Pavia was at one time an important Roman city (*Ticinum*). Little remains, though the municipal museums in Castello Visconteo contain finds from Roman times and early Pavia. On an upper floor you will find the picture gallery with works by, among others, Bellini and Van der Goes, the latter one of the most important of the Flemish Renaissance painters.

The most noteworthy monument to visit is the Certosa di Pavia, a remarkable, highly decorative Renaissance monastery complex, just on the outskirts of town. A tour will take in the vestibule, the cloisters and the church with Gothic, Renaissance and baroque decoration.

Back in the town, Leonardo was partially responsible for the design of the Duomo, begun in 1488, and in addition to the cathedral, there are about six other churches worth seeing.

i Via Fabio Filzi 2

▶ *Take the **SS35** back to Milano, about 35km (22 miles).*

Pavia, capital of the Lombard kings for two centuries

SCENIC ROUTES

The most scenic parts of this tour are the following:
– From Sacro Monte Varese, drive to Monte delle Tre Croci (the Mount of the Three Crosses) where you will have wonderful views of the surrounding countryside. Another 200m (220 yards) further up, at Campo dei Fiori – a long ridge – an even wider panorama can be enjoyed.
– From Stresa on Lago Maggiore, take a cable-car to Mount Mottarone and see the views to the Alps and to Lake Garda.
– On the west shore of Lago di Como, at Argegno, there are views to the northern snowy mountains.
– The SS45bis for the last 11km (7 miles) before you reach Riva del Garda on Lago di Garda, is one of the most spectacular stretches of road on the lake, should you elect to drive rather than take the steamer.

TOUR 3

La Grassa – the 'Fat' Country

This tour reveals two of the finest Romanesque churches in Italy, well-preserved fortified cities, great Renaissance painting and sculpture, grand opera, thermal spas, Parma ham and a sparkling local wine – Lambrusco – which is never at its best outside the region. Bologna is the most cosmopolitan city on the tour. It has a huge, ancient university, its shops mirror those of Milan and it has a wide range of excellent restaurants giving it its nickname 'La Grassa' – 'Bologna the Fat'.

3 DAYS • 378KM • 234 MILES

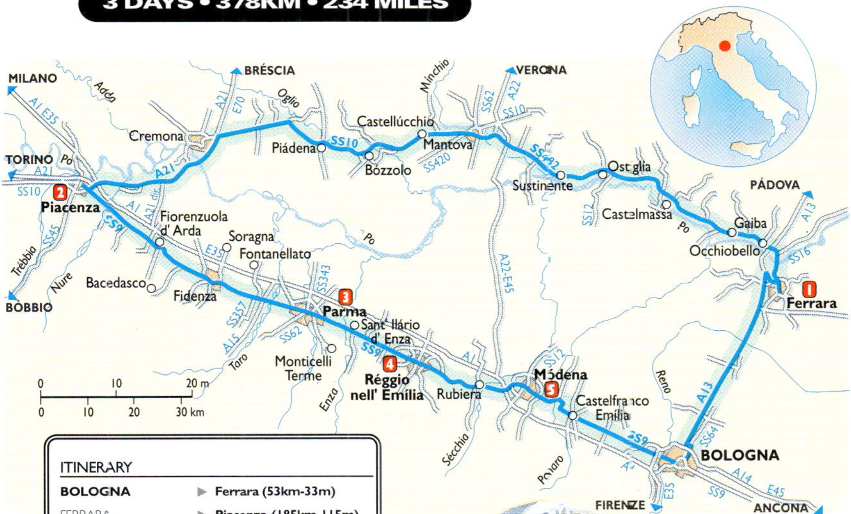

ITINERARY

BOLOGNA	▶ **Ferrara (53km-33m)**
FERRARA	▶ **Piacenza (185km-115m)**
PIACENZA	▶ **Parma (49km-30m)**
PARMA	▶ **Reggio nell'Emilia (28km-17m)**
REGGIO NELL' EMILIA	▶ **Modena (24km-15m)**
MODENA	▶ **Bologna (39km-24m)**

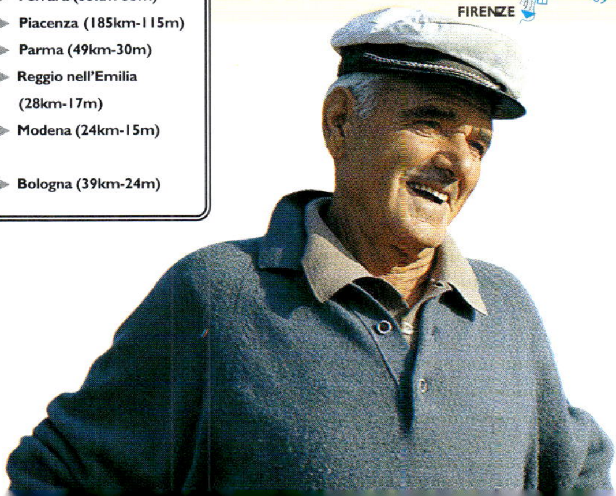

TOUR **3** **La Grassa –** the 'Fat' Country

i *Galleria d'Accursio, Piazza Maggiore 6, Bologna*

▶ *The autostrada* ***A13*** *goes north from Bologna until the Ferrara Nord exit.*

1 Ferrara, Emilia-Romagna
The centre of Ferrara is dominated by a vast castle, the Castello Estense. Begun in 1385, it was the backdrop to the splendid court of the Este family, the rulers of Ferrara. It was designed to ward off any potential threat to this little city state, and its moat, drawbridge and military bulwarks are still formidable and do nothing to relieve its prisonlike appearance. A tour round the castle includes the dungeons in which Nicolò III d'Este imprisoned his lovely young wife Parisina Malatesta and her lover before they were beheaded. After these, the various decorated chambers of the castle are a welcome relief. Nicolò III's son Ercole I (1471–1505) was responsible for an addition to the medieval town known as the 'Herculean Addition', making Ferrara the first 'modern' town in Europe. At the heart of the Herculean Addition is the extraordinary Palazzo dei Diamanti whose façade is studded with 8,500 stone 'diamonds', the Este badge.

Castello Estense, Ferrara, is heavily fortified with moat and drawbridge

On the other side of the castle is the Duomo (cathedral). Begun in 1135, it has a lovely sculpted portico, with scenes from the Last Judgement. Inside, look for the painted *Martyrdom of St Lawrence* by Guercino in the south transept. The cathedral museum has some splendid works, including a marble *Madonna of the Pomegranate* (1408) by Jacopo della Quercia, the greatest Sienese sculptor of the early Renaissance. The museum is housed in the church of San Romano. Back outside in the Piazza Trento e Trieste, you come down to earth at the colourful market. There is also the Museo Archeologico (National Archaeological Museum), housed in the Palazzo di Ludovico il Moro, with a collection of vases from the Greek and Etruscan necropolis of nearby Spina. See also the Palazzo Schifanoia with its lovely Renaissance frescos by Cosimo Tura.

i *Castello Estense Largo Castello*

FOR CHILDREN

There are few activities specifically designed for children in this part of Emilia-Romagna; your best bet is to take them to see the displays of puppets and dolls for sale in Ferrara, in the Circus Atelier in Via Mazzini.

▶ *Leave Ferrara on the* ***SS16*** *going north. After crossing the Po, turn left towards the* ***A13****. Cross the motorway and continue west to Ostiglia, 56km (34½ miles). The* ***SS482*** *continues to Mantova, another 33km (20 miles). From Mantova, the* ***SS10*** *continues west for 62km (39 miles) to Cremona immediately before which the autostrada* ***A21*** *branches southwest for 30km (19 miles) towards Piacenza. Leave the autostrada at the*

Piacenza Est exit and follow the signs into the city.

SCENIC ROUTES

For the most scenic drives between towns on this tour, you must really veer off the given route and take to the mountains immediately to the south. Among the mass of the Apennines, which follow the route from Piacenza to Bologna, you are never very far from deep wooded valleys and views to the snow-covered highest peaks of these.

Frescos from Parma's baptistery – a glimpse of medieval Italy

2 Piacenza, Emilia-Romagna
This is a town that visitors to Emilia-Romagna tend to ignore unwittingly: its treasures and attractions are less obvious and less well known than those of other places. It has an interesting old centre filled with churches including a 12th-century Romanesque Duomo with a bell tower topped by a gilded angel and interior frescos by Guercino, a notable baroque illusionist painter of the 17th century. The cathedral stands at the top of the Via XX Settembre looking down to the Piazza Cavalli, named after its equestrian statues of Alessandro Farnese and his brother Ranuccio. These early 17th-century statues by Francesco Mocchi, a pupil of Giambologna, who was the most famous sculptor in Florence after the death of Michelangelo, are the pride of Piacenza. The 16th-century Palazzo Farnese is a huge unfinished palace of the Farnese family which houses the Museo Civico (Civic Museum) containing works by Botticelli and the school of Botticelli. It also has another very peculiar relic known as *Il Fegato di Piacenza*, 'Piacenza's Liver', an Etruscan bronze sheep's liver marked with the names of local deities.

To the south of the Piazza Cavalli, in a warren of little streets near the cathedral, is an early 19th-century theatre, an elegant neo-classical building still used during the various seasons of chamber and orchestral music and ballet. It has an eccentric little museum attached to it containing relics from the theatre's past. Near by the Galleria d'Arte Moderna Ricci Oddi (Ricci Oddi Gallery) is worth a visit. It has works from the 18th century to the present day.

i Piazzetta dei Mercanti 7

► *Leave Piacenza by the **SS9** which runs directly to Parma 49km (30 miles).*

3 Parma, Emilia-Romagna
Parma is built on the flat so visiting its monuments is not such a strain on the calf muscles. Bigger than either Piacenza or Ferrara it has much more to see. If you start in the heart of the city, in the Piazza del Duomo, you will see the two buildings for which Parma is best known – the 11th-century Duomo and the 12th-century baptistery alongside it. The exterior of the cathedral is richly patterned, and the interior contains work of the painter Correggio, who was influenced by Michelangelo. His *Assumption* (1526–30) can be seen in the vault of the dome: the painted 'architecture' and the apparently three-dimensional clouds and angels almost seem a part of the real world.

In the Church of San Giovanni Evangelista, just behind the cathedral, you can see Correggio's *Vision of St John* (1520), also in the dome. While you are here, take a look at the work of Parmigianino, a pupil of Correggio, which can be seen in the first two chapels on the northern side of the interior. In the Camera di San Paolo you can see Correggio's very earliest documented works, painted in about 1518 for the abbess of the now defunct convent of San

Paolo. The little Church of SS Placid e Flavia is one other place to see his work and so is the Pinacoteca (National Gallery), housed in the Palazzo della Pilotta. Back in the Piazza del Duomo, the baptistry is well worth a visit.

For a complete change of scenery, visit the Teatro Regio, one of Italy's great theatres. The great conductor, Toscanini, who was born in Parma, played in the orchestra here. His birthplace in Via R Tanzi has a fascinating collection of items and an audio-visual presentation relating to his musical career. Another theatre in Parma is called the Teatro Farnese. Built entirely of wood by Aleotti (a pupil of Palladio) in 1618, it is part of the Palazzo della Pilotta, along with the Museo Archeologico Nazionale (National Museum of Antiquities). In its majestic interior performances took place in honour of the ruling family of Parma – the Farnese. Have the local speciality, prosciutto di Parma (Parma ham) as an antipasto for lunch.

i Via Melloni 1

▶ *The **SS9** leaves Parma going southeast to Reggio nell'Emilia 28km (17 miles).*

FOR HISTORY BUFFS

In the province of Parma are two interesting castles that would make a detour from Parma more than rewarding. Northwest of the city, at Fontanellato (take the A1 westwards for 20km/12 miles, as far as the Fidenza-Salsomaggiore Terme exit), is the moated Castello di Sanvitale. It has good frescos by Parmigianino, and is open to the public.

Just to the north of this, at Soragna (only 8km/5 miles), is the furnished and frescoed Palazzo di Soragna. The castle, begun in the 8th century and converted into a palace in the 19th century, contains fine period furniture and art. This is also open to the public.

4 Reggio nell'Emilia,

Emilia-Romagna

This town, almost halfway between Parma and Modena, is a centre of Parmigiano (Parmesan) cheese manufacture. Here, so good is the cheese, and so well does it mature, that it goes up in value. People buy huge cakes of it as an investment. Reggio nell'Emilia, sometimes known as Parmigiano-Reggiano, is a thriving, bustling little capital. You would not really need to spend more than a morning here. Like the rest of this part of the region, it is completely flat. Also, like the other towns, it is built of characteristic small red bricks. Perhaps the most interesting – and the oldest – historic relic to be seen here is the mysterious 'Venus of Chiozza', reputedly 12,000 years old. You can see it in the Museo Civico (Civic Museum), which incorporates a number of collections on diverse themes.

Reggio was once an important Roman city, *Regium Lepida*, which was cut in two by the great ancient Via Emilia, also built by the Romans. In the

Piazza Prampolini in Reggio nell'Emilia

public gardens behind the theatre is a Roman family tomb (Monument of the Concordii), dating from AD 50.

The A and L Parmeggiani Gallery houses a fine collection of paintings, sculpture, tapestries, furniture and various other items.

Reggio nell'Emilia's Duomo (cathedral), while as old as any others on the tour, has fewer artistic treasures. However, the Church of the Madonna della Ghiara is full of the work of the Emilian painters, particularly those of the 17th century. All over town there are unexpected architectural treasures, such as the courtyard of the baroque Palazzo Sormani-Moretti and the Palazzo Spalletti-Trivelli. There are also a great many beautiful neo-classical buildings from the 19th century, including the Palazzo Corbelli and the municipal theatre, which stages a season of opera, concerts and plays running from December to March.

i Piazza Prampolini 5/C

▶ *From Reggio nell'Emilia, the **SS9** runs straight to Modena.*

BACK TO NATURE

The floodplain of the River Po is an area of rivers, wetlands and cultivated rice fields. The latter are especially rewarding for the bird-watcher: look for little egrets, grey herons, purple herons and squacco herons.
Harvested fields attract ducks and wading birds, including lapwings, snipe, ruff and spotted redshanks.

5 Modena, Emilia-Romagna
Modena vies with Parma for status as the most prosperous city in the region, though Modena has a head start over Parma due to the existence of the Maserati and Ferrari car works on its territory. Modena was once an Etruscan colony, then a Roman city, but the earliest apogee of its power was under the 11th-century Canossa Countess Matilda, a powerful ally of the Pope. Until the middle of the 19th century, the Este family, through a variety of judicious marriages, were its rulers. The Duomo, dedicated to San Geminiano, built between 1000 and 1200, was constructed largely from material taken from the old Roman city. The external sculptures are worth examining in some detail particularly those on the west portal and on the apse. The tomb of the patron saint of the city, San Geminiano, is in the crypt, and a wooden statue of the saint lurks in the shadows of the north aisle.

Close to the cathedral is the medieval Ghirlandina Tower, which contains an eccentric relic in the form of an old wooden bucket which, as an act of rivalry, was stolen by the people of Modena during a 14th-century raid on Bologna. If you want to see it, you may have to ask for the key to the tower at the Comune.

Most interesting is the town's Palazzo dei Musei. This contains the Biblioteca Estense which has a famous collection of illuminated manuscripts including the Bible of Borso d'Este. In the same building is the Galleria Estense, with a fine collection of paintings, including works by El Greco, Correggio, Velázquez and Tintoretto, as well as a bust

The sculpted tomb of St Dominic in the Church of San Domenico, Bologna

of Francesco I d'Este by Bernini. Here, too, is the Museo d'Arte Medievale e Moderne e Etnologia.

i Piazza Grande 17

▶ *From Modena, return to Bologna on the **SS9** – 39km (24 miles).*

SPECIAL TO...

Modena has an important Antiques Fair on the fourth Saturday and Sunday of every month, held in the Piazza Grande. It is advisable to go early in the morning, firstly so that you can spot the hidden treasures before anyone else does, and secondly to avoid the crowds, who come into the town from all over the countryside to stroll among the stands.

RECOMMENDED WALKS

If you want some of the best walks in Emilia-Romagna (60 per cent of which is flat and rather uninteresting to look at), drive from Modena to Sestola, just off the SS12 about 50km (30 miles) to the south.
Here, at the base of Mount Cimone, the tallest peak in the Northern Apennines, there are lovely walks in mountain scenery. You could even stay at Sestola – it has a reputation as a good mountain resort.
The Great Apennine Excursion is a 400km (250-mile) path, but short sections can be followed that are accessible by car.

TOUR
4

Of Mosaics, Sun & Sea

With one or two exceptions, the towns on this tour are the antidote that every trip needs to a surfeit of culture. Whereas the interior of Emilia-Romagna contains the cultural capitals, the coast has all the playgrounds. Restaurants, night-clubs and hotels are in good supply, particularly at Rimini. And there is still plenty of sightseeing to do.

2/3 DAYS • 258KM • 160 MILES

ITINERARY	
RIMINI	▶ **Cesenatico (22km-14m)**
CESENATICO	▶ **Ravenna (30km-19m)**
RAVENNA	▶ **Comacchio (37km-23m)**
COMACCHIO	▶ **Faenza (81km-50m)**
FAENZA	▶ **Brisighella (13km-8m)**
BRISIGHELLA	▶ **Forlì (28km-17m)**
FORLÌ	▶ **Rimini (47km-29m)**

[i] Piazza Fellini 3, Rimini

► *From Rimini, the coast road, the **SS16**, leads north to Cesenatico.*

> FOR CHILDREN
>
> There are plenty of very safe beaches on this tour, where the water is shallow for a good stretch from the shoreline. In particular, San Mauro a Mare, about 4km (2½ miles) south of Cesenatico, and Bellaria-Igea Marina (just further on) are ones to aim for. Gatteo a Mare, just south of Cesenatico, has a special games park for children.

1 Cesenatico, Emilia-Romagna

Just a short way from Rimini on the Adriatic coast, Cesenatico was built in 1302 as the harbour of Cesena, a town about 14km (9 miles) inland. It seems to have spent its days being destroyed by the enemy, each time being faithfully rebuilt. Cesare Borgia did much to prevent the sea knocking down the fortifications. These were built to the plans of Leonardo da Vinci, the originals of which are kept in the National Library in Paris.

Cesenatico nowadays is a seaside resort often crowded in the summer with people attracted by the fact that the beach gently slopes into the water, making for good swimming. There are in fact about 6.5km (4 miles) of sandy beach, sometimes 200m (650 feet) in width, giving plenty of room for everybody. While this stretch of beach has the usual array of high-rise hotels, the old town has nice shady streets and a lively and colourful market.

The town was once a canal port and here you can still see the yellow and brown sails of the *bragozzi*, flat-bottomed boats with colourful designs painted on them. Brightly painted fishermen's houses with canvas canopies leaning out over the pavement line the

Colourful boats line the lively harbour in the town of Cesenatico

waterfront. Hidden among them are the Museum of Antiquities, the Maritime Museum (reopening late 2005) and a variety of typical restaurants selling unpretentious local food.

[i] *Viale Roma 112*

▶ *From Cesenatico, the* ***SS16*** *goes straight towards Ravenna.*

2 Ravenna, Emilia-Romagna
This is the most important place in Italy for mosaics of the Byzantine era (5th and 6th centuries). They adorn the interiors of the octagonal Church of San Vitale, the Mausoleo (mausoleum) di Galla Placidia, and the Church of Sant'Apollinare Nuovo, built by Theodoric. There are more in the Battistero degli Ortodossi or Neonian Baptistery (named after Bishop Neon who commissioned the mosaics) and the Oratorio di Sant'Andrea. Even if you see nothing else but the mosaics, you will not leave town disappointed. San Vitale's are the best and they include the portraits of Emperor Justinian and his wife Theodora, located in the apse. Justinian offers a gift to the new church; his wife is covered in extravagant jewellery and both are surrounded by servants. The Mausoleum of Galla Placidia is a jewel-like little building. Inside is one of the most beautiful mosaics in the world, taking up the entire interior – geometric patterns and flowers, animals and religious imagery. There are also three hefty tombs, one of which contains the remains of Galla Placidia's second husband Constantius III. Galla Placidia was one of the patronesses of early Ravenna, though she was in fact buried in Rome.

Sant'Apollinare Nuovo has two long mosaic processions running the length of its nave – male and female martyrs. Other sights include, not far from the central Piazza del Popolo, Il Sepolcro di Dante (the tomb of Dante), housed in a little neoclassical mausoleum. Italy's greatest poet Dante died here in exile in 1321. There is also a variety of little museums, including the Museo dell'Arcivescovado which contains the exquisite 6th-century ivory throne of Maximian and the silver cross of Sant'Agnello. The Museo Dante has rather erratic opening hours, and you might have difficulty getting in. The Municipal Gallery has works from the 14th to 20th centuries and an exhibition of contemporary mosaics. The Museo Nazionale, next to San Vitale, has a fine collection of artefacts dating back to ancient times.

Mosaic splendour fills Ravenna's Mausoleum of Galla Placidia

FOR HISTORY BUFFS

The Church of Sant'Apollinare in Classe is worth the short detour from Ravenna, and completes the tour of Ravenna mosaics. In particular it has a wonderful apse with a depiction of the Transfiguration of Christ attended by Sant'Apollinare.

The Arch of Augustus in Rimini, where ghosts of the past rub shoulders with sun-seekers

[i] Via Salara 8–12

SPECIAL TO...

At Ravenna is a summer school teaching the art and technique of mosaic. Details are available at the local tourist office or on www.sisamravenna.it.
The market, on the third weekend of every month, is an antiques fair which sells a huge variety of things, from carved wooden angels to gilded clocks to wooden breadboards from the 19th century.

▶ *From Ravenna, the* ***SS309*** *goes north for about 32km (20 miles) to the turning for Comacchio, a further 5km (3 miles).*

3 Comacchio, Emilia-Romagna

Comacchio is situated a few miles from the coast, just north of Ravenna. It is a kind of little Venice with the town sitting among a series of canals. Even its bridges, of which the most famous is the Trepponti that spans three of the waterways, have a Venetian look about them. But the resemblance stops here. Comacchio is a rural place, home to fishermen who sail down the canals, past the lagoon to the sea at Porto Garibaldi. It is famous for its eels: they are farmed in the nearby Valli di Comacchio and you can have them cooked with tomatoes or grilled and washed down with a Trebbiano wine called Vino di Bosco. You can watch the fishermen catch the eels in huge square nets suspended in the water. The season for eels is October to December. Grey mullet and bass, produce of the lagoons and canals of the area, are also often found on the menu at Comacchio, and you can visit the Peschiera (fish market), housed in a restored 17th-century building. Until the beginning of the 16th century the town was a flourishing place with a healthy commercial life. Fearing competition, the Venetians destroyed it, but it was later rebuilt. Thus the look of the town today is fairly uniform because many of the buildings were constructed more or less at the same time Find time to visit the churches of the Carmine and Del Rosario and the restored Cathedral of San Cassiano.

▶ *The quickest way to Faenza is to go back towards Ravenna on the* ***SS309*** *and to continue on to the* ***SS309dir,*** *which quickly becomes the* ***A14dir.*** *Turn left on to the* ***A14*** *and exit at the Faenza turn-off. Follow the signs to Faenza.*

BACK TO NATURE

The Valli di Comacchio, a vast wetland area, is the haunt of breeding terns, gulls and waders. Coots and great crested grebes commonly nest among the waterside vegetation and small flocks of penduline tits can be found in reedbeds. View this area from any accessible part of its perimeter.

4 Faenza, Emilia-Romagna
Faenza has been one of the most important centres of the ceramic industry in Italy for about 1,000 years and gave its name to the type of glazed pottery called faience. Early faience ware is much sought after and nowadays is the kind of thing found gracing the cabinets of international museums, not least of which is the Museo Internazionale delle Ceramiche (International Museum of Ceramics) in Faenza itself, one of the most comprehensive ceramics collections in Italy. Here there are examples with designs by Picasso, Chagall and Matisse. Faience ware is a majolica with characteristic yellow and blue patterns. There are traditional versions of it, modernist reinterpretations of it and you can eat off it, drink out of it or simply put it on a shelf and admire its colour and texture. You can even decorate your house with it as did the owners of the Art Nouveau Palazzo Matteucci, using ceramic tiles of decorative patternwork including flowers and plants. There are shops selling it all over town, and the workshops are interesting to visit. There is even an Institute of Ceramics where works have been documented and technology tries to discover new and exciting ways of manipulating the raw material.

If you can tear yourself away, visit the cathedral, which contains some excellent Renaissance sculpture, and the Palazzo Milzetti with its 18th-century Pompeian-style ceiling decorations by Felice Gianni.

▶ *Close to Faenza is Brisighella, 13km (8 miles) to the south-west on the* ***SS302****.*

5 Brisighella, Emilia-Romagna
In the last century, the discovery of the therapeutic efficacy of the waters in the nearby Lamone Valley put Brisighella back on the map. It is a pretty little town, dwarfed by the great quarries that produced the clay for the Faenza workshops. It never grew much in size but it is the proud possessor of one or two interesting and unusual monuments. Perhaps the most noteworthy is the strange little Romanesque Pievo del Tho, a church which incorporates Roman fragments.

Above the town is the 12th-century castle, the Rocca, which was built to guard the Lamone Valley. It was radically modified by the Venetians, who added cylindrical towers. Nowadays it contains the Museo del Lavoro Contadino (Museum of Country Life), covering the Lamone, the Senio and Marzeno river valleys.

▶ *Return to Faenza, then follow the* ***SS9*** *for about 15km (9 miles) as far as Forli.*

6 Forli, Emilia-Romagna
Forli, the administrative capital of the Romagna, is another old brick town with an ancient Roman heritage. Once known as the Forum Livii, it was an important post on the old *Via Emilia* which still bisects the town. A large part of Forli still retains something of its old character, but much of it suffered under Mussolini.

Still, you can ignore the surroundings and visit the interiors of the Romanesque Basilica of San Mercuriale, the cathedral and the Church of Santa Maria. The first of these three churches has a lovely red brick interior. If you can get into the crypt, look out for the remains of the 11th-century

View over Brisighella

SCENIC ROUTES

The road from Ravenna to Classe and to Cervia has a remote eerie flatness which is very typical of this stretch of the coast. Here there are pine groves. On the road from Brisighella to Faenza, the countryside is dramatically different around each of these towns; the former is deep in the Apennines, the latter on the plain. The road weaves through the Lamone Valley's pretty mountain scenery.

Ravenna's fine Basilica di San Vitale, built in 547

church. The Cathedral of Santa Croce has been much rebuilt and most of what you see now dates from the middle of the 19th century. A piece of the old fabric of the church survives in the apse and is adorned with a huge tempera painting of the *Assumption* by Cignani. The San Mercuriale Museum in Piazza Saffi is undergoing a refurbishment at the time of going to print, but there are lots of other museums and galleries to explore. The Museo Archeologico (Archaeological Museum) contains the finds from a variety of prehistoric and Roman sites in and around Forli.

RECOMMENDED WALKS

South of Forli, in the Emilian Apennines, there is the famous Campigna forest, a vast parkland of beech, maple, fir, hornbeam and chestnut. This is an idyllic place to walk. To reach it, take the SS67 going south from Forli. At Rocca San Casciano (about 28km/17 miles), follow the signs to Santa Sofia, about 16km (10 miles). From there take the SS310 to Campigna (about 14km/8½ miles).

[i] *Piazzetta Novanta Pacifici*

► *From Forli, take the* ***SS9*** *back to Rimini, bypassing Cesena, a total distance of 47km (29 miles).*

SPECIAL TO...

The Adriatic coast has a huge number of very popular beaches. The best among these are the Marina di Ravenna, with its backdrop of pine woods, and Cervia, with possibilities for windsurfing, sailing and other summer sports.

TOUR
5

The Gentle Veneto

This tour takes you through one of the most popular parts of the Italian peninsula. If travellers are not chasing the memory of a famous writer or painter, they are in search of the sublime beauty of Venice and its islands. Asolo, where the tour begins, claims Robert Browning as its most famous inhabitant. From Asolo you can visit the Renaissance villas among the vineyards that produce some of Italy's most characteristic white wines.

3 DAYS • 274KM • 169 MILES

ITINERARY	
ASOLO	▶ **Possagno (12km-7m)**
POSSAGNO	▶ **Feltre (31km-19m)**
FELTRE	▶ **Conegliano (56km-35m)**
CONEGLIANO	▶ **Treviso (28km-17m)**
TREVISO	▶ **Venezia (31km-19m)**
VENEZIA	▶ **Murano (4km-2m)**
MURANO	▶ **Burano (6km-4m)**
BURANO	▶ **Torcello (3km-2m)**
TORCELLO	▶ **Venezia (return) (13km-8m)**
VENEZIA	▶ **Castelfranco Veneto (66km-41m)**
CASTELFRANCO VENETO	▶ **Asolo (24km-15m)**

▶ *From Asolo going north, follow the signs to Possagno.*

FOR HISTORY BUFFS

You cannot go on this tour and not visit at least one villa designed by the great architect Andrea Palladio. His designs, based on the architectural principles of the ancient world, were immensely influential throughout Europe and in the United States. Indeed, this influence is apparent in neo-classical buildings built even in the present century.

The Villa Barbaro at Maser, about 10km (6 miles) east of Asolo, is the very best of his houses. Still a private residence, it has fabulous frescos by Veronese, as well as original furnishings and lovely gardens. There are other villas; in fact you could go on a special villa route, seeing most of them.

Grand Canal, Venice's main thoroughfare, runs for two miles (3km) through the city

1 Possagno, Veneto
The first thing you will notice about Possagno is the huge mausoleum, the Tempio, of the sculptor Canova, who was born here in 1757 and died here in 1822. You can see this building for miles around. It sits on a hill overlooking the town with the snow-covered heights of Mount Grappa looming behind it. Designed by Canova himself, the Tempio is based on the Pantheon in Rome. Canova's house is not far away, at the bottom of a wide straight road leading down from the Tempio. His rooms are preserved in the pretty courtyard house, now partly an art gallery, and there is a Gipsoteca (gallery of casts) where examples of his work, as well as full-scale plaster models for pieces now in museums or abroad, can be seen, including the *Three Graces*.

▶ *From Possagno, follow signs for about 9km (6 miles), then branch north on* ***SS348*** *along the River Piave, to Feltre, about 22km (13 miles).*

2 Feltre, Veneto
You enter old Feltre, squatting on a low incline, through the Imperial Gate. From here, a road rises gradually to the Piazza Maggiore, passing on the way a series of palaces some of which, like the Casa Franceschini, have frescos by Morto da Feltre painted on their external façades. The Piazza Maggiore itself is full of old buildings, mainly from the 16th century. Apart from the Church of San Rocco and a lovely central fountain by Tullio Lombardo there are the remains of the town's old castle with its clock tower. Surveying the entire scene is an enormous column on top of which stands the Lion of St Mark, the symbol of Venice.

A large ornate palace to one side is the Palazzo Municipale, which has a striking Palladian portico of a type fairly common in this part of Italy. Beyond the piazza is the Palazzo Villabruna in which is the Museo Civico (Civic Museum). Here you will see paintings representative of the region's famous art history, in particular works by Cima da Conegliano and Gentile Bellini. The Museo Rizzarda contains a collection of wrought-iron work, much of it locally made by Carlo Rizzarda. Just below the spur on which Feltre is situated, and close to the site of the weekly market, is the Duomo (cathedral) with a 15th-century façade. Make a point of seeing the Byzantine cross of AD 524 housed here. It is carved with 52 scenes taken from the New Testament.

i *Piazza Trento e Trieste 9*

▶ *Go back to the* ***SS348*** *and follow it south to Fener, at which turn left on to the Strada del Vino Bianco to Conegliano, a total of 56km (35 miles).*

3 Conegliano, Veneto
Conegliano is the centre for a wine-producing region. It was also the birthplace of the painter Cima da Conegliano, the great rival of Bellini. Cima's home is restored and filled with copies of his greatest work, and in the Gothic Duomo is one of the originals – an altarpiece dated 1493. Near by is the Sala dei Battuti, a guildhall whose walls are covered in 16th-century frescos by, among others, Francesco da Milano. The details are extraordinary.

Above the town, standing on a cypress-covered hillock, is the castle, now a museum and art gallery. This is full of interesting works of art, including paintings by Palma il Giovane, who once worked in Titian's studio, and sculptures by the Florentine sculptor Giambologna.

▶ *From Conegliano, the* ***SS13*** *goes straight down to Treviso, about 28km (17 miles).*

4 Treviso, Veneto
Treviso is a bright, busy provincial capital, crossed by canals that once fed the moat. There is plenty to see, although the town suffered much damage during World War II. In the Duomo di San Pietro (St Peter's Cathedral), which has seven domes, is an *Annunciation* by the greatest Venetian painter, Titian, who died in 1576 at the age of 99. The Diocesan Museum of Religious Art includes the cathedral treasury, with chalices, tapestries, vestments and a silver statue of St Liberale. In the Museo Civico (closed temporarily), housed in a former monastery, is the town's art gallery with works by Venetian artists such as Bellini, Guardi and Tiepolo.

Of Treviso's churches, perhaps the large Dominican Church of San Nicolò, with its fine apse and decorated columns, is the most interesting. In the restored 13th-century Church of San Francesco you will see the tomb (1384) of Francesca, daughter of the poet Plutarch. Out in the streets of Treviso the arcades are full of cafés.

i *Piazzetta Monte di Pietà 8*

None of Venice's grandeur on Burano, but plenty of colour

SPECIAL TO...

In Conegliano is the Strade del Vino Bianco (the Road of White Wine), a 42km (26-mile) wine route that encompasses some of the main vineyards between Conegliano and Valdobbiadene.
There is also a Strada del Vino Rosso which starts at Conegliano.

▶ *From Treviso, take the* ***SS13*** *towards Mestre, about 18km (11 miles), then via the* ***SS14*** *and the* ***SS11*** *to Venezia. Here you must leave your car in a specially provided garage.*

5 Venezia, Veneto

Venezia (Venice) is one of the great 'art cities' of Italy, and its churches and galleries are still crammed with magnificent paintings. To see the city's many treasures, you must take to the water – the *vaporetto* (water bus) is the main means of transport through the canal system and the lagoon. In Piazza San Marco (St Mark's Square) is the Basilica di San Marco, the chief glory of Venice, which was built after the original burned down in 976. Mosaics, coloured marbles, ancient columns and the famed bronze horses of St Mark are its chief attraction. The latter are copies of the 3rd-century BC originals, kept in the Basilica's Museo Marciano. Next door is the Palazzo Ducale (Doge's Palace) which took on its present appearance in about 1309. It has a lovely façade of lacy Gothic tracery and decorative brickwork. Look for the two reddish pillars on the front, said to have acquired their colour from the tortured corpses that used to hang there.

Behind the palace is the Ponte dei Sospiri (Bridge of Sighs) leading to the prison. Just across the water of the Giudecca canal and standing on a separate little island, is the Church of San Giorgio Maggiore (1565), built by Palladio, one of Italy's most influential architects. Other great sights are the Ca' d'Oro, a former palace on the Grand Canal with a picture gallery, the Ponte di Rialto (Rialto Bridge) across the Grand Canal, and the Galleria dell' Accademia, with some of the greatest masterpieces of Venetian art.

Amid all the historical magnificence and classical artworks is one of the greatest collections of modern art in the world. The Peggy Guggenheim Collection has works by the likes of Picasso, Mondrian and Magritte – along with paintings by the eccentric patroness's own protégé, Jackson Pollock – all displayed in state-of-the-art galleries within a palazzo on the Grand Canal.

[i] *Castello 4421*

SPECIAL TO...

In Venice the great Carnevale festival is held annually in the days preceding Lent, when the streets are thronged with people dressed in wild, extravagant costumes and masks. In the streets there are concerts and dancing and there are more formal concerts in the Teatro La Fenice (Fenice Theatre), now rebuilt and reopened following a fire in 1996.

▶ *From Venezia take a* vaporetto *from Fondamenta Nuova to the island of Murano.*

BACK TO NATURE

The bird life of the Venetian lagoons is a high spot on this tour. Boat tours and ferries allow an interesting range of birds to be seen in the Valli Venete. Mediterranean gulls are a conspicuous feature of the area but also look for black terns and whiskered terns and waders and herons on any exposed areas of mud.

FOR CHILDREN

This tour does not especially favour children. However, the Lido, just southeast of Venice, is a popular holiday resort with sandy beaches.

6 Murano, Veneto

Murano has been famous for its glass-blowing workshops since the early 13th century. Many palaces in Venice contain elaborate multicoloured chandeliers from this island and nowadays you can visit the descendants of the glass-blowers in their forges and workshops. In the Museo Vetrario (Museum of Glass) are

Murano is known for its exceptional glassware which can be found all over the town

the best examples of the work of the Murano glass-blowers and its annexe, the Modern and Contemporary Glass Museum, contains more up-to-date pieces. There are even fine pieces from Roman times. Glass objects can be purchased here in a large variety of shops. In the Church of Santi Maria e Donato, built at roughly the same time as St Mark's in Venice itself, you can see fragments of Murano glass in the 12th-century mosaic floor.

▶ *Murano and Burano are connected by boat. You can do a round trip that includes both, or else you can visit either on a single trip from Venice. The distance from Murano to Burano is about 6km (4 miles).*

Attila's Chair, outside Torcello's Church of Santa Fosca

7 **Burano,** Veneto

Lace-making is to Burano what glass-blowing is to Murano. All over the island you will find exquisite examples of it for sale. In the Museo dei Merletto at the lacemaking school you can see fine samples of work. This school was established late in the 19th century to rejuvenate the craft, which had all but died out. Burano is a very pretty island and its town, also called Burano, is like a miniature Venice. In the Church of San Martino is a *Crucifixion* by Tiepolo, the last of the great Venetian painters. While here, you could visit the little island of San Francesco del Deserto, about 20 minutes by ferry to the south of Burano. This is the location of the little monastery with beautiful gardens said to have been founded by St Francis of Assisi in 1220.

▶ *From Burano, the boat goes to the island of Torcello, a few miles further north.*

8 **Torcello,** Veneto

All that remains of this once great city, the first settlement in the lagoon in the 5th century AD, and once a serious rival to Venice itself, are two beautiful churches. One, the Byzantine-style Duomo di Santa Maria dell'Assunta, founded in 639 but rebuilt in about 1008, has splendid mosaics covering the floor as well as the walls. The *Last Judgement*, done by Greek artists in the 11th century, is particularly noteworthy. In the apse, the mosaic of the Madonna on a stark gold background, is one of the finest examples of Byzantine art anywhere.

The other church, 11th-century Santa Fosca, standing in the shadow of the cathedral, is just as ancient. In the garden outside is a stone seat known as 'Attila's Chair', the exact origins of which are unknown. Near the cathedral is the Museo dell'Estuario which contains finds from the ruins of the old city and is worth a visit. There is a silver altarpiece from the cathedral and some Roman remains from the ancient city of *Altinum*, which once stood near the present-day town of Mestre (seen on the way to Venice). Malaria virtually wiped out the population, bringing life in Torcello to an end.

▶ *From Torcello, return to Venice. Here take the* ***A4*** *to Padua (35km/22 miles), then go north on the* ***SS307*** *to Castelfranco Veneto, about 31km (19 miles).*

9 **Castelfranco Veneto,** Veneto

This little town's claim to fame is that it was the home of Giorgione, one of the most mysterious and elusive painters of the Venetian Renaissance. Little is known of him and few of his works survive (nobody knows why): those whose

authorship has been authenticated are very precious. You can see one in the town's duomo (cathedral). The *Madonna and Child with Saints*, often called the *Castelfranco Madonna*, dated 1504, is set in a typically lyrical Venetian landscape.

The old town of Castelfranco was once surrounded by a battlemented brick wall. One chunk of this – the Torre Civica – survives in the centre of town, and there is another length of moated wall to the west.

Visit the Casa del Giorgione (Giorgione's house); also see if you can get inside the pretty 18th-century Teatro Accademia.

▶ *From Castelfranco, the* ***SS307*** *leads northwards to Caerano di San Marco, about 15km (9 miles), where you turn left on the* ***SS248*** *to Asolo, another 9km (6 miles).*

RECOMMENDED WALKS

There are some good, pretty walks in the foothills of the Dolomites around the little town of Asiago – about 32km (20 miles) from Bassano del Grappa, a town within easy reach of both Possagno and Asolo.

If you have time, spend as long as you can walking around the islands of the Venetian Lagoon – Murano, Burano, and Torcello. Torcello in particular has little paths leading through the ghostly remains of what was once a large and important city.

Torcello's cathedral of Santa Maria Assunta is noted for its magnificent 11th- and 12th-century Byzantine mosaics

SCENIC ROUTES

The countryside is fairly flat on this tour. However, it has its scenic parts:

– the exit from Conegliano on the SS13: the profile of the town and its little mountain is idyllic;

– the scenery looking out over the Trevisian Plain from the castle at Asolo;

– the boat trip from Venice, to the islands of Murano, Burano and Torcello, with views of the lagoon and back over Venice.

TOUR
6

Beyond Venice – Inland Veneto

Many of the towns in this part of the Veneto have at least one architectural gem worthy of attention. Most often it is a church or a palace by Andrea Palladio, the greatest Italian architect of the 16th century. Verona, the starting point, is second only to Venice in the importance of its cultural treasures.

ITINERARY

VERONA	▶ **Montecchio (43km-27m)**
MONTECCHIO	▶ **Vicenza (13km-8m)**
VICENZA	▶ **Marostica (28km-17m)**
MAROSTICA	▶ **Padova (49km-30m)**
PADOVA	▶ **Arqua Petrarca (23km-14m)**
ARQUA PETRARCA	▶ **Monselice (7km-4m)**
MONSELICE	▶ **Este (9km-6m)**
ESTE	▶ **Verona (84km-52m)**

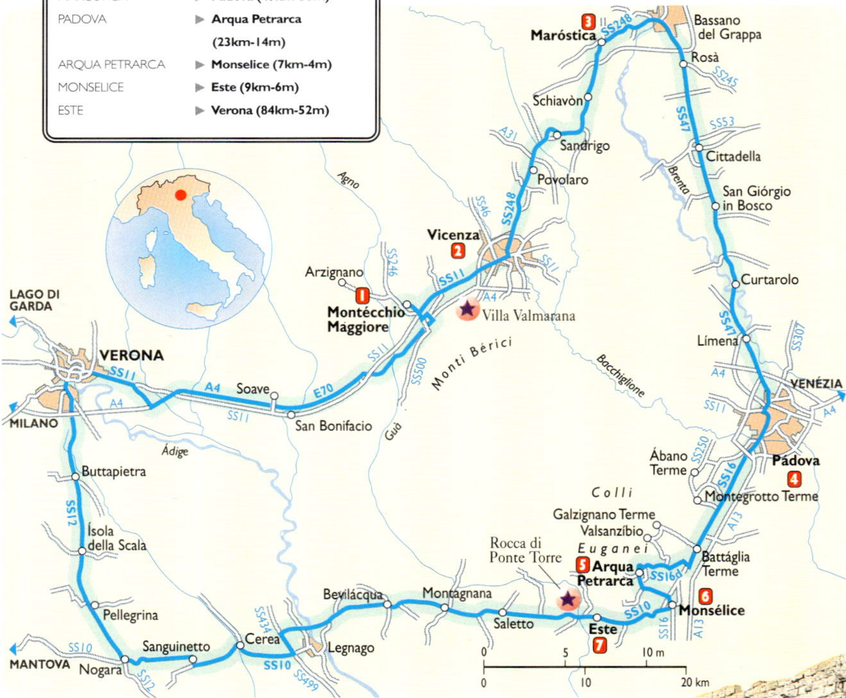

2/3 DAYS • 256KM • 158 MILES

i Via degli Alpini 9, Verona

BACK TO NATURE

To the west of Verona is Lago di Garda, a fine place to forget art and architecture for a while and do some bird-watching. Herring gulls haunt the shores of the lake in the summer and great crested grebes and ducks can be seen on the open water. Migrant waders – notably sandpipers and plovers – can be found around the margins in spring and autumn.

▶ *Take the **A4** going east from Verona as far as the Montecchio Maggiore turning.*

1 Montecchio Maggiore, Veneto

Montecchio Maggiore was one of the strongholds of the legendary Montagues of *Romeo and Juliet* fame, but now it's a quiet backwater. The two castles here are restored, and the G Zannato Museum, housed in the 19th-century Villa Lorenzoni, has a splendid collection. It has Roman finds from the necropolis of Carpane and from Campestrini, some amazing fossils and over 300 gemstones. About 6km (3½ miles) away is the castle of Arzignano, whose mighty black stone walls are still intact.

▶ *Return to and take the **SS11** to Vicenza.*

2 Vicenza, Veneto

Vicenza is known as the 'City of Palladio' because many of its buildings were designed by the great architect, who was born here. His works include the Basilica and the justice building, in the Piazza dei Signori, with classical statuary along the top and a two-tiered arcade along the front. In the same square is his Loggia del Capitano, built in 1571 to celebrate the Venetian victory at the battle of Lepanto. The Corso Palladio contains his Palazzo Chiericati, now the Museo Civico (Civic Museum) housing an art gallery in which you can see Van Dyck's *The Four Ages of Man*. But Palladio's masterpiece is the Teatro Olimpico, modelled on the theatres of ancient Rome. Half-moon shaped, it has a permanent wood and stucco stage set of an imaginary city in fake perspective. This is supposed to be the ideal Renaissance dream city. Just beyond the confines of the city, but within walking distance, are the Villa Valmarana ai Nani, renowned for its flamboyant decoration, and La Rotonda, Palladio's most famous villa and the inspiration for many buildings in Britain and France.

SPECIAL TO...

Vicenza is home to the International Palladio Study Centre which offers summer courses in architecture. In the neighbourhood of Padova are the thermal baths at Abano Terme, 9km (5½ miles) away, with 100 thermal swimming pools and a much venerated mud therapy. Others are at nearby Galzignano, Battaglia and Montegrotto.

Padova's Church of Santa Giustina

i Piazza Matteotti 12

► *From Vicenza, take the **SS248** northwards for about 28km (17 miles) to Marostica.*

3 Marostica, Veneto
Marostica preserves its medieval fortifications almost intact. Not a very big town, it is centred around the large oblong called Piazza del Castello. In the square is the battlemented castle building, now the town hall and the location of the Museum of Chess Game Costumes (see panel below). All along the length of the walls are towers placed at regular intervals. The biggest, at the top of the hill, was supposed to have been the very last resort for the town's people in times of war.

South of Marostica is Cittadella, another remarkable town whose walls are circular and extremely high. They are punctuated by brick towers; from one of these, the Tower of Malta, political prisoners were once flung to their deaths.

► *From Marostica, continue to Bassano del Grappa, then branch south on the **SS47** via Cittadella to Padova.*

FOR CHILDREN

Try, if you are there on the second weekend in September, to take the children to see the open-air chess game at Marostica, called the Partita a Scacchi, which dates from 1454. The players, dressed in 15th-century costume, play on a 22m (72-foot) square board and the event is supposed to commemorate a contest for the hand of the daughter of the lord of Marostica. Plenty of local children are involved in the chess match and the parade, in which they are dressed as ambassadors, noblemen, bejewelled ladies. This is a popular and lively spectacle.

Old-fashioned craft fair, Piazza dei Signori, Vicenza

4 Padova, Veneto
Shakespeare set *The Taming of the Shrew* in Padova (Padua), and although the city was badly damaged during World War II, much of its southern quarters retain the kind of setting that Shakespeare might have found appropriate for his play. Arcaded streets, fountains, orange brick churches and, above all, one of the oldest and most revered universities in Italy (founded 1222), survive to be looked at and walked through.

But the city's real treasure is the 14th-century Cappella degli Scrovegni (Chapel of the Madonna dell'Arena), which contains the most revolutionary paintings in the early history of Renaissance art. In order to preserve the famous frescoes, a system has been instigated to limit visitors to 25 at a time for a maximum of 15 minutes. Visitors pass along a special 'technological body' which extracts dust and pollutants before they enter the chapel.

Near by is the hermits' church, Chiesa degli Eremitani, with more early Renaissance works, this time by Mantegna.

The Museo Civico (Civic Museum) in the old Eremitani convent contains Greek and Roman finds from the area. Tours are conducted around the seat of the university, the Palazzo del Bo'. Here you can see the old Anatomical Theatre (1594). Other places of interest are the Palazzo de Capitano in the Piazza dei Signori, with Italy's oldest astronomical clock (1344), and the domed Basilica di Sant'Antonio in whose treasury you can see, in a precious reliquary, the tongue and larynx of Sant'Antonio of Padova, who was canonised in 1232.

SCENIC ROUTES

The little country roads leading through the Euganean Hills around Arqua Petrarca, Monselice and Este are laced with vineyards. Volcanic mounds, they are quite out of character with the surrounding area, which is flat.

[i] Riviera dei Mugnai 8

► *From Padova, take the **SS16** south for about 18km (11 miles) until the turning on the right, the **SS16d** for Arqua Petrarca. Follow the signs for about 5km (3 miles).*

5 Arqua Petrarca, Veneto

The second part of this town's name derives from the fact that it became the home, in his last years, of Francesco Petrarca (Petrarch), one of the greatest early Italian writers. He died here in 1374, and apart from being able to visit his tomb in the courtyard in front of Arqua's parish church, you can visit his house, the Casa del Petrarca, as well. It contains furniture contemporary with his period, and it even has a stuffed cat which you will be told belonged to the great man himself.

The town itself thrives on the memory of this illustrious past resident. It is pretty, well restored and has one or two chapels worth a visit.

RECOMMENDED TRIP

At Valsanzibio in the Euganean Hills, just a few miles north of Arqua Petrarca, is a magnificent 18-hole golf-course, good for a game or a leisurely walk. Close by is the Villa Barbarigo with a lovely garden, park and labyrinth all open to the public.

► *From Arqua Petrarca, a road leads to Monselice, 7km (4 miles) to the southeast.*

6 Monselice, Veneto

Monselice dominates the lovely Colli Euganei (Euganean Hills) on the edge of which it stands. Its position made it a natural fortress which was none the less fortified with castles and walls in the Middle Ages. Not very much of these survive because the town lost its military function in the 15th century. However, there is a lovely 16th-century fortified palace in the town, the Ca'Marcello, with a magnificent collection of Renaissance arms. There is one other palace at Monselice: Villa Duodo, designed towards the end of the 16th century by Scamozzi, the most important of Palladio's immediate followers. Only the gardens are open.

Rising up the hill beside it is the curious Via Sacra delle Sette Chiese (Sacred Way of the Seven Churches), also designed by Scamozzi, with seven chapels spaced along it. It is linked to the Romanesque duomo (cathedral).

► *From Monselice, the **SS10** goes straight to Este, 9km (6 miles).*

7 Este, Veneto

Este is one of the more beautiful walled towns in this part of the Veneto. Its fortifications – crenellations and towers – date from the 14th century. The walls were once over 1,000m (3,000 feet) long and there were 14 towers, of which only 12 remain. The castle became a pleasure palace of the Mocenigo family in the 16th century, and today its park is open to the public. Este was once protected by other out-of-town strongholds.

One of these, the Rocca di Ponte Torre, is the most interesting. It lies just outside town on the west side. There is also the town's Torre Civica (Civic Tower), which was transformed from a far earlier building in 1690 into a clock tower. In the Duomo is a painting of St Tecla by the artist Tiepolo.

One of Italy's best archaeological collections is in the Museo Nazionale Atestino here, housed within the Palazzo Mocenigo. Note particularly the 5th- and 6th-century bronze statuettes.

► *From Este, continue along the **SS10** for 53km (33 miles) until Nogara, at which branch north on the **SS12** to Verona, 31km (19 miles).*

The magnificent 1st-century AD amphitheatre in Verona's Piazza Brà has survived in remarkable condition despite a 12th-century earthquake

FOR HISTORY BUFFS

If you want to see some of the best preserved medieval fortifications in Italy, then go to the little town of Montagnana, 15km (9 miles) west of Este on the SS10. The walls were built in the 13th century by the Paduan tyrant Ezzelino da Romano. Look out for the two wonderful original gateways into the town through the wall. Also medieval, they look like mini castles.

LIGURIA & TUSCANY

The Apennines, skirting the Gulf of Genova and the Ligurian coast, link the Maritime Alps on the Italian-French border with the mountains of Tuscany. But this, together with deep, wooded valleys and an idyllic climate, is all that Liguria and Tuscany have in common.

Liguria is better known as the Italian Riviera with, to the north of Genoa, the Riviera di Ponente – famous for flowers and olives – and to the east the Riviera di Levante, with dramatic cliffs and pretty fishing villages. Justly famous, its attractions range from throbbing seaside resorts to lonely isolated coves hidden on one of the most spectacularly beautiful coastlines in Europe.

The great undiscovered secret of Liguria is, however, the hilltowns hidden among the Apennine valleys further inland. Built in inaccessible places in the Middle Ages, mostly as defence against Saracen attack from the sea, their little houses clustered together around the parish church are now mostly silent and empty. Yet, strangely, even the most under-visited of these is only, at the most, one and a half hours' drive from the coast. Mountain passes lead to them whilst providing incredible views down through the valleys to the sea.

Parts of Tuscany enjoy the same isolation as the Ligurian hinterland. And the beauty of this region is legendary. As the Apennines sweep down towards Firenze, much of the countryside is folded into hills and valleys which hide villages and castles, known only to the few. The Mugello, in the northeast of the region, is one of these places, characterised by thick woodland. By contrast, the Chianti region, producing Italy's most famous wine, between Firenze and Siena, is immensely popular and is a fixture on most travellers' itineraries.

Firenze's Duomo

It is difficult to appreciate that this peaceful landscape was, from the 11th to the 15th century, the backdrop to fierce wars between the independent city-states of the region before they were united as the Grand Duchy of Tuscany under the infamous Medici rulers. Remarkably, a great many towns and villages have preserved their cultural heritage intact. You can find, in remote country churches, paintings of the Madonna and saints from the very earliest days of the Renaissance, still in their original positions. Considering that so many wars, despots, invaders and calamities have each in their turn wrought havoc in this particular region, it is surprising that anything has managed to survive at all.

Tuscany's Chianti region is justly famous for its wines

San Remo

There are two distinct parts to San Remo: a modern metropolis and a quaint medieval town. Vestiges of a more aristocratic period in its history survive in the grand old hotels lining the seafront, and the promenade backed by palms. But today, bustling, modern San Remo, with its glossy shops, cafés and its very popular Casino, has taken over. San Remo is a fairly costly place, but if you go into the old town (La Pigna) you will find less expensive restaurants. Up here the character of the old town has survived amongst the tangle of cobbled lanes and tunnel-like alleys.

Genova

Many travellers bypass Genova (Genoa), but by doing so, they miss out on not only one of the most lively cities in northern Italy but also on some unexpected monuments – little wonder, then, that this was Europe's Culture Capital in 2004. In addition to the typically Genoese cathedral there are proud palaces which date from the 16th century when Genova was at the height of its power. For art lovers, the National Gallery in the Palazzo Spinolo contains some important work.

In Italy's small towns, the priest is an important figure

Pisa

Pisa contains some of the most magnificent buildings in Italy. Everyone knows about the Leaning Tower where Galileo conducted his experiments on the velocity of falling bodies. This, together with the cathedral, baptistery and the cemetery known as the Campo Santo (Holy Field) make up the Campo dei Miracoli (Field of Miracles) in the heart of Pisa. But what about the tiny Church of Santa Maria della Spina, one of the supreme examples of the Italian Gothic style? Pisa is full of surprises. In the Borgo Largo and Borgo Stretto districts there are ancient twisting alleys and an old market; here you will also find handsome squares and majestic palaces, such as the Palazzo dei Carovana and the Palazzo dell'Orologio.

Firenze

Firenze (Florence) is Tuscany's capital and the undisputed centre of the Renaissance. In its heart, the Piazza del Duomo, is the great Duomo (cathedral), crammed with paintings, sculpture and frescos by early masters, and the Baptistery, a strange little building in green-and-white marble with its famous and much imitated 15th-century sculpted bronze doors by Ghiberti. From the art in the Galleria degli Uffizi (Uffizi Gallery) to the numerous notable churches and palaces and the antique shops, markets and restaurants, Florence's reputation rests on the fact that it can offer everything that is best about Italy.

The Ligurian Hilltowns

The Ligurian interior is wild and mountainous. The remote townships, once the home of rural communities, are empty now but are worth visiting for the magnificent views from them. By contrast, San Remo is a lively, if old-fashioned, resort full of 19th-century villas, hotels and places to swim and to eat.

ITINERARY	
SAN REMO	▶ **Dolceacqua (22km-14m)**
DOLCEACQUA	▶ **Apricale (6km-4m)**
APRICALE	▶ **Pigna (10km-6m)**
PIGNA	▶ **Castel Vittorio (3km-2m)**
CASTEL VITTORIO	▶ **Triora (29km-18m)**
TRIORA	▶ **Ceriana (44km-27m)**
CERIANA	▶ **Taggia (19km-12m)**
TAGGIA	▶ **San Remo (11km-7m)**

2 DAYS • 144KM • 90 MILES

FOR CHILDREN

San Remo's beaches are very popular, and there are swimming pools here and at other resorts along the coast. If you go to the part of the town, by the sea, called the Lungomare Vittorio Emanuele XI, you will find the beach is protected by breakwaters, which means it is suitable for children. Small 'natural' sea-pools are created free from waves.

i Largo Nuvolini 1, San Remo

► *Take the coastal **SS1** going west from San Remo for about 12km (8 miles) to Bordighera, at which follow the signs to Dolceacqua, about 10km (6 miles) via Camporosso.*

1 Dolceacqua, Liguria
This is one of the prettiest towns of the Ligurian countryside. A wide stretch of the River Nervia divides it into two parts: the higher section, dominated by the ancient castle of the Doria family, is the most interesting. If you happen to be in Dolceacqua in August, and are spending a few nights there, look out on the castle ramparts for the ghost of an unfortunate girl murdered by a Doria baron in the Middle Ages, when she refused him his *droit de seigneur*. The castle was partially destroyed by artillery fire in the Austrian War of Succession and

The Casino in San Remo, one of Italy's most elegant resorts

Remote Apricale is typical of Liguria's semi-deserted hilltowns

is now a ruin. The Doria moved into a small palace in the main square down by the Nervia, where Napoleon visited them in 1796.

Behind the palace, narrow medieval stone-paved streets, lined by tall houses, straggle up to the castle gates. The atmosphere is all the more evocative for the fact that cars are not allowed into the narrow streets. A curious single-arched medieval bridge links the two districts of the town, the section below the castle called Borgo, the other Terra. There are interesting little churches to visit in each. But the real reason for coming to Dolceacqua is to sample the local wine called *Rossese di Dolceacqua* – a favourite of Napoleon – which can be found for sale or for tasting in any of the little shops and bars slotted into the walls of the Borgo district.

SPECIAL TO...

In Dolceacqua is a festival linked to primitive agricultural rites. On 20 January, St Sebastian's Day, a man carries in procession a tree heavily laden with communion hosts of different colours. The hosts allude to Christian sacrifice but also to bread and fruits of the earth, and the man, half hidden by the tree, becomes a 'tree man', infusing the plant with his life force.

▶ *Continue along the same unnumbered country road, along the Nervia River, branching right at Isolabona, for 6km (4 miles) to Apricale.*

2 Apricale, Liguria

You can see Apricale from miles around, lodged on the top of a hill covered in olive trees, way above the upper reaches of the Nervia River. Like most of the mountaintop settlements in the region, it was built on high as defence against attack from Saracen pirate raids in the Middle Ages. These were the scourge of Ligurian life at the time; if the Saracens struck, women and children were carried off and enslaved – or worse.

The ruined castle was another place that belonged at one time to the Doria barons. From this lair they could survey the comings and goings in the surrounding countryside. Not a great deal of it is left but its presence none the less gives Apricale, with its narrow dark alleys and streets, a dour air, all the more oppressive because much of the town is no longer inhabited. There is an interesting little Romanesque church dedicated to Sant'Antonio and there is also the Chapel of Santa Maria Alba.

▶ *Retrace your route to Isolabona on the Nervia River, then continue to Pigna.*

3 Pigna, Liguria
Pigna's name derives from the fact that, according to the locals, it resembles a pine-cone. Pigna's reputation as a picturesque town is matched by the views from the medieval gates across the valley to the little town of Castel Vittorio. In its tightly packed centre of old stone houses are the Romanesque Church of San Tommaso, the parochial Church of San Michele, and some pretty buildings in the main square in the local vernacular style. San Tommaso is in ruins, but enough architectural detail survives to be able to note that it was once an important building. San Michele is in better condition. Dating from 1450, it contains a painted wood altarpiece by Giovanni Canavesio hanging in the choir. You can see frescos, dated 1482, by the same artist, covering the walls of the Chapel of San Bernardino, not far away.

The oldest part of Pigna is also the highest. Up here is a small covered square which was used as an assembly point by the local parliament, with its old stone measures used in the sale of oil and grain.

▶ *Continue to Castel Vittorio.*

4 Castel Vittorio, Liguria
In the past this hilltown had a variety of names. It was known as Castel Dho, Castel Doy and Castelfranco, only becoming Castel Vittorio in the middle of the 19th century in deference to the ruling house of Savoy, one of whose members was Vittorio Emanuele XI, King of Sardinia and later the first king of a united Italy. Today it is more a village than a town, though it is recorded as having once possessed a fortress with four towers. None of this remains, but Castel Vittorio still merits a grinding detour in second gear to its high ramparts.

Look out for the openings under the houses where the locals kept their goats and pigs. You might well see this old tradition still being carried on. If you come to Castel Vittorio early enough in the morning you will see old women in black leading their livestock down into the terraced countryside. Chickens are shooed out into the streets and there is a pungent smell of dung and hay. In the winter, logs are dragged down the covered alleys and streets and bundled into the undercrofts for use while the countryside all around is clogged with snow.

▶ *Retrace your route back towards Pigna then continue in the opposite direction for 27km (17 miles) to Triora.*

5 Triora, Liguria
Triora is one of the most fascinating towns on the tour. It is in the upper valley of the River Argentina which it overlooks from its precipitous site, 1,240m (4,070 feet) above sea-level, on the side of Monte Trono. Like so many other remote towns in Liguria, it is practically empty, many of its ancient houses locked and deserted. However, it is an interesting place to wander through. Many streets are covered over with stone vaults, the upper limits of which have been blackened by the woodsmoke of the ages. Here and there you will see carved door lintels: some are decorated with figures of saints and there are others with past owners' initials.

Pigna's chapel of San Bernardino has frescos by Giovanni Canavesio

Triora was an important walled fortress in the Middle Ages. It once had five towers but only three of these remain. In the centre of the town is a large square. It seems almost too big for a town of this size until you realise that beneath it is a vast cistern capable of holding enough water to enable the population of the town to withstand a siege for several months.

Also in the square are two important churches: the Church of Our Lady contains one of the oldest dated paintings in the district, a panel called the *Baptism of Jesus Christ*, by Taddeo di Bartolo da Siena, 1398; the Church of San Giovanni Battista (St John the Baptist), smaller and older, has its own curiosity, a late 17th-century statue of its dedicatee, known to the locals more colloquially as San Zane. The statue is the centre-piece of an annual procession that takes place in the town in June.

Like an Italian version of Salem, Triora is renowned for the witch trials held here in the 16th century, a story that is portrayed perhaps a little too realistically in the Museo Etnografico e della Stregameroa (Museum of Enthnography and Witchcraft).

FOR HISTORY BUFFS

Between Ceriana and Taggia is the ruined town of Bussana Vecchia. This was devastated in the 19th-century earthquake which killed a large proportion of its inhabitants.
Today you can visit it and poke about the quaint ruined streets and marvel at the fact that a colony of artists and artisans have established a community here and are carefully restoring the buildings.
Look in particular at the ruins of the parish church which collapsed on that fateful Ash Wednesday in 1887.
Incongruously, there is a very good restaurant here.

BACK TO NATURE

In the hills and valleys immediately surrounding Triora, you will find dense but beautiful forests of chestnuts, pines and firs – good places for picnics. If you are lucky, walking through this remote landscape you will see wild boar (but take care, they can be very aggressive) and birds of prey including golden eagles.

► *Return to Castel Vittorio, then follow the signs to Ceriana, 44km (27 miles).*

6 Ceriana, Liguria

Ceriana was founded in Roman times by the Celiani family. It stands on a wooded promontory covered in olive, pine and chestnut trees and is full of interesting ancient monuments. Although this spot was inhabited way before the Middle Ages, Ceriana only enters the written records in the 11th century, when it is mentioned in the history of San Remo for the courageous part its population played in the struggles against Genova's supremacy.

Of special interest are the churches of SS Pietro e Paolo and of San Salvatore, both of which lie on the outskirts of the town. SS Pietro e Paolo, once called Santo Spirito, is early Romanesque, and has a lovely entrance portal. Inside, the church is divided in half by a low wall running across the nave. The front part was reserved for the men, the back for the women. San Salvatore is an immense building with outside buttresses supporting its weight. Ceriana still preserves its labyrinthine streets and alleys – often the coolest places to be at the height of the summer. Some are lined with arcades and most are still paved with flagstones.

► *The country road leads back to the coastal* ***SS1*** *(follow the signs). Then follow the signs to Taggia via Arma di Taggia, a total distance of 19km (12 miles).*

7 Taggia, Liguria

Being very close to the coast, Taggia was forever being attacked by the Saracens. In the 16th century, their attacks were so prolific that the prior of the local Dominican convent led a team of monks and townspeople in the construction of a massive fortress near the mouth of the River Argentina. This, and the defensive walls of Taggia itself, repelled the raiders so successfully that no subsequent raids were recorded there. The castle, the walls and also the courageous prior's convent all survive today. Modern Taggia is surrounded by olive groves and fields of flowers (the cultivation of which is this area's particular plus point). Right at the centre of the town are characteristic streets (some of which are arcaded), long vaulted flights of steps, little Romanesque

churches, one or two tiny baroque palaces and an assortment of carved stone portals.

Walk down the Via Soleri with its 15th- and 16th-century palaces; through the entrance portals you can glimpse ancient staircases and vaulted ceilings, most with old dappled glass in their windows.

Off the Via San Dalmazzo are two very steep streets which lead up to the castle. At the top of these you can still see a huge stone, said to have been rolled down the hill to crush invaders intent on climbing to the citadel – then, presumably, rolled back up to the top in readiness for the next hostilities.

The Convent of San Domenico (1490) lies just outside town. It has an interesting library and its church contains works by Giovanni Canavesio and the 15th-century Ligurian School painter, Ludovico Brea, who also painted the frescos in the library of the monastery. There are also various illuminated manuscripts and *incunabula* (books printed before 1501).

Castel Vittorio no longer has the fortress from which it derived its name

SCENIC ROUTES

Liguria is a very mountainous area and much of this tour is scenic. Particularly worth watching out for are:
– the approach to Triora on the road from Pigna; you come from the other side of the valley, above the Argentina River, level with Triora, then the road dives to the bottom of the valley only to rise gradually in a series of devious hairpin bends;
– around Apricale, where there are ever-changing distant views of other little hilltop villages and towns. Choose a particular view, park the car and sit and have a picnic among the wild flowers at the roadside.

RECOMMENDED WALKS

Make your way to the Sanctuary of San Zane on the summit of Mount Ceppo on the other side of the Argentina River. Park the car here, where, apart from the magnificent views, there are acres of woodlands of chestnuts, beech, alder, Turkey oak and hazelnut in which to walk.

Taggia's mid-July festival of St Mary Magdalen is centred around the life-giving powers of the lavender blossom. Two men perform a Dance of Death in which the saint is 'brought back to life' by the miraculous perfume of the blossom, thus renewing the fertility of the countryside.

[i] *Via Boselli*

► *Return to San Remo via the town of Arma di Taggia and the coastal* ***SS1***.

TOUR **8**

The Riviera di Levante

The shoreline of this part of Italy is the most popular riviera on the peninsula. It is also the most beautiful. Away from the clamour of the bigger ports, there are hidden villages. These are places where you could sit all day on a restaurant terrace, washing down seafood with sparkling local wine. Genova (Genoa), on the other hand, is Liguria's biggest city, though its old centre still has the flavour of a small seaport. It has big department stores as well as little traditional markets where the locals all know each other.

3 DAYS • 267KM • 166 MILES

ITINERARY	
GENOVA	▶ **Camogli (23km-14m)**
CAMOGLI	▶ **Portofino (14km-9m)**
PORTOFINO	▶ **Rapallo (8km-5m)**
RAPALLO	▶ **Monterosso al Mare (69km-43m)**
MONTEROSSO AL MARE	▶ **Vernazza (17km-11m)**
VERNAZZA	▶ **Portovenere (27km-17m)**
PORTOVENERE	▶ **Genova (109km-67m)**

[i] *Via Roma 11, Genova*

▶ *Take the coastal **SS1** from Genova to Recco, branching off right on the minor road to Camogli, 23km (14 miles).*

1 Camogli, Liguria
Camogli is one of a series of little fishing ports which dot the Ligurian coastline. Tall, brightly painted houses crowd on to the quay overlooking rows of fishing boats and small yachts. Space being at a premium along this steep crowded coastline, everything is tightly packed together. Streets are narrow and tortuous and some are really only flights of steps tunnelled beneath the buildings. The tangy smell of the sea is everywhere and so are the fishing nets, buoys, and the up-turned, brightly painted dinghies, while strollers are constantly tripping over the lines being repaired by old, bronzed seamen. Explore the town in the morning, then lunch on the terrace of a restaurant, of which Camogli has many.

The Museo Archeologico contains all the finds from old Camogli, beginning with the very earliest settlement on this seaside spot (Bronze Age). There are also a number of items recovered from the water, including rare Roman silver coins from about the 3rd century BC. The Museo Marinaro (Maritime Museum) concentrates on the maritime traditions of the town. It illustrates various aspects of Camogli's once-important fleet. There are journals, navigational equipment, maps, pictures, prints and votive offerings. There are also objects from Roman ships. The Garibaldi section is devoted to this famous national figure and his followers.

Perched on a rock near the port is the 12th-century Castello Dragono (Dragono Castle). It once provided for the defence of the town and now it contains the Acquario, a seawater aquarium full of indigenous fish in specially re-created 'natural' habitats.

Genova's Palazzo Reale

[i] *Via XX Settembre 33*

▶ *From Camogli, continue to rejoin the **SS1** for a short distance before branching off right to Santa Margherita Ligure, about 9km (6 miles), at which turn right on to the coastal **SS227** for Portofino.*

SPECIAL TO...

Camogli holds its annual fish festival on the second Sunday in May. Here fish are cooked in the largest frying pan in the world, then freely distributed to all and sundry.

2 Portofino, Liguria
Portofino is one of the tiniest ports on the coast. It is also one of Europe's costliest playgrounds. Previously a meeting place for sailors and coral fishermen, whose former homes have been transformed into sumptuous weekend retreats, Portofino

The charming, steep cobbled streets of Manarola run down to the sea and its delightful harbour

restaurants and bars. Another lovely Ligurian Riviera town, this one was fortified by the Genoese in the early 12th century; it has a ruined fortress and remote, windswept sanctuary to be visited. The latter is dedicated to St Peter (San Pietro), the patron saint of fishermen, and is supposed to stand on the site of an ancient temple dedicated to Venus, who may have given her name to the town itself. She, too, was the protectress of fishermen. The sanctuary is one of the most beautiful churches – more of a chapel really – along the Ligurian coastline. Built in 1277, it is constructed in black and white marble. The other coloured marble that shows through dates from a 6th-century building that once stood on the spot. From the sanctuary you can see across to the little islands of Palmaria and Tino.

Just below the sanctuary, very slippery steps lead down to the rocky shoreline and a cove associated with Lord Byron – it is thought to be the spot from which he swam across the sea to Lerici. Look in the Church of San Lorenzo and see the town's most precious relic, the Madonna Bianca (White Madonna), which is said to have floated into town in the 13th century, encased in a cedar log (also on view).

FOR CHILDREN

The little beach at San Fruttuoso (see For History Buffs, page 52) is very small and should be safe for young children to bathe from. Its scale means that toddlers cannot wander out of sight.

▶ *Trace your route to La Spezia, then follow the **SS1** to Carrodano where you join the autostrada **A12** back to Genova, a distance of 109km (67 miles).*

SPECIAL TO...

The Cinque Terre (Five Lands) are noted for wines which are among the best you will find anywhere in Italy.

Two produced here are DOC (*Denominazione d'Origine Controllata*) wines, considered to be of particular reputation and worth. The *Cinqueterre Bianco secco* is a dry white, good with seafood and liver. *Cinqueterre Sciacchetra* is rarer: it has a golden colour and varies from being sweet to almost dry. There are lots of others: look out for *Vermentino, Albarola* and *Trebbianco*.

Treasures of Tuscany

Most of the towns on this tour made a contribution to the unique artistic achievements of Toscana (Tuscany). A rich heritage of monuments survives covering a time-span ranging from the Etruscan period to the Renaissance. Pisa, one of the region's principal cities, competes with Florence as a showcase for the region's artistic accomplishments.

3 DAYS • 314KM • 194 MILES

ITINERARY	
PISA	▶ **Viareggio (21km-13m)**
VIAREGGIO	▶ **Lucca (28km-17m)**
LUCCA	▶ **Pistoia (43km-27m)**
PISTOIA	▶ **Prato (18km-11m)**
PRATO	▶ **Poggio a Caiano (10km-6m)**
POGGIO A CAIANO	▶ **Artimino (7km-4m)**
ARTIMINO	▶ **Empoli (28km-17m)**
EMPOLI	▶ **Certaldo (27km-17m)**
CERTALDO	▶ **San Gimignano (13km-8m)**
SAN GIMIGNANO	▶ **Volterra (29km-18m)**
VOLTERRA	▶ **Pisa (90km-56m)**

The skyscrapers of San Gimignano: once there were scores of towers

i Piazza del Duomo, Pisa

SPECIAL TO...

After nearly 12 years of repair work, Pisa's famous leaning tower reopened in December 2001, with strictly controlled guided tours.

▶ *From Pisa, take the* ***SS1*** *going north for about 21km (13 miles) to Viareggio.*

FOR HISTORY BUFFS

A few kilometres to the south of Viareggio is Torre del Lago Puccini, on the edge of Lago (Lake) di Massaciuccoli. Here you can visit the home, now a museum, of the composer Puccini, who wrote most of his operas here.

1 Viareggio, Toscana

This coastal resort's scale is matched by its popularity in summer. The biggest resort on the north Tuscan coast, it has two pretty promenades beside the sea, a tremendous sandy beach and the kind of night-life that people drive miles to indulge in. It has a small dock-yard dominated by a 16th-century tower and in the centre of the town is a museum housed in the old Palazzo Comunale. Lido di Camaiore, Marina di Pietrasanta and Forte dei Marmi are other popular bathing resorts along the coast; the latter, in the shadow of an 18th-century fortress, is the most fashionable.

i Piazza Mazzini

▶ *From Viareggio, take the* ***A11*** *about 28km (17 miles) to Lucca.*

SPECIAL TO...

Viareggio has a carnival which precedes Lent. Throughout the week there are costume balls, parties and performances, the whole spectacle topped by the parade of gigantic floats which generally present a satirical view of current politicians and events.

FOR CHILDREN

The beaches from Viareggio to Forte dei Marmi are popular for swimming. The beach disappears gently into the water which is shallow for some distance.

2 Lucca, Toscana

Strangely, this is one of the more under-visited Tuscan cities. Lucca is small and compact – mostly contained within massive walls – and is undoubtedly one of Italy's most beautiful cities. It has the most impressive bastions in Italy and three of its early gates are still intact. Porta San Pietro (St Peter's Gate), on the south side, has preserved its portcullis, Porta San Donato is decorated with statues of San Paolino and San Donato, while Porta Santa Maria, the oldest, is decorated with a 16th-century sculpture of the *Madonna and Child*. The city you walk – or cycle (as most people do) – through today has preserved its Roman street plan, betraying its origins. The outline of the vanished amphitheatre is now the Via dell'Anfiteatro which, lined with medieval houses, follows its original shape. The Romanesque and Gothic Duomo di San Martino (cathedral), is a masterpiece in the Pisan style. In it you can see a crucifix said to have been carved in New Testament times by the Jewish high priest Nicodemus and supposedly an accurate portrait of Christ.

Other places to see are the Museo Nazionale, housed in the Palazzo Mansi, with paintings commissioned by the Medici family, including some by Bronzino; the Museum in Palazzo Guinigi, which is still being established, and devoted to the Resistance period (1943–5); and the Museo della Cattedrale.

i *Piazzale de Verdi*

▶ *From Lucca, the **A11/E76** runs directly to Pistoia, about 43km (27 miles).*

RECOMMENDED WALKS

North of Lucca (take the SS12 going up the River Serchio) is the mountainous Garfagnano region. At Borgo a Mozzano, go left along the SS445 to Barga – a pretty town with good views, and a good starting point for walks into the Garfagnano.

3 Pistoia, Toscana

Pistoia's reputation rests on its Piazza del Duomo, the medieval square at its ancient heart. It is overshadowed by a Romanesque cathedral, a 14th-century baptistery and two magnificent Gothic palaces. In the Duomo (cathedral) you can see a clutch of paintings and sculpture by Tuscan artists, and the Dossale di San Jacopo (Altar of St James), made of solid silver. Started in 1287 and not completed until the late 15th century, it weighs over a ton. Adjacent is the Museo San Zeno with other treasures. The Gothic Palazzo del Comune, just beside the cathedral, has a huge collection of paintings, some of which you should go out of your way to see, for instance the *Madonna and Child* by Domenico Beccafumi.

Beyond the magnificent heart of this city, famous in the past for the manufacture of weaponry, are countless churches. Among the most characteristic is San Bartolomeo in Pantano, where you can see a remarkable pulpit which stands on the backs of humans and lions. The pulpit in the Church of Sant'Andrea, by Giovanni Pisano, is one of Tuscany's finest, with scenes from the Life of Christ depicted on it.

i *Piazza Duomo 4*

▶ *From Pistoia, the **A11** continues to Prato, about 13km (11 miles).*

4 Prato, Toscana

Prato is a centre for textiles and an extensive textiles collection forms part of the Municipal Museum. As such it has been important for the last 600 years, though its stature nowadays is obscured by its more illustrious neighbour, Florence. Its principal attraction is the Duomo (cathedral), a great green and white striped building. The choir is decorated with frescos by Filippo Lippi, a 15th-century monk who abducted a nun by whom he had a son called Filippino, also a great painter. If you have time to wander about Prato's quiet, deserted streets, look in at the fortress built by the Emperor Frederick II, the Castello dell'Imperatore. The

The rolling countryside between San Gimignano and Volterra

Prato's Romanesque Duomo with its green and white marble stripes

Municipal Museum and Art Gallery (closed for restoration) in the Palazzo Pretorio contains more Lippis (father and son), while the Museo dell'Opera del Duomo (Cathedral Museum), in addition to yet more Lippis, contains the fine panels carved by Donatello for the pulpit which stood at the cathedral's west front. The Museo Pittura Murale contains minor artworks from churches in and around Prato.

▶ *From Prato, follow the signs going south for about 10km (6 miles) to Poggio a Caiano.*

5 Poggio a Caiano, Toscana
Poggio a Caiano is a small rural town, no more distinguished than any other in Tuscany except that in its midst is a colossal late 15th-century Medici villa built by Guiliano da Sangallo for Lorenzo il Magnifico (the Magnificent). Its (mostly empty) rooms, open to the public, have frescoed scenes painted to the glorification of members of the Medici family by Andrea del Sarto and his assistants; incidents in Roman history are depicted as events in the lives of Cosimo il Vecchio (the Old) and Lorenzo il Magnifico. There are lovely views from a wide terrace, on a colonnade that encircles the villa – you look down into formal gardens and a park.

▶ *Follow the signs to Artimino – about 7km (4 miles) away.*

6 Artimino, Toscana
Artimino is famous for another magnificent Medici villa, this one built a little later (1594) for Ferdinand I de Medici by Bernardo Buontalenti. The villa faces Artimino village, standing a little way outside of it at the end of a long tree-lined avenue. Its position is spectacular – from its front windows you look out over the valleys and hills beyond. It now houses an archaeological museum.

Artimino, more a hamlet really, is a walled enclosure in which only a handful of families now live. Its other notable monument is a Romanesque church, a short way out of the village, on the opposite side of the ridge from the route by which you approached Artimino. It is a pleasant, short walk to this building which seems to have been constructed from the stones of a nearby Etruscan cemetery (7th-century BC), discovered only in 1970.

▶ *Follow the signs to Signa then, having crossed the Arno, continue west on the **SS67** to Montelupo Fiorentino. After that, it is only about 7km (4 miles) further to Empoli.*

7 Empoli, Toscana
The oldest part of Empoli dates from the Roman era, though today's town centre grew up around the Church of Sant'Andrea (sometimes known as the Collegiata) in the 12th century. This little church has a beautiful, typically Florentine Romanesque façade – when in Florence, compare it with the Church of San Miniato al Monte – in green and white marble. To the right of the church is the Museo Collegiata where you can see paintings by the ever prolific Filippo Lippi and other important Renaissance artists, such as Masolino and Lorenzo Monaco.

The musician, Ferruccio Busoni (1866–1924) was born in Empoli, and his birthplace is now a museum and musical study centre, with exhibits relating to music from around the turn of the 20th century.

▶ *Take the cross-country road going southwest until you run into the **SS429**. Certaldo is 22km (14 miles) further on the latter.*

two museums, one of which contains local ecclesiastical works of art, jewels and vestments. The other exhibits the finds from nearby Etruscan sites.

If you can absorb any more religious artworks, go to the Museo Civico (Civic Museum) in the Palazzo del Popolo adjacent to the cathedral. Here in the Pinacoteca (art gallery) are works by Benozzo Gozzoli and Filippino Lippi. From the piazza, the Via Matteo, littered with fine medieval buildings including the Church of San Bartolo, leads down to the Church of Sant'Agostino with frescos by Gozzoli.

SPECIAL TO...

San Gimignano has scores of wine shops all over town in which you can buy the local brew – in particular the white *Vernaccia di San Gimignano*, a wine with an ancient pedigree, drunk by Dante and Boccaccio.

8 Certaldo, Toscana

Certaldo is one of the most dramatic hilltowns in the region. Its silhouette is the kind that immediately springs to mind when you think of a medieval Tuscan hilltown – orange-red buildings, towers and castellations crammed together on the pinnacle of a defensive outcrop. It has two principal buildings: the crenellated Palazzo Pretorio and the Casa del Boccaccio. The Palazzo Pretorio's outside walls are covered in coats of arms, made of majolica or painted on to the wall surface, belonging to the local notables of long ago. Those on the façade above the entrance are still very brightly coloured. The Casa del Boccaccio was the home, until he died, of one of Italy's greatest writers, Giovanni Boccaccio (1313–75). Author of the *Decameron*, he had a profound influence on the English poet Chaucer. His home is preserved as a museum. Boccaccio was buried in the Church of Santi Michele e Jacopo – he himself wrote the inscription on his tomb.

▶ *Cross the Elsa River and follow the signs to San Gimignano, about 13km (8 miles).*

9 San Gimignano, Toscana

San Gimignano is known as the City of Towers; though only 14 remain out of an original 72, it is for these that it is remembered even today. They were built for protection by the feuding families of San Gimignano. The town is easily seen at a leisurely pace in one morning. Enter at the medieval Porta San Giovanni, the gate which opens the way to the heart of town. Here in the Piazza del Duomo is the town's largest church, the Collegiata, in which are spectacular frescos by early Sienese artists including Taddeo di Bartolo. Attached to this church are

▶ *Take the road via the hamlet of San Donato to Castel San Gimignano, then go west on the* ***SS68*** *to Volterra.*

10 Volterra, Toscana

Once a rival to Florence, Volterra was one of the most important centres in Italy for over 2,000 years. It was already an inhabited site in the 9th century BC, and was most favoured by the Etruscans for its defensive hilltop position. Their presence survives in the Museo Etrusco Guarnacci, one of the most important of all Etruscan museums, whose collection includes carved sarcophagi and a large array of funerary urns. To continue the leaps through history, you can visit the remains of the Roman occupation of the town: the ruins of an amphitheatre survive, as do those of the baths.

The rest of the town is predominantly medieval. Enclosed by fearsome walls (in

BACK TO NATURE

Parco Naturale Migliarino San Rossore lies to the west of Pisa. This large area of coastal forest – mainly stone pines – together with *macchia* (scrub) vegetation and wetlands, is excellent for birds, butterflies and reptiles.

which you can see the best preserved Etruscan gateway in Italy – the Porta dell'Arco), it has a large 15th-century castle, the Fortezza Medicea, and the oldest town hall in Tuscany, the Palazzo Minucci Solaini, which dates from 1208.

Despite its heavy Etruscan influences, Volterra has fine Roman remains

FOR HISTORY BUFFS

Rather more off the beaten track, near the village of Artimino, (or go from Empoli, whichever is more convenient) is Vinci, birthplace of Leonardo da Vinci. It has a castle and a museum dedicated to the great painter, sculptor, architect and engineer, whose birthday (15 April) is celebrated there by annual festivities.

This contains Volterra's art gallery, the Pinacoteca Comunale, whose prized possession is an *Annunciation* by Luca Signorelli. Other places to see are the 15th-century cathedral, with its fine frescos by Gozzoli, and the earlier octagonal baptistery.

SCENIC ROUTES

Particularly scenic is the steep road between Artimino and Poggio a Caiano: Artimino is on the top of the hill, Poggio a Caiano at the bottom, on a small hillock. Just before you reach Artimino, stop and look back down to Poggio a Caiano. The A12 between Viareggio and Lucca is a beautiful stretch of motorway. As you leave Lucca, look to the right at the rugged Apuan Alps.

i *Piazza dei Priori 20*

► *From Volterra, continue along the **SS68** towards the sea, then branch on to the **SS206** which goes back to Pisa.*

The Cradle of the Renaissance

The city of Firenze (Florence), the cradle of the Renaissance, was the brilliant new world which succeeded the murk of the Dark Ages. Visiting Florence first gives a foretaste of the other great monuments of art and architecture to be seen in such places as Siena and Arezzo.

3 DAYS • 456KM • 282 MILES

ITINERARY	
FIRENZE	▶ **Colle di Val d'Elsa (50km-31m)**
COLLE DI VAL D'ELSA	▶ **Siena (24km-15m)**
SIENA	▶ **Montalcino (41km-25m)**
MONTALCINO	▶ **Monte San Savino (89km-55m)**
MONTE SAN SAVINO	▶ **Cortona (42km-26m)**
CORTONA	▶ **Arezzo (34km-21m)**
AREZZO	▶ **Bibbiena (31km-19m)**
BIBBIENA	▶ **Caprese Michelangelo (35km-22m)**
CAPRESE MICHELANGELO	▶ **Poppi (41km-25m)**
POPPI	▶ **Pratovecchio (8km-5m)**
PRATOVECCHIO	▶ **Firenze (61km-38m)**

The Cradle of the Renaissance

i *Via Manzoni 16, Firenze*

▶ *From Firenze, take the* ***SS2*** *going south for about 43km (27 miles) to Poggibonsi. Two kilometres (1 mile) further on, branch right to Colle di Val d'Elsa.*

1 Colle di Val d'Elsa, Toscana

Colle di Val d'Elsa is a small town sloping down the side of a steep ridge. There are two parts to it: the Colle Alto (upper town) was always the religious and administrative centre, while the Colle Basso (lower town) was home to artisans and their workshops. While the buildings in the former are still almost uniformly Renaissance, the latter has changed with the times, and today there are factories producing excellent glassware and crystal.

In the upper town, the Castello is still walled by grim fortifications in which is a massive castellated gate called the Porta Volterrana (or Porta Nuova). Beyond, crammed in among dark stone alleyways lined with brooding medieval houses, are the Duomo (cathedral) – go inside and see the 16th-century bronze crucifix over the altar – and ancient administrative buildings, including the Palazzo dei Priori (the Civic Museum) and the Palazzo Vescovile (the Museum of Religious Art). The most interesting museum is the little Antiquarium in the Piazza del Duomo, with its collection of objects from the Casone Necropolis, in use from the late Iron Age to the last days of the Romans. Colle di Val d'Elsa was the birthplace of the architect Arnolfo di Cambio (died *c*1302), who designed the bell tower of the cathedral in Florence. His house is marked with a plaque.

i *Via Campana 18*

FOR HISTORY BUFFS

From Colle di Val d'Elsa, go to Monteriggione (about 8km/5 miles), a fortified hamlet that survives with its walls and 11 of its huge towers intact. It has a little church and sits on its own like an island in a sea of olive groves.

Siena's main square, Piazza del Campo, is one of the finest in Italy

▶ *From Colle di Val d'Elsa, the road leads in a southeastwards direction towards Siena, a distance of about 24km (15 miles).*

2 Siena, Toscana

After Florence, Siena is the most interesting city in Tuscany. Its most memorable characteristic is the Campo, a sloping semi-circular piazza dominated by the mighty Palazzo Pubblico. This late 13th-century Gothic building is topped by a 102m (335-foot) high tower, the Torre del Mangia, from the top of which there are amazing views of the surrounding countryside. Nearer at hand, it looks down over the Campo crammed with the tables of open-air cafés, and other important Sienese landmarks, including the Duomo (cathedral), sited at the city's highest point. This Romanesque building was added to over the centuries and restored in the 19th century. The most ambitious part of it is the polychrome marble façade designed in the 13th century by Giovanni Pisano. There is also a magnificent rose window in the upper façade, which was added in the next century, and the pinnacles of the gables are decorated with 19th-century mosaics. This remarkable decorative display is matched inside by black and white bands on the columns and walls. Before leaving the building look at Nicola Pisano's fantastic pulpit, 1265–8, with New Testament scenes in relief. One of Siena's greatest works of sculpture is in the Battistero San Giovanni (baptistery) under the cathedral. This is a baptismal font, the bronze relief panels of which are by some of the greatest exponents of Renaissance art – Ghiberti, Donatello and Della Quercia.

As with Florence, it would take days to explore Siena fully. Nearly any church you see is worth entering, though San Francesco, with 14th-century frescos by the Lorenzettis, is among the best. For a closer look at the original works from the cathedral go to the Museo dell'Opera Metropolitana. The Pinacoteca Nazionale (art gallery) is in the 14th-century Palazzo Buonsignori; here there

The 'icing sugar' fantasy of Siena's magnificent cathedral

is an excellent survey of Sienese art from its beginnings to the 17th century. Pre-eminent here are the works of Guido da Siena, the best of the earliest Sienese painters, and the work of Pietro and Ambrogio Lorenzetti. Others to look out for are the works of Beccafumi, born 1484, a High Renaissance artist and contemporary of Raphael, and the works of Il Sodoma, born in 1477, the leading mannerist painter in Siena. You can see other works by him in the nearby Church of Sant'Agostino.

While in Siena make sure you allow some time for wandering through the back streets, away from the main tourist spots. It is here that you will find its medieval houses, ancient alleyways and little churches. The Church of San Domenico contains the head of Saint Catherine in a golden reliquary. She, like St Francis, received the *stigmata*. Not far away is Casa di Santa Caterina (Saint Catherine's house), now a museum and a shrine to this mystic reformer, one of the co-patrons of Italy. Also near by is the medieval Fonte Branda, a fountain which was once an important source of water for Siena's inhabitants.

If you have time, go out of Siena on the SS2, south, and after about 27km (16½ miles) branch right on the SS451 to the remote Abbey of Monte Oliveto Maggiore which is still inhabited by monks. Chief among its treasures is the huge cloister with a fresco cycle depicting the life of St Benedict, partially by Luca Signorelli (born *c*1441), and by Il Sodoma. There is a lovely early 15th-century church here, and the entrance gate is decorated by fine della Robbia terracottas. The abbey is set in a striking position and is considered one of the chief attractions of the Sienese locality (you could go here on the way to the next town, Montalcino).

SPECIAL TO...

Siena hosts the Palio, a horse race between the *contrade* (districts) of the city, which takes place twice a year on 2 July and 16 August. It is preceded by parades in medieval costume and takes place in the Campo, which is always filled to the brim with spectators.

i *Piazza del Campo 56*

Taking a quiet moment from the daily chores in Cortona

▶ *From Siena, take the* ***SS2*** *south as far as Buonconvento, 27km (17 miles) then, 2km (1 mile) further on, branch on to the smaller country road that leads to Montalcino.*

3 Montalcino, Toscana
The most memorable thing about Montalcino is the number of wine shops scattered around what is a rather small town. They make sightseeing difficult because their attractions are hugely popular. Montalcino is the home of *Brunello di Montalcino* and perhaps the best place to taste this wine is in the café in the old Rocca, the 14th-century castle at the top of the town.

Montalcino is a hilltown surrounded by medieval walls. Its precipitous streets straggle up to a lovely medieval Palazzo Comunale in the Piazza del Popolo, while higher up is the Romanesque Church of Sant'Agostino with a good rose window in its façade. There are two collections of Sienese paintings in the town, one in the Museo Civico (Civic Museum), the other in the Museo Diocesano (Diocesan Museum).

Montalcino is a good place from which to visit a collection of other lovely, typically Tuscan towns and villages. It should take an extra afternoon or morning. One of these, Castelnuovo dell'Abate, just 8km (5 miles) to the south, has the lovely 12th-century Benedictine Abbazia di Sant'Antimo which is supposed to have been founded by Charlemagne. Just to the north of Montalcino, also about 8km (5 miles), is the little town of Pienza, famous for having been the birthplace of one of the greatest popes of the early Renaissance, Pius II (Aeneas Sylvius Piccolomini). During the Pope's lifetime it became something of a centre for art. Pius' family home, the Palazzo Piccolomini was designed by Bernardo Rossellino in 1460, one of the great Renaissance architects. It now houses a museum and a superb library.

To the east of Montalcino is San Quirico d'Orcia, another well preserved town with a good Romanesque church.

i Costa del Municipio 8

▶ *Return to the* ***SS2****, turn right and continue southeast for about 14km (9 miles) on this road to San Quirico d'Orcia. From here, take the* ***SS146*** *to Pienza and Montepulciano and then follow the signs to the* ***A1*** *via the* ***SS326*** *and the* ***SS327****. Go north on the* ***A1*** *to the exit for Monte San Savino.*

4 Monte San Savino, Toscana
Monte San Savino is another of Tuscany's most characteristic hilltowns. It is a quiet, pretty place that comes alive early in the morning, the shopping hours, and late in the afternoon when everyone takes their evening stroll. The most inter-

esting things to see here are the monuments that were either designed or restructured by Andrea Cantucci, a sculptor who was born here in 1496, and subsequently nicknamed Sansovino. His is the Loggia dei Mercanti in the Corso Sangallo and he was responsible for altering the 14th-century Church of Sant'Agostino. Some of his sculptural works can be seen in Santa Chiara. It was Antonio da Sangallo the elder, an architect who built some of the masterpieces of Renaissance architecture, who designed the Palazzo Comunale early in the 16th century. The museum, housed in a 14th-century castle, has a particularly good collection of ceramics.

Not far from Monte San Savino (take the SS73), is the little walled village of Gargonza. Turned by its owners into a hotel, the castle was once frequented by Dante and is an interesting and beautiful spot to stay. It has a little church dedicated to the saints Tiburzio and Susanna, and the buildings behind the north wall are dominated by a medieval tower.

▶ *Go back down the **A1** for 14km (9 miles) as far as Val di Chiana, then follow the signs via Foiano di Chiana and Monsigliolo to Cortona.*

RECOMMENDED WALKS

A lovely walk is one that takes in the estate surrounding the castle of Gargonza, just outside Monte San Savino. It is even better if you stay in the castle hotel here. Routes are planned and laid out on paths through the woods and gardens and there are good views out over the plain to Monte San Savino.

5 Cortona, Toscana

Cortona, one of the oldest towns in Tuscany, is also one of the highest. It featured in the film *Under the Tuscan Sun*. There is a lot to see and do here but be prepared for your calf muscles to bear the brunt of your sightseeing. Cortona is perched on the side of Monte Egidio and all the streets, like the medieval Via del Gesù with its overhanging houses, and the steps leading to and from the central piazza, are immensely steep. The Duomo (cathedral), poised above a steep drop to the valley below, is perhaps the least interesting building in this medieval town. Originally Romanesque, it underwent later alterations that left it leagues behind the 13th-century Church of Sant'Agostino, and the 14th-century San Niccolò, which contains a *Deposition* by Luca Signorelli. More works by Signorelli, who was born in Cortona, are in the Museo Diocesano (Diocesan Museum) alongside other precious Renaissance paintings, most notably those by Fra Angelico and Pietro Lorenzetti. Relics of the Etruscans can be seen in the museum in the Palazzo Casali, while the Etruscan walls, nearly obliterated by the Roman and medieval ones, can be seen around the Porta Colonia (the Colonia Gate).

At the top of the town is the forbidding Fortezza Medicea, not far from the Basilica di Santa Margherita da Cortona, which contains a fine Gothic tomb. Cortona is a lovely place to be in the late afternoon when the townsfolk emerge after their siesta. They loiter in the main square eating ice-creams and gossiping, or else indulge in the universal Italian pastime – *la passeggiata*. This is the leisurely evening stroll backwards and forwards up the piazza, down the other side, then along one of the side streets and back again. Overlooked by ancient buildings, this scene can not have changed much over the centuries.

[i] *Via Nazionale 42*

▶ *From Cortona, return to the SS71, west of Cortona, which leads to Arezzo, about 29km (18 miles) further on.*

SCENIC ROUTES

The most scenic parts of the route are:
– the road from Montalcino to Montepulciano. This is the classic Tuscany that attracts visitors, richly agricultural with wheatfields, vineyards and distant hill villages and castles;
– the SS2 from Siena to Buonconvento, typical Chianti landscape with trails of cypresses following each other in a line up to the crest of a hill. Look out for the characteristic Tuscan farmhouses;
– the views from Cortona to the Lake of Trasimeno. These are among the highest and most far-reaching in this part of the region. Look first at the Renaissance landscapes in the art galleries, then look at the views from Cortona. The perspectives, the detail and colours are the same;
– the views from Stia across the Casentino to Poppi and Caprese Michelángelo. In this unspoilt landscape you can see each of these towns – over a distance of about 40km (25 miles).

6 Arezzo, Toscana

Arezzo, birthplace of the poet Petrarch, is another Tuscan city with a medieval air about it. Piazza Grande is its most magnificent square, lined with an assortment of medieval houses, some of which are attached to castellated towers. The piazza slopes downwards from Giorgio Vasari's 16th-century loggia – built in the style of an ancient Greek stoa or portico – of the Palazzo delle Logge on the right of which is the Palazzo della Fraternità dei Laici topped by a clock tower. Just below this building, also on the right, is the apse of the Romanesque Church of Santa Maria della Pieve. The entrance to this church is at the other side, by way of a most extraordinary façade consisting of a three-tiered loggia. Inside is Pietro Lorenzetti's famous polyptych (1320) of the *Madonna and Saints*. The Gothic Duomo is further up the hill past the Palazzo Pretorio, whose façade is decked with the coats of arms of imperial and Florentine governors of the city. The best things about the cathedral, begun in 1277, are the 16th-century stained glass, by the Frenchman Guillaume de Marcillat, and the tomb of Bishop Guido Tarlati, who died in 1327, an enormous sculpted monument.

Above all, do not miss the Church of San Francesco which contains one of the finest fresco cycles to have emerged from the Renaissance. The work of the great Piero della Francesca, it depicts the *Legend of the Cross*, and is generally accepted as one of the world's greatest paintings. Piero, of the Florentine school of painting, produced his masterpiece between 1452 and 1466, but its drama, colour and light speak across the centuries.

Other places to visit are the Casa del Vasari, the house of the painter and early art critic Giorgio Vasari (1511–74) which is now a museum; the nearby Museo Statale d'Arte Medioevale e Moderna, which houses a collection of works by local artists that spans five centuries; the remains of a Roman amphitheatre down near the station; and the Museo Archeologico next door, containing the relics of the city's more ancient past.

SPECIAL TO...

In Arezzo there is an antiques fair on the first Sunday of every month. One of the best in Italy, it has items ranging from statues to old brass beds. Arezzo also has an annual medieval festival called the Giostra del Saracino (the Joust of the Saracen). It takes place on the first Sunday in September, in Piazza Grande with the contestants dressed in 14th-century costume.

i *Piazza della Repubblica*

▶ *From Arezzo, take the* ***SS71*** *going north to Bibbiena for 31km (19 miles).*

7 Bibbiena, Toscana

Bibbiena is in the heart of the Casentino area of Tuscany, the lovely wooded valley in which the River Arno rises. It is the biggest town in the area, a typical hilltown where the pace of life is slow and easy. Here is the 15th-century Church of San Lorenzo which contains terracottas attributed to the school of della Robbia.

The 12th-century Church of SS Ippolito e Donato has a triptych painted by Bicci di Lorenzo (1435), as well as the remains of some late medieval frescos. Most interesting of all is the 16th-century Palazzo Dovizi, with a dramatic façade lining the main street in the centre of town. This was the home of Cardinal Bibbiena (1470–1520), friend of the painter Raphael.

From Bibbiena (take the SS208) it is easy to get to the Abbey of La Verna, high above the town, the site of which was given to St Francis in 1213; it was here that he received the *stigmata* (Christ's wounds).

▶ *Take the* ***SS208*** *to Chiusi della Verna, from where follow signs to Caprese Michelangelo, a total of 35km (22 miles).*

BACK TO NATURE

A wide variety of wild orchids grace the countryside of Tuscany from March until May. Seemingly dry and barren areas are often surprisingly good, especially if the soil is undisturbed and the bedrock is limestone. Look for numerous members of the bee orchid family – the flowers resemble small, furry insects – as well as tongue orchids, lizard orchids and giant orchids.

8 Caprese Michelangelo, Toscana

This tiny hamlet, birthplace of Michelangelo, occupies a rock site with the source of the Tevere (Tiber) River that runs through Rome, just to the east, and the upper reaches of the Arno River to the west. Everything there is to see here has something to do with Michelagniolo di Lodovico Buonarroti – Michelangelo – perhaps the greatest artist that Italy ever produced. You can

Pieve di Romena church near Pratovecchio, a Romanesque gem

visit his birthplace among the chestnut trees; the Casa del Podestà, where his father was the Florentine governor, is now a museum. There are also the remains of a castle and the little Chapel of San Giovanni Battista where Michelangelo is said to have been baptised.

▶ *From Caprese Michelangelo, return to Bibbiena. Turn right on the* ***SS70****, which leads after 6km (4 miles) to the turning for Poppi.*

9 Poppi, Toscana
You can see Poppi from miles around. It stands high above the plain of Campaldino, where an important battle was fought in 1289 (at which the poet Dante was present). Dante's bust faces the piazza in front of the Palazzo Pretorio which dominates the town and the countryside. This was once home to the Guidi counts who, in the Middle Ages, dominated the entire Casentino hill region. Today it houses some frescos from the 15th century and a chapel decorated a century earlier. Poppi is very pretty indeed. Its main street is arcaded and lined with medieval houses. Nothing stirs here, not even the cats lying in the sun when you walk past.

From Poppi cross over to the Abbey of Camaldoli, about 8km (5 miles) to the north. Its buildings date mostly from the 17th and 18th centuries – visit the monks' old pharmacy, and also the little baroque church about 2.5km (1½ miles) above the abbey. Here, housed in cells, lived (and still live) hermit monks in complete isolation.

i *Piazza Amerighi*

▶ *From Poppi, return to and turn left on to the* ***SS70****. Turn right within 2km (1 mile) on to the* ***SS310*** *to Pratovecchio, a further 6km (4 miles).*

10 Pratovecchio, Toscana
Pratovecchio, like other places in the area, is associated with the poet Dante. It serves as a base from which to visit places of interest in the immediate vicinity. For example, a short way out of town is Stia, from whose lofty position you can see right over Casentino to Poppi and Caprese Michelangelo. In the centre of this village, and at its highest point, are the remains of a castle which also belonged to the Guidi counts and in which Dante was imprisoned for a while.

Near by, and just above Pratovecchio, is the Castello di Romena, which has a museum of archaeology and weapons, and a country church, the Pieve di Romena, one of the most beautiful Romanesque buildings in the region. Ask for the key at the neighbouring farmhouse, go inside, and examine the carvings on the columns lining the nave.

Enjoying a quiet moment in Montalcino's Piazza del Popolo

▶ *From Pratovecchio continue north on the* ***SS310****. After 2km (1 mile), branch left on to, and follow, the* ***SS556*** *via Stia until it cuts the* ***SS67*** *which leads back into Firenze.*

FOR CHILDREN

Show the children true Tuscan cooking. Take them to a barbecue Tuscan style (by doing so you are following the real tradition of Tuscan cuisine) and eat juicy wild boar sausages or a steak *alla Fiorentina* grilled on the open flame. The latter is a steak on the bone with a drop of olive oil added once it is cooked. Fish, too, is delicious. Follow the whole lot with the best ice-cream in Italy – from Vivoli's in Florence.

UMBRIA & THE MARCHES

Even though it is so close to Tuscany, Umbria is remarkably under-visited. It is green and fertile, a land of saints and artists, a gentle region whose towns have on the whole been left alone by the march of progress. The Marches (so called because they were a border province of the Holy Roman Empire), lying just to the east and bordering the Adriatic Sea, are a lesser version of the same thing. But whereas Umbria has been opened up by the great central valley running through its midst from Città di Castello to Todi, the hilly landscape of The Marches has been miraculously preserved from development, since a large portion of its terrain is difficult to negotiate. Access to The Marches is easier by way of the coastal autostrada; as a result, few visitors to the region venture beyond the easily reached coastal resorts to explore the ancient cities further inland.

It is the Apennines, the mountainous backbone of Italy, that are responsible for the region's varied scenery. They continue their southward march from Firenze towards Perugia in Umbria, becoming increasingly more rugged as they approach The Marches. But by the time they reach the coast the landscape has transformed itself entirely into a gently rolling coastal belt which falls away to the sandy beaches of the Adriatic.

Most of the Umbrian towns you will visit have, hidden in the gloom of a church or palace, a fresco of a dewy-eyed Madonna or a scene in the life of a local saint, on a wall or inside a niche. Umbria was hit badly by the earthquake of 1998, and while many country villages were damaged, restoration is currently being undertaken very quickly. Churches are reopening one by one; this is the most sophisticated task of restoration ever undertaken in Italy.

But if Umbria is under-visited, then The Marches region is Italy's best kept secret. Quiet, small towns, packed with magnificent art and architecture, punctuate the mountain valleys, just waiting to be discovered by the more adventurous traveller. And in the north, in Urbino, the region can boast a city on a par for beauty and interest with such towns as Lucca or Siena in Tuscany.

Left: sunflowers clothe the Umbrian landscape

Perugia

Perugia, capital of Umbria, is a treasure-house of art, centre for industry and commerce, medieval hilltown, and home of two universities. As Umbria's major city – and surrounded by motorways – its old character could have been ruined, but this is not so. Indeed, the dominant face that it presents to the world is its medieval one. Perugia was a flourishing commercial centre in the Middle Ages, and its major buildings, the Duomo, the Palazzo dei Priori and the Corso Vannucci lined with fortified palaces (now shops and cafés), date from this period or shortly after. The narrow cavernous back streets contribute to this old-world character. In addition, Perugia has the region's finest paintings in the Galleria Nazionale dell'Umbria (National Gallery of Umbria) in the Palazzo dei Priori.

Ancona

Ancona, the capital of The Marches region, was the ancient Greeks' northernmost Adriatic settlement. Its oldest quarters sit on a promontory which juts out into the Adriatic, with the half-moon of the harbour below. Although much of it was destroyed during World War II, with further damage caused by an earthquake and landslide in 1972, a large-scale restoration effort has meant that there is once again plenty to see and do here. There are one or two churches with fine Romanesque façades (Santa Maria della Piazza is one, with entertaining carvings), and the cathedral was built on the site of a very much more ancient temple of Venus.

Urbino

Urbino is dramatically placed overlooking the Metauro River. It is a perfect – and rare – example of a Renaissance city that has survived intact, complete with surrounding walls. Dominating all is the huge Palazzo Ducale (Ducal Palace) that seems, even though it was never finished, almost like a city within a city. Started in 1444, this was once home to the Montefeltro dukes of Urbino whose cultured court was the envy of the rulers of many other Italian city-states during the Renaissance. At the time, it contained an enviable art collection and, although the Montefeltro family no longer exists, a part of the collection does and you can see what survives in the palace, now, in part, an art gallery – Galleria Nazionale delle Marche. Raphael, one of the greatest artists of the later Renaissance, was born in Urbino in 1483, and you can visit his home. A quiet walk around the town, preferably after dark, through the cobbled lanes lined with ancient houses, is an evocative experience, transporting you back in time very nearly to the period of the Montefeltro family.

The little church of Santa Maria Maggiore once served as Assisi's cathedral

TOUR
11

The Green Heart of Italy

Umbria is best observed from the ramparts of the ancient hill-towns crammed into its central valley. Its hills and lower slopes are covered with olive groves, pines and grapevines and the towns in this magical region are among the most evocative in Italy. Perugia is an imposing city with a grand central square, Gothic cathedral and magnificent 13th-century fountain.

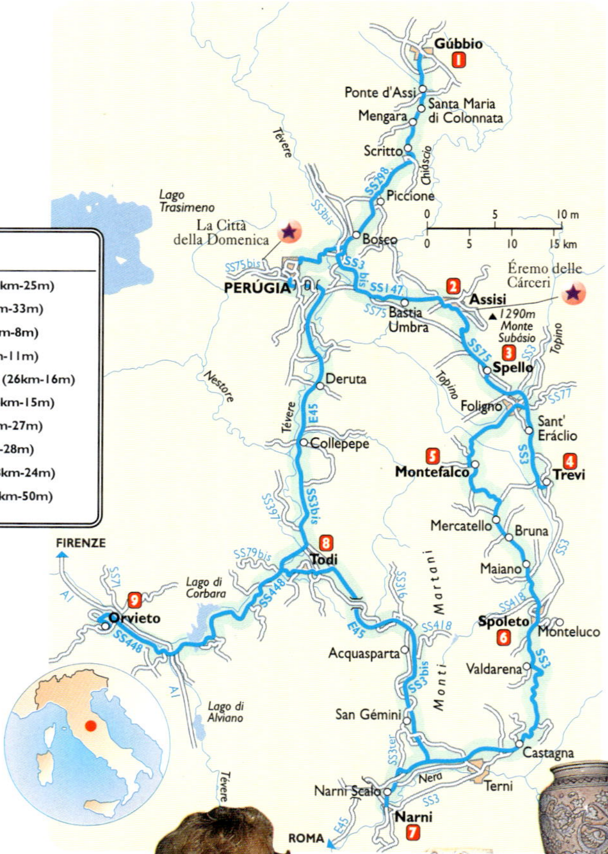

ITINERARY	
PERUGIA	▶ **Gubbio (40km-25m)**
GUBBIO	▶ **Assisi (53km-33m)**
ASSISI	▶ **Spello (13km-8m)**
SPELLO	▶ **Trevi (18km-11m)**
TREVI	▶ **Montefalco (26km-16m)**
MONTEFALCO	▶ **Spoleto (24km-15m)**
SPOLETO	▶ **Narni (43km-27m)**
NARNI	▶ **Todi (45km-28m)**
TODI	▶ **Orvieto (38km-24m)**
ORVIETO	▶ **Perugia (81km-50m)**

3 DAYS • 381KM • 237 MILES

[i] Piazza IV Novembre 3, Perugia

FOR CHILDREN

La Città della Domenica is a Disney-style playground 8km (5 miles) west of Perugia, just off the SS75bis. The 200-hectare (500-acre) park has a zoo, archaeological zone, games rooms, bumper cars and a variety of buildings based on fairy-tale themes, such as 'Snow White's House'.

▶ *Take the **SS298** going north-east from Perugia to Gubbio.*

1 Gubbio, Umbria
Beautifully situated at the mouth of a gorge and rising up the slopes of Mont'Ingino, Gubbio has managed to preserve much of its medieval appearance. In the Middle Ages it was one of the fiercest and most warlike places in Umbria, and the 14th-century Palazzo dei Consoli, a massive Gothic battlemented structure of dressed stone, in Piazza della Signoria, still dominates the town. It now houses a museum and art gallery. Among its many exhibits are the famous *Tavole Eugubine* (Gubbio Tablets), seven 2nd- to 1st-century BC bronze plaques with inscriptions in Umbrian and Latin, which are the most important evidence extant of the Umbrian language. The Palazzo Ducale, built in 1476 for Federico da

Steep winding streets in the hilltop town of Spello

Montefeltro, Duke of Urbino, by Luciano Laurano, has a delightful Renaissance courtyard and charming rooms with unusual architectural fashions, carved doors and 16th-century fireplaces.

As you wander through the town look out for the Porte del Morto (Doors of Death or Deadman's Gates). Many houses still have two doorways. The lower one, according to tradition, was where coffins were removed from the house after death. In the lower part of the town is the Gothic Church of San Francesco, whose simple façade is adorned with a great

Fine frescos in Todi's Romanesque and Gothic Duomo, Piazza del Popolo

rose window, creating a striking effect. Inside is a notable fresco depicting the *Life of the Virgin*, painted by Ottaviano Nelli in the early 1400s.

Gubbio's 1st-century AD Roman theatre is one of the largest surviving of its kind. It is in an excellent state of preservation, and hosts performances in the summer.

SPECIAL TO...

In Gubbio, the Corsa dei Ceri (Feast of Candles), takes place every year on 15 May and begins with a picturesque procession through the streets to the Abbey of Sant'Ubaldo on Mont'Ingino, just outside the town. The festival is centred round a dramatic race in which three teams of sturdy men each carry a huge, heavy, candle-shaped pillar up the hill to the abbey in honour of St Ubaldo, whose mortal remains are preserved in an urn beneath the main altar. Legend has it that the venerable saint intervened in a battle against Perugia, giving the victory to the outnumbered Gubbians. If you don't care to walk, the abbey can be reached by car or funicular.

i Piazza Oderisi 6

▶ *Return towards Perugia on the* ***SS298****. Just before Perugia turn south on the* ***SS3bis****, then on to the* ***SS75*** *eastwards for a short distance before taking the* ***SS147*** *to Assisi.*

2 Assisi, Umbria

Nestling on the slopes of Monte Subasio, Assisi has hardly changed since St Francis, born here in 1182, the son of a wealthy merchant, walked its streets, and its ancient character has helped to preserve his cult. Little, winding, stone-paved streets, lined with old houses, lead from the base of the town to the various monuments. Almost everything worth seeing is in some way associated with the saint. Art-lovers should head for the Basilica di San Francesco, which consists of two fine 13th-century churches, one on top of the other. Here there are frescos celebrating the life of St Francis. Most important is the series of 28 by Giotto, the first major artist of the early Renaissance, in the basilica's upper church. The rest of the basilica is equally interesting, and includes exquisite scenes from the life of St Martin by the Sienese painter Simone Martini (1322) in the Chapel of St Martin. There are a number of relics belonging to the saint, among them his sandals and his patched grey cassock.

You cannot avoid the religious life in Assisi: the streets are full of nuns and monks. Other churches well worth visiting include the 13th-century Santa Chiara which enshrines St Clare's body. Even though she died nearly 750 years ago, her intact body, blackened by time, lies open to view in the crypt. One of St Francis' earliest and most enthusiastic supporters, St Clare founded the order of the Poor Clares.

It is well worth the stiff walk up Via San Francesco to the Piazza del Comune. Here you can see the remains of the Temple of Minerva, a good example of Roman architecture dating from the 1st century AD and now the Church of Santa Maria della Minerva. There are also several fine medieval buildings: the Palazzo del Capitano del Popolo, and the Torre and Palazzo del Comune, the latter containing the Pinacoteca Civica (Civic Picture Gallery).

Work continues on the transformation of the Rocca Maggiore from 14th-century fortress into a splendid art gallery, and though most of it is closed, it is worth heading up there for the panoramic views.

i Piazza del Comune 27

▶ *Take the road southeast from Assisi to the **SS75**, which runs for 3km (2 miles) before the turning to Spello, 13km (8 miles) from Assisi.*

> **FOR HISTORY BUFFS**
>
> For those interested in the life of St Francis, and who have the stamina, a walk up Monte Subasio, offering magnificent panoramas of the surrounding countryside, brings you to the Eremo delle Carceri, the saint's favourite retreat. The hermitage, cut out of the rock, is set in the dense woodland covering the mountain, 5km (3 miles) behind Assisi. Most of the miracles recounted in St Francis' *Fioretti* ('Little Flowers') took place in these woods.

3 Spello, Umbria

Clinging to the southern slopes of Monte Subasio, Spello has changed little since the Middle Ages. History lies all around you here, as you will find if you pick your way through its streets: if not Roman, then it is bound to be medieval or, at the very latest, Renaissance. The town was under the influence of the Romans for much of its history. Look for the Porta Venere, a fine old Roman gateway which survives in the town's walls. Near the station you will find another, the Porta Consolare, with three statues from the Roman theatre whose ruins can be seen just before entering the town.

Steep winding streets lead from it and up into the town, past higgledy-piggledy medieval shops and houses to the centre and the Church of Santa Maria Maggiore. The church's magnificent Cappella Baglioni (Baglioni Chapel) contains frescos (1501) by Pinturicchio, which tell the life of the Virgin in a fresh and lively way. An important Renaissance artist, whose work can be seen in the Sistine Chapel in the Vatican, Pinturicchio was assistant to Perugino.

Villa Fidelia is a fine 17th-century mansion in formal gardens, and it is home to the Straka-Coppa Collection of paintings and furniture.

▶ *Rejoin the **SS75** heading southwest and turn right on to the **SS3** round Foligno to Trevi.*

4 Trevi, Umbria

Magnificently situated on the slopes of a steep hill,

Ancient Narni, on Umbria's border, was once a fortress-city

dominating the Spoletino plain, Trevi is set so high up that from the approach road you cannot see it from the car windows. It is a lovely, undiscovered place with pavements that are speckled with mosaic-like arrangements of cobbles, and a maze of winding streets and blind alleys is contained within two sets of medieval walls.

The former convent of San Francesco is the location of the town's Pinacoteca (art gallery), and it contains a mixture of Renaissance paintings by Pinturicchio and Lo Spagna, Roman remains, sculptures and ceramics. You can see Lo Spagna's fresco of the *Life of St Francis* (1512) in the Church of San Martino in Via Augusto Ciufelli on the edge of town. This is thought to be his best painting and it is particularly fascinating to see the contemporary view of Assisi in its background.

It is contemporary art that features in the Trevi Flash Art Museum, which opened in 1994. Its collection includes works by international artists, and temporary exhibitions are also staged.

A modern sample of Gubbio's centuries-old pottery industry

▶ *Return to Foligno via the **SS3**, then follow signs to Montefalco.*

5 Montefalco, Umbria

The pretty little walled hilltown of Montefalco – which means 'Falcon's Mount' – once boasted more saints than any other town in the region, earning itself the title of 'a little strip of heaven fallen to earth'. With a population of only 6,000, this was a remarkable achievement!

The Church of San Francesco, founded in 1336, contains 15th-century frescos by Benozzo Gozzoli, as well as work by other Umbrian painters. These frescos are considered so important that the church has been deconsecrated and the building has become a museum.

Other churches to see are the Gothic Church of Sant'Agostino with its fine selection of Renaissance frescos by local artists, and the baroque Church of Santa Chiara di Montefalco. Here you can see the crumbling remains of Santa Chiara's heart. Montefalco is a tranquil, peaceful place, often called the 'Balcony of Italy'; you should take time to sit in one of its cafés and sample the famed *Sagrantino* wine or take in the delightful views of the surrounding countryside.

▶ *Head across country, via Mercatello and Bruna, to Spoleto.*

6 Spoleto, Umbria

Spoleto, shadowed by its 14th-century Rocca (castle), is a very old city, rich in evidence of a history that began centuries before the Roman occupation. It has survived sieges, earthquakes, plagues, a period of misrule by the notorious Lucrezia Borgia and World War II bombing. The Duomo (cathedral), built in 1067 but restored in the 12th century, with its splendid doorway and Renaissance porch surrounded with mosaics, is without doubt the most beautiful in Umbria, though the churches of San Gregorio Maggiore, Sant'Eufemia and San Pietro come close. Be sure to visit them all, particularly the latter (just out of town), with its extremely early relief sculptures.

Among Spoleto's many Roman ruins is a partially restored theatre in the vicinity of Piazza della Libertà, which is still used for concerts, and the 1st-century AD Arch of Drusus, in an excellent state of preservation. The imposing Ponte delle Torri (Bridge of the Towers) was erected in the 13th century as an aqueduct over a river gorge (pedestrians only now), and links the town with neighbouring Monteluco. Built of stone, with 10 arches, it is 230m (755 feet) long and 81m (265 feet) high and was probably constructed on the foundations of an earlier Roman aqueduct.

Spoleto can get very busy at peak times, so it is best to plan your visit to avoid these. It is one of the liveliest towns in the region, helped by the annual Festival dei Due Mondi (Festival of the Two Worlds) that takes place here. The festival, in June and July, presents the latest trends in art, music,

The Duomo in Orvieto: detail from the much-admired carved façade

theatre, painting and sculpture against the magnificent setting of the ancient town.

i Piazza della Libertà 7

RECOMMENDED WALKS

The countryside round Spoleto is particularly picturesque and quite accessible by foot. For spectacular views follow the road at the eastern end of the Ponte delle Torri for 1km (half a mile) to the Church of San Pietro (one of the finest achievements of Umbrian architecture and sculpture). A little further afield, for those who have the stamina, another road from the east end of the Ponte delle Torri winds its way up the hillside for 6km (3½ miles). Here, at the top of thickly wooded Monteluco, you will find a monastery founded by St Francis, with enchanting views of the valley.

► *Take the **SS3** south. Bypass Terni, and head for Narni, entering on the **SS3ter**, 43km (27 miles).*

7 Narni, Umbria

Narni, crammed on its hilltop, is so constricted that it has hardly expanded since Roman times. This solid, stone-built town has an interesting, though ruined, 14th-century Rocca (castle), with fine views in most directions, and the odd-looking Palazzo del Podestà, which was created by joining three fortified tower houses together. Palazzo Vescovile houses the local art gallery whose greatest treasure is a *Coronation of the Virgin* by the 15th-century master Ghirlandaio. See the fine inlaid choir stalls and early marble screen in the Duomo (cathedral), which, with the Podestà Palace, provides a splendid backdrop to the Corso dell'Anello, a spectacular costumed pageant enacted each May, when horsemen representing the town's rival quarters joust for a coveted prize.

Just below Narni, on the line of the ancient Via Flaminia, are the ruins of the Roman Ponte d'Augusto (Bridge of Augustus) which was originally 120m (400 feet) long and carried the road almost 30m (100 feet) up over the River Nera.

► *From Narni, head back towards Terni, turning north on **SS3bis** to Todi, about 45km (28 miles).*

SCENIC ROUTES

Most of the route along this tour of Umbria offers an outstanding range of scenery, but there are certain stretches of road where the views are particularly spectacular.
Perugia to Gubbio – along the SS298 between Piccione and Santa Maria di Colonnata;
Gubbio to Assisi – the last 13km (8 miles) of the SS147 before Assisi;
the roads in and around Montefalco;
Todi to Orvieto – the SS448 round the south shore of Lake Corbara and in to Orvieto;
Orvieto to Perugia – the SS3bis from Deruta to Perugia.

8 Todi, Umbria

Todi occupies a triangular site, still partly surrounded by its rings of Etruscan, Roman and medieval walls, on a ridge above the Tevere (Tiber) valley. The Piazza del Popolo, at the centre of town, is the kind of place where you could sit all day in the sun at one of the cafés and do nothing but watch the world pass by. On one side of the piazza is the Romanesque Duomo (cathedral), on the site of a former Roman temple to Apollo, while the remaining sides are bounded by a variety of other medieval buildings, in particular the 14th-century Palazzo del Capitano. The sleepy charm of this place is enlivened early in the evening when the residents pour into the piazza for the daily stroll and a chat: then it seems like a drawing room with a party in progress.

You should not leave Todi without visiting Santa Maria della Consolazione, inspired by Bramante's plan for St Peter's in Rome. This domed church on the plan of a Greek cross, is much admired as one of the finest creations of Renaissance architecture. Started in 1508, it took over 100 years to complete.

i Piazza Umberto I

▶ *Leave Todi on the* ***SS448****, and head southwest, around Lago di Corbara, to Orvieto.*

9 Orvieto, Umbria

Orvieto's commanding position on a great square rock makes it an amazing sight, visible from miles around. An ideal site for a fort, it was first settled by the Etruscans (who called it Volsinii), but they could not withstand the might of the rising new power, and eventually Orvieto fell to Rome. It is a dark, brooding town, dominated by its glorious Gothic-style Duomo (cathedral), which was started in the late 1200s, supposedly to the designs of Arnolfi di Cambio, famed for his Duomo and Palazzo Vecchio in Florence. It was built in alternate courses of black basalt and greyish-yellow limestone, and decorated by the finest artists of the day, to commemorate the Miracle of Bolsena (when the Host started to bleed during a celebration of Mass in the town of Bolsena). The façade, adorned with elaborate sculptures and coloured mosaics, was designed by Lorenzo Maitani of Siena. To appreciate fully, you should view it in bright sunlight, when the effect is quite stunning. Inside, magnificent frescos in the lovely Cappella della Madonna de San Brigio are largely the work of Fra Angelico and, later, Luca Signorelli. The town abounds in interesting monuments: the 11th-century Palazzo Vescovile, an old papal residence; the 12th-century Palazzo del Capitano del Popolo; and the churches of San Domenico, San Lorenzo, Sant'Andrea and San Giovenale are among the best buildings.

Orvieto is famous for its wine, particularly the whites. Signorelli, when painting the Duomo, is said to have asked that part of his contract be paid in wine, and the rock beneath the city is honeycombed with caves used to ferment the grapes for the Orvieto vintages.

i Piazza del Duomo 24

▶ *Take the* ***SS448*** *back towards Todi, then turn left on to the* ***SS3bis*** *to Perugia.*

FOR HISTORY BUFFS

On the east side of Orvieto, you can descend into Pozzo di San Patrizio (St Patrick's Well), a vast cylinder cut through the rock on which Orvieto stands. Built in the 16th century, this 62m (200-foot) deep well was commissioned to ensure the town's water supply in times of siege. It was constructed with two separate spiral staircases winding around the shaft – one for the descent and the other for the ascent of the donkeys which were sent down to bring the water up to the surface. Near by are the remains of an Etruscan temple, and there is an exhibition of Etruscan artefacts unearthed from tombs in the area in the Museum of Archaeology in the town.

BACK TO NATURE

While you are travelling in Umbria you will undoubtedly notice the kind of countryside which naturalists call *macchia* (*maquis*). This is the characteristic Mediterranean habitat of evergreen trees with a shrubby understorey. As well as its distinctive wild flowers, including several species of orchid and the much more easily spotted, but no less pretty, rock-roses, this habitat contains such creatures as praying mantids, wall lizards and green lizards (look for them basking in the morning sunshine) and lots of snakes (don't worry, they are likely to see you a long time before you see them and beat a quiet retreat!). You probably will not see, but will almost certainly hear, Scop's owls. Their call, delivered for most of the night – usually from trees – is a quite uncanny and unnatural sound, likened by some to sonar bleeps.

View over the heart of Perugia, capital of Umbria

TOUR **12**

Italy's Best Kept Secret

It takes hours to get through the Marches region of central Italy on the little country roads but there are breathtaking views. Ancona is the biggest port in the region, running along a natural promontory in the shadow of Monte Conero. Severely damaged by World War II bombs and in a later earthquake, its charms are well hidden.

3/4 DAYS • 406KM • 252 MILES

ITINERARY	
ANCONA	▶ **Portonovo (11km-7m)**
PORTONOVO	▶ **Sirolo (10km-6m)**
SIROLO	▶ **Loreto (13km-8m)**
LORETO	▶ **Macerata (29km-18m)**
MACERATA	▶ **Fermo (49km-30m)**
FERMO	▶ **Ascoli Piceno (66km-41m)**
ASCOLI PICENO	▶ **Tolentino (100km-62m)**
TOLENTINO	▶ **Camerino (32km-20m)**
CAMERINO	▶ **San Severino Marche (22km-14m)**
SAN SEVERINO MARCHE	▶ **Cingoli (21km-13m)**
CINGOLI	▶ **Ancona (53km-33m)**

TOUR

12 **Italy's Best** Kept Secret

Though mountainous, the Marches region is extremely fertile

[i] *Via Thaon de Revel 4, Ancona*

▶ *Take the coast road from Ancona going south for about 11km (7 miles) to Portonovo, which itself is 1km (½ mile) off the main road.*

1 **Portonovo,** Marche

One of the most beautiful stretches of coastline along the Adriatic begins just south of Ancona. Called the Riviera del Conero, it is made up of sheltered beaches which alternate with cliffs dropping straight down into the ocean. The first port of call among the pines and the holm-oaks lodged into the crevices of this area, is Portonovo, a minute settlement whose major attraction, apart from its shoreline and attendant campsites, is the ancient Church of Santa Maria di Portonovo. Built in 1034, it sits among the olives and the scrubland not far from the shore. This Romanesque building is in very good condition and you can clearly see Byzantine influences on its design. It has always been regarded as an architectural gem – the poet Dante mentions it in his *Divina Commedia* (*Divine Comedy*). Also at Portonovo is a reconstructed Napoleonic fortress erected in 1808 and an early 18th-century watch-tower, where the writer Gabriele D'Annunzio often stayed.

▶ *Return to the main road, which winds further south to Sirolo, 10km (6 miles).*

SPECIAL TO...

At Camerino, not far from Portonovo and Sirolo, is Aspio Terme, one of The Marches' important thermal springs. There are six of them on this spot – cold salt-bromo-iodic water good for the treatment of jaded livers, dodgy stomachs and biliary tract diseases.

2 **Sirolo,** Marche

Monte Conero, 572m (1,877 feet) separates Portonovo from Sirolo which is bigger and better equipped as a holiday place. There is a handful of hotels, restaurants and one or two nightclubs and, because this is still the Riviera del Conero, there are also little coves and places to swim. Sirolo has a medieval fortress of the Counts Cortesi, and the local Franciscan convent, now a villa, has two elms planted, according to legend, by St Francis himself on a visit to the town in 1215. In the Church of the Sacrament you will find a lovely local painting of the *Madonna of the Misericordia*, about 1500.

Not far away at Numana, about 1.5km (1 mile) further south, go to the Santuario del Crocefisso (Sanctuary of the Cross) and see the venerated Byzantine *Crucifixion*.

▶ *From Numana follow the signs to the* ***SS16****. Turn left on to the* ***SS77*** *for 5km (3 miles) before taking the turn-off for Loreto.*

3 **Loreto,** Marche

This town has the incredible reputation of being the point at which the Madonna's house, transported by angels from Nazareth to Italy, came down to earth late in the 13th century. This much-venerated relic, which is a simple brick building containing traces of medieval frescos inside, is the final destination of a pilgrimage undertaken by thousands of Italians each year. The Santa Casa (Holy House) is kept in the Santuario della Santa Casa (Sanctuary of the Holy House) and is placed directly under its dome. It is worth noting that the church's baroque façade is one of Italy's finest. Nobody

knows who designed the façade, but a whole host of other great names worked on the building: for instance Giuliano da Sangallo was responsible for the cupola and Bramante (one of Italy's greatest Renaissance architects) designed the side chapels.

In the Piazza della Madonna in front of the building is a beautiful loggia designed by Bramante in 1510, and in the middle of the square is a large fountain by Carlo Maderna, one of the architects of St Peter's in Rome. The sanctuary is brimming over with great works of art. Look out for the frescos by Angelica Kauffmann, who was a founder member of the London Royal Academy, in the right transept chapels. Bramante designed the beautiful marble screen in front of the Santa Casa itself and there are statues by Baccio Bandinelli.

i Via G Solari 3

▶ *From Loreto, take the* ***SS77*** *across country, via Recanati, to Macerata, about 29km (18 miles).*

4 Macerata, Marche

Macerata is one of the oldest university towns in Italy. It crowns a series of low hills and is a quiet place, full of bookshops and hidden restaurants, with narrow streets and stairways. Mostly medieval, everything is built of terracotta-coloured brick, and the homogeneity of its appearance is the town's most striking feature. But there is a host of monuments, mostly Renaissance and baroque. Apart from the 11th-century Duomo (cathedral), there is the even earlier Santa Maria della Porta – look for the Gothic doorway. The Basilica della Misericordia has an interior by Vanvitelli. The Museum and Art Gallery adjoining the Church of San Giovanni contains works by local 'Marchegiani' artists, as well as a collection of carriages and equestrian items.

In the courtyard of the Palazzo del Commune there are items from the 2nd-century AD settlement of Helvia Ricina. The site itself (freely accessible) lies on the banks of the River Potenza, 5km (3 miles) north of the town near the junction with the SS571, and remains include a huge amphitheatre, tombs and a section of paved roadway.

i Via Garibaldi 87

FOR HISTORY BUFFS

In the Via Manzoni in Macerata is the Palazzo Compagnoni-Marefoschi, scene of the marriage in 1772 of the 'Young Pretender' to the British throne, Bonnie Prince Charlie, to Louise of Stolberg. Charles, at 52, was no longer 'young' or 'bonnie', and the marriage was a failure.

▶ *From Macerata, go southeast for about 6km (4 miles) to the* ***SS485****, then head back towards the coast for 21km (13 miles). Branch south again on the* ***SS16*** *for 15km (9 miles) to Porto San Giórgio before turning right on to the* ***SS210****, which leads up to Fermo, 7km (4 miles), further.*

5 Fermo, Marche

Fermo is a very pretty hilltown poised above the Adriatic. It has tremendous views over Monti Sibillini and the Gran Sasso peaks in the Abruzzo to one side, and to the sea on the other. As in Macerata, almost everything is of terracotta-coloured brick, in this case primped and cleaned in recent restoration programmes.

Fermo was a relatively important town during Roman times.

In the Via degli Aceti you can see the remains of the 1st-century Piscina Epuratorio, an underground reservoir designed to hold and to clarify rain water. Above ground again, the Duomo has a lovely 13th- to 14th-century façade, although most of the rest of the building was rebuilt in the 18th century. Look at St Thomas à Becket's chasuble, woven from Moorish silk in 1116. It was left here by a bishop of Fermo to whom Becket presented it. In the Palazzo dei Priori is a small gallery which contains a painting of the *Adoration of the Shepherds* by Rubens. On this building's façade is a weird statue of Pope Sixtus V, once a bishop of Fermo.

Other places of interest are the Teatro dell'Aquila (1780) and the Church of San Domenico (1233).

[i] *Piazza del Popolo 5*

► *From Fermo, return to the coastal **SS16** and continue south along the coast for 32km (20 miles) until Porto d'Ascoli, at which branch inland on the **SS4** and continue to Ascoli Piceno.*

6 Ascoli Piceno, Marche

Ascoli Piceno is one of the great towns of The Marches region. There is a lot to see, most of it confined to the Piazza del Popolo, which lies at the centre of town. The early 13th-century Palazzo del Popolo has a later façade by Ascoli Piceno's best known artist, Cola dell'Amatrice. Also in the square is the Church of San Francesco (about 1262) with a statue of Pope Julius II over the south door, and there is the Franciscan Chiostro Grande (Great Cloister) of the mid-16th century, which is now used as a market. The Loggia dei Mercanti was built by the Wool Corporation in the early 1500s.

In the Piazza dell'Arringo you will find the Duomo della Sant'Emidio (cathedral), a largely 12th-century building with an unfinished façade, also by Cola dell'Amatrice. Look in the chapel on the right of the nave and you will see a beautiful painting by Carlo Crivelli – thought to be his finest work. The treasury contains a silver altar-frontal and an opulent silver reliquary by Pietro Vannini. Beyond the cathedral is the Palazzo Comunale gallery containing works by, among others, Titian and Crivelli.

[i] *Piazza Arringo 7*

► *Retrace your route to, and join, the **SS16** travelling northwards to Civitanova, at which take the **SS485** going inland past the turning to Macerata, continuing for 19km (12 miles) to Tolentino.*

SPECIAL TO...

In Ascoli Piceno a festival is held in August in which local townsfolk don the costumes of 15th-century musicians, soldiers, lords and ladies, and parade through the medieval streets of the town before the tournament known as the Quintana. In this jousting tournament, in which the rules go back to the 14th century, horsemen ride at a figure representing a Saracen.

Palazzo del Popolo, a 13th-century town hall with a graceful Renaissance courtyard, in the heart of Ascoli Piceno

RECOMMENDED WALKS

To the north of Ascoli Piceno, beyond its walls, is the valley of the River Tronto, a pleasant area for walks and picnics – ideal for the family as the terrain is gentle.

7 Tolentino, Marche
Tolentino's medieval centre is far more interesting than its outskirts, which are mostly modern. An ancient bridge known as The Devil's Bridge leads the way to the Basilica di San Nicola da Tolentino, the main reason for visiting the town, which has a beautiful early 15th-century portal by Nanni di Bartolo. In the crypt beneath the church is the tomb of St Nicholas of Tolentino who died in 1305. A great many miracles were attributed to him and in a large chapel on the right side of the basilica you can see his statue by Giorgio da Sebenico. The basilica has three museums, the Vestry, the Ex-Voto and a ceramics collection. In the Palazzo Sangallo is the Museum of Caricatures, with hundreds of satirical cartoons from all over the world.

► *Continue west from Tolentino via the **SS77** for 23km (14 miles) to a turning on the right for Camerino.*

8 Camerino, Marche
At Camerino is a massive fortress built by Cesare Borgia, one of the most hated figures of early Italian history. There are also the remains of the Rocca Varano, an early 13th-century castle built by the Varano family, who held the fiefdom of Camerino for about 300 years until 1539. Churches to see include the Duomo (cathedral) San Venanzio with its beautifully executed Renaissance doorway, and the little Church of the Annunziata. The Museo Diocesano (Diocesan Museum), in Camerino's main square, is closed for refurbishment. The Art Gallery (Pinacoteca) and Museum is filled with works by local 15th-century painter, Girolami di Giovanni.

The University Botanical Garden, established in 1828, surrounds the ducal palace and includes a huge physic garden.

► *Go north on the **SS256** and just before Castelraimondo, turn right on to the **SS361**, going through the town and along the river, to San Severino Marche.*

St Nicholas' Basilica's 13th- to 14th-century cloisters, Tolentino

9 San Severino Marche, Marche
The 16th-century anatomist Bartolomeo Eustachi was born in San Severino Marche. He is best known as the man after whom the Eustachian tube (in the ear) was named, but there is not much in the town to remind you of this fact. You will, however, see the work of a local painter who achieved great fame at the beginning of the 15th century – Lorenzo Salimbeni, who was also born here. Some of his frescos can be seen in the old cathedral, in the old upper town. The Duomo Nuovo in the lower town contains a striking painting of the *Madonna* by one of the great Mannerist painters, Pinturicchio. Look in at the art gallery in the Palazzo Comunale where there are works by contemporary artists.

The Tacchi Venturi Municipal Gallery has a collection of 14th- and 15th-century art, including works by the Salimbeni brothers and another local artist – Lorenzo d'Alessandro.

► *The **SS502** goes north from San Severino Marche to Cingoli.*

10 Cingoli, Marche
Cingoli is a very ancient town famous for its views. Crammed on to the top of a hill, its nickname is 'The Balcony of The Marches'. There is no single great masterpiece to be viewed here, but the little town's small early Renaissance palaces, particularly the Palazzo Castiglione in the Corso Garibaldi and those in the Polisena Quarter, appeal, with their carved entrance portals, their old window surrounds and their general air of antiquity. Narrow stone-paved streets, cupolas and belfries are the predominant characteristics of the town. Look into the church of San Francesco, the proud possessor of a lovely 16th-

BACK TO NATURE

Migrant birds – especially songbirds and birds of prey – pass through Italy each spring and autumn on their way to and from their breeding grounds in northern Europe and the wintering grounds in Africa.
Many species follow the coast on their journeys and the Ancona headland is an excellent observation area. Unfortunately, countless millions are shot or trapped in Italy for 'sport'. Warblers and turtle doves suffer particularly badly.

century wooden crucifix, and the church of Sant'Esuperanzio, an ancient vaulted structure founded in the 12th century by the Benedictines. It contains frescos from the 15th and 16th centuries, and a *Flagellation* by Sebastiano del Piombo, one of the greatest of the Venetian painters and a contemporary of Michelangelo.

i *Via Luigi Ferri 17*

▶ *From Cingoli, the* ***SS502*** *continues northwards (for 20km/12 miles) towards Jesi. Turn right on to the dual carriageway, which goes back to Ancona, about 33km (20 miles).*

SCENIC ROUTES

For the loveliest coastal views, nothing in The Marches will beat the Riviera del Conero, its cliffs and sheltered coves contrasting with the uninteresting straightness of the east Italian seaboard elsewhere.
From Camerino, to the south of Cingoli, you will be able to see the great Gran Sasso ranges of mountains which actually lie in the south of the Abruzzo.
The most scenic part of this tour is undoubtedly to be seen from the SS502 in and around Cingoli, about 650m (2,130 feet) above sea-level.

San Severino Marche, a modest town but worth a halt

The Northern Marches

In the 15th century many of the towns in this part of The Marches were in the orbit of the powerful Federico di Montefeltre, Duke of Urbino. Monuments to his reign are scattered around the region. Luckily he was an enlightened individual and there is little from the time of his rule that is not worth visiting or contemplating.

3/4 DAYS • 410KM • 255 MILES

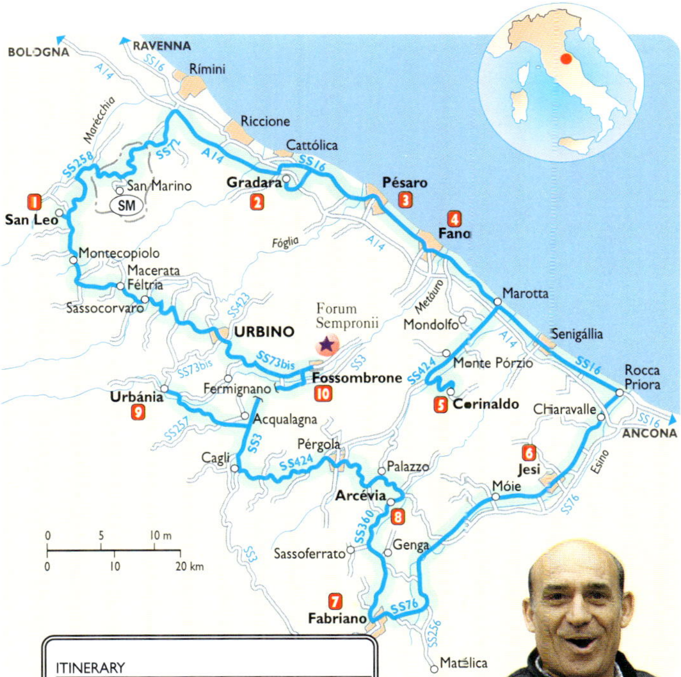

ITINERARY

URBINO	▶ **San Leo (52km-32m)**
SAN LEO	▶ **Gradara (63km-39m)**
GRADARA	▶ **Pesaro (15km-9m)**
PESARO	▶ **Fano (12km-7m)**
FANO	▶ **Corinaldo (35km-22m)**
CORINALDO	▶ **Jesi (43km-27m)**
JESI	▶ **Fabriano (42km-26m)**
FABRIANO	▶ **Arcevia (25km-15m)**
ARCEVIA	▶ **Urbania (72km-46m)**
URBANIA	▶ **Fossombrone (32km-20m)**
FOSSOMBRONE	▶ **Urbino (19km-12m)**

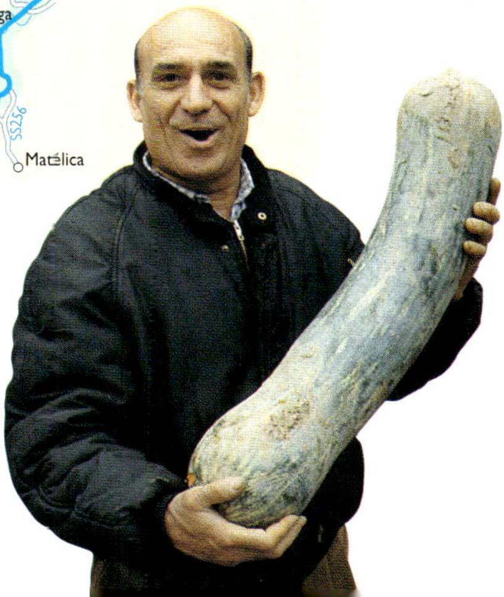

The countryside around Urbania has changed little over the years

From San Leo, follow the signs to San Marino, then towards Rimini on the **SS72** *(about 39km/24 miles). Then take the autostrada* **A14** *southwards for 16km (10 miles) leaving it at the Cattolica exit. Join the* **SS16** *travelling south for 5km (3 miles) before branching right on the minor road to Gradara.*

FOR HISTORY BUFFS

The fortress in San Leo once housed, in its prison, the infamous Giuseppe Balsamo, better known as Count Alessandro di Cagliostro, a conman who, in the 18th century, duped countless gullible people all over Europe into believing that he had discovered a way of turning base metals into gold. Ugly women came to him in the belief that he could make them more beautiful. He was eventually condemned for freemasonry and ended up in San Leo where he died in 1795.

i *Via Puccinotti 35, Urbino*

RECOMMENDED WALK

One very pleasant walk from Urbino – go west for about half and hour – is to the little Church of San Bernardino which is thought to have been designed by Bramante. Inside are the black marble tombs of the Montefeltro dukes.

The best way to San Leo from Urbino (about 52km/32 miles) is to go cross-country via Sassocorvaro, Macerata Feltria and Montecopiolo.

1 San Leo, Marche

San Leo is accessible by a single road cut into the rock. It is a tiny place, poised way above the Marecchia river on a kind of rocky lump. The Renaissance fortress, in its present state dating from the 15th century, is even higher, dramatically placed on the edge of a cliff overlooking the town. It is currently being turned into a museum, which will bring to life the most momentous events in its history.

Remarkably well preserved, the little town confines most of its interesting monuments in and near to the central Piazza Dante, including a museum of Sacred Art housed in a Renaissance palazzo. The 12th-century Duomo (cathedral) was erected in honour of St Leo. Its interior is dark, solid and unadorned, its mighty structure in a wonderful state of preservation. La Pieve (the parish church), which backs on to the main square, is the oldest church in the vicinity (9th-century possibly). San Leo has good restaurants and the seats in the square's cafés are great for a couple of hours' coffee-drinking and watching the world go by.

SPECIAL TO...

The provinces of Urbino and Pesaro hold annual weekend 'gastronomia' events, in which chosen restaurants in a variety of locations (San Leo is one) agree to produce a specific menu of local dishes on an agreed date. This keeps obscure culinary traditions going and usually results in a delicious feast. Check the details in the local tourist office.

2 Gradara, Marche

You will be able to see the whole of Gradara in about two hours. The old town only contains about 25 buildings and a fortress, the whole lot contained within 14th-century walls which are mostly still intact. You can go inside the castle and see the rooms in which one of the great tragedies of medieval Italy was enacted. The beautiful young Francesca fell in love with her very ugly, and older husband's younger brother, Paolo. This was almost inevitable, as Paolo had stood proxy for his older sibling at the marriage ceremony. A servant reported the two young lovers to the husband, who murdered them. You can visit the scene of the murder – an event immortalised by Dante in the *Divine Comedy* and by Tchaikovsky in his fantasy overture *Francesca da Rimini*.

Once you have strolled around the castle, peered over its walls to the patchwork countryside all around, and looked in at the glazed terracotta relief by Andrea della Robbia (1435–1525) in the castle chapel, you will have seen all there is to see.

▶ *Return to the **SS16** and travel southeast to Pesaro.*

3 Pesaro, Marche

Pesaro is proud of the reputation of Rossini, the composer, who was born here in 1792. It preserves his birthplace at Via Rossini 34, which you can visit, and it holds a series of concerts and operas during the annual Rossini festival held towards the end of the summer. You can also go and look at his manuscripts and other memorabilia in the Tempietto in Piazza Olivieri.

Pesaro is a large, bustling city a seaside resort brimming over with people in the summer, as well as a commercial centre. It has some quirky old streets in its older quarters but, because of heavy bombing during World War II, which laid waste large tracts of the city, its monuments are no longer very exceptional. However, the Museo Oliveriano contains local finds from the Etruscan and Roman periods – inscriptions, bronzes, coins; and the Museo Civico has some lovely majolica as well as a *Coronation of the Virgin* by Giovanni Bellini.

i Via Mazzolari 4

▶ *From Pesaro, the **SS16** leads to Fano, about 12km (7 miles) away.*

4 Fano, Marche

Fano is much better preserved than its less fortunate neighbour. It was an important Roman town and you can still see the Arco d'Augusto (Arch of Augustus), a triumphal arch dating from the 1st century AD. Nearby buildings were constructed over the centuries using material stolen from this Roman relic.

In particular, and interesting in its own right, is the 15th-century pawnshop, the Logge di San Michele, at the end of the street named after the arch. The old Church of San Michele, another structure made from recycled antique building materials, preserves a relief carved on to its façade showing what the arch looked like in the 15th century.

In the Church of Santa Maria Nuova are fine altarpieces by Giovanni Santi, Raphael's father, and Perugino, Raphael's teacher. There is also a little panel painting supporting the work of the young Raphael

A massive fortress defended Gradara in medieval times

(Raffaelo Sanzio) himself. The Museo Civico (Civic Museum) has precious works of art, with pieces by Santi Senior, Domenchino (1581–1641), and the 17th-century artist Mattia Preti.

i *Via C Battisti 10*

▶ *Continue along the* ***SS16*** *for 14km (9 miles) to Marotta, then turn inland on* ***SS424****, to follow signs to Corinaldo.*

5 Corinaldo, Marche

Corinaldo is famous as the centre of production of the *Verdicchio* wine, one of the most popular Italian white wines. Behind its 15th-century walls, in which you can still see massive bastions, towers and old gateways, the village is intact and compact, hardly spreading down the hillside at all. From the Porta di Sotto a massive stairway takes you into the village, ascending steeply between the little houses and lateral alleys. The churches of Sant'Agostino and San Francesco are both interesting. The latter dates from the 17th century and contains paintings by Claudio Ridolfi.

▶ *The quickest way to Jesi is to go back to the* ***SS16*** *and continue along it for 24km (15 miles) as far as Rocca Priora, then branch inland on the* ***SS76*** *and continue to Jesi.*

The cloisters of the Church of Santa Maria Nuove in Fano

6 Jesi, Marche

Jesi sits on the plain by the River Esino. Another walled town, it has houses built outside the walls. It is a picturesque place, best known as the birthplace of Emperor Frederick II (1194–1250) whose empire included Germany and Sicily. If you look on the external façade of the Palazzo Comunale, you will see, carved on stone, the text of a letter Frederick wrote to the townspeople confirming Jesi's ancient privileges. This old curiosity is by no means Jesi's only treasure.

In the town's Municipal Museum there is a fine collection of art and antiquities, including a mosaic floor and statuary from the 1st century.

Don't be deceived by the rather plain exterior of the Palazzo Pianetti in via XV Settembre. Not only does it have a magnificent rococo interior with intricate stucco work in its long gallery, but it also houses the civic art gallery (pinacoteca) with, among other treasures, an important collection of works by Lorenzo Lotto.

FOR CHILDREN

When bored with the countryside and 'Great Art', youngsters can go skating at Jesi and Fabriano.
Boating at Pesaro is another attraction, while places for riding can be found at Urbino, Urbania, Jesi and Fabriano.

Before you leave Jesi, you should take a look at the 14th-century frescos in the Church of San Marco.

▶ *Follow the* ***SS76*** *to Fabriano.*

7 Fabriano, Marche

The paper watermark was invented in Fabriano and this little town has been an important centre for paper-making since the Renaissance. Today banknotes are manufactured here. A small museum, in the old Convent of San Domenico, reveals details of the craft. The town was the home of Gentile da Fabriano (1370–1427), whose paintings were important examples of the International Gothic style that was to influence the Florentine Renaissance.

The Grand Museum has an eclectic collection covering toys, weapons (including those used by Native Americans), musical instruments and a section on special effects used in sci-fi and horror movies.

The baroque Church of San Benedetto has an extravagant gilt and stucco interior comparable to the elaborate decoration of the nearby Oratory of the Gonfalone. In particular, this building has a deeply coffered ceiling of the 17th century, with figures of gilded saints and tiny figures of the Apostles. There is gold everywhere – quite out of proportion with the building's very tiny scale.

i *Piazza Manin 11*

▶ *From Fabriano, a country road leads northeast to join the* ***SS360****. Continue northeast on the* ***SS360*** *to Arcevia.*

8 Arcevia, Marche

Arcevia sits on a spur of land about 535m (1,755 feet) above sea level. The site has been inhabited since prehistory, though the oldest remains in evidence today are those from the late Middle Ages to the Renaissance. As usual, the town is fortified, and its 15th-century walls are mostly intact. Walk

Part of the 14th-century walls enclosing the old town of Jesi

down the Via Ramazzani and look at the range of small country palaces – Palazzi Anselmi, Pianetti and Manneli-Pianetti. The parish Church of the San Medardo, rebuilt in 1644, can be regarded as the local art gallery, so precious are its contents. Here you can see works by Signorelli, della Robbia and Ridolfi, as well as a variety of works by local artists. Giovanni della Robbia's glazed terracotta altar (1513) is the most stunning piece. Sitting on it is the Madonna crowned beneath glazed fruit and flowers. Behind her is the blue glaze, so typical of the della Robbia family's work.

▶ *Make your way from Arcevia via Pergola, about 27km (17 miles), to the **SS424** and follow the signs to Cagli, 19km (12 miles). Here, take the **SS3** as far as Acqualagna, about 9km (6 miles), then follow the signs to Urbania.*

9 Urbania, Marche

About the size of Arcevia, Urbania is a centre for the production of blue jeans – which seems an unlikely activity for this small walled medieval town. Its other activity is the production of majolica (a type of earthenware with coloured decoration on an opaque white glaze), a craft for which it has always been famous. However, it is for neither of these that people tend to come to Urbania. For here, in the old Palazzo Ducale (Ducal Palace), is the famous library of the dukes of Urbino, which is full of drawings and engravings. The palace also contains an art gallery and a small museum. Look in also at the Chiesetta dei Morti (the Little Church of the Dead) where rows of mummies lie embalmed in the shadows.

▶ *Retrace your steps to the **SS3**, joining it once again at Acqualagna, and continue northeast for 16km (10 miles) to Fossombrone.*

10 Fossombrone, Marche

Fossombrone lies on the lower slopes of a hill near a crumbling fortress and the River Metauro. For a town of its size, it has a remarkable number of things to visit and admire. First of all there are the ruins of the old Roman town, Forum Sempronii (which, corrupted, gives 'Fossombrone'), about 3km (2 miles) downstream in San Marino. There are five churches including the Duomo (cathedral) and there is an elegant Palazzo Vescovile (Bishop's palace) dating from the 15th century, as well as a museum housed in a mansion which once belonged to the dukes of Urbino. Modern art is displayed in the Cesarini Picture Gallery, along with furniture and art from the inter-war years.

▶ *From Fossombrone, the **SS73bis** leads directly to Urbino, about 19km (12 miles).*

SCENIC ROUTES

This is one of the most scenic tours in Italy. In particular, look out for the sudden views from the road, towards San Leo and Gradara as you approach them.

At dusk, the views from the parapets of Urbino are magical and in the half light the landscapes of local Renaissance painters are never far from the mind.

BACK TO NATURE

The Adriatic Sea is not only a beautiful stretch of water popular for seaside holidays, but is also rich in wildlife. Shorelife is difficult to observe because of the poor tidal range, but out to sea, Cory's and the Mediterranean race of Manx shearwaters can be seen along with gulls, cormorants and dolphins.

LAZIO, CAMPANIA, ABRUZZO

Lazio is centred on Italy's capital, Roma (Rome), home to half the region's population. The landscape surrounding this ancient metropolis ranges from the hills and mountains of the Apennines to the most important lakes in the southern half of Italy – Bolsena, Bracciano, Vico and Nemi. Each of these was once a volcanic crater and the countryside all around them shows signs of turbulence. To the west of Rome is a plain that extends southwards along the Tyrrhenian Sea and here are Lazio's sandiest beaches.

The ancient origins of Italy are closely linked with the history and fortunes of Lazio. Those mysterious early Italians, the Etruscans, had important settlements in the area. Abutting Lazio on the east side is the Abruzzo region where the Apennine peaks reach as high as 2,000m (6,500 feet) above sea-level. This is an essentially rustic zone, a large chunk of which is protected by legislation as a National Park. Much of Abruzzo is territory unseen by conventional travellers to Italy. Close to Rome and easily accessible (there are two motorways), it has none of the star attractions of a Florence or a Milan. Yet hidden in the hills of its awe-inspiring landscape, the region offers glimpses into a fascinating version of normal Italian life.

Campania, Lazio's neighbour to the south, is often known simply as 'the Naples countryside'. Centred on this sprawling city, the region presents two distinct faces to the world – an idyllic coastal belt along the Tyrrhenian Sea and, inland, rough mountain terrain. The Romans considered the Bay of Napoli one of their country's most beautiful spots. The emperors had their villas on its coast and scattered among its islands, and some of the principle attractions of Campania today are those left behind by the Romans. In the brooding shadow of Mount Vesuvius, coastal Campania is still a stunning part of Italy.

A few kilometres inland, however, the contrasts are enormous. Here the mountains and valleys are less visited; travellers, spoiled by the coastal luxuries, never make it to the ancient cities of the Campanian countryside, well worth the effort of the trek inland.

Roma

The ancient capital of the Roman Empire (and now the capital of Italy) was built on seven hills – the Palatine, the Capitoline, Esquiline, Viminal, Caelian, Aventine and Quirinal. Much of its ancient construction survives; you could easily spend a week just visiting the ruins of such imperial splendours as the Colosseum, the Forum and the Baths of Caracallá. In fact, you could divide Rome up into historical periods, spending a week investigating each one. The city centre is full of baroque churches and convents of great magnificence, and countless palaces. Renaissance and baroque, some of them are now galleries or museums; and then there is the Vatican City with Bernini's magnificent Piazza San Pietro (St Peter's Square) and the huge and sumptuous Basilica di San Pietro. The Vatican museums give access to Michelangelo's Sistine Chapel, but they include many other museums and galleries with paintings and sculpture from all periods. Visitors will also find that Rome is a noisy, breathlessly busy city.

Napoli

Napoli (Naples) has one of the most important archaeological collections in the world housed in the Museo Archeologico Nazionale (National Museum). Here are displayed treasures and everyday items – silver and gold objects, household utensils and gladiator's weapons – from Pompeii, Ercolano and all the other ancient sites which proliferate throughout the Campania region. But Naples is also a great seething metropolis where daily life takes place against an ever-present background cacophony of car horns and revving engines. Anarchic traffic jams, headily scented vegetable markets, a vast royal palace (Palazzo Reale) from the 17th century, overdecorated baroque churches the like of which you will never see anywhere else on the Italian mainland – all are facets of this unforgettable city. And here you can dine at pavement cafés on the best pizzas you will taste anywhere – this now universal fast-food dish was Naples' most important gastronomic contribution to the world. A word of warning: Naples is an unruly city as far as traffic is concerned. Buy a detailed map of the city but do not be clever and take short cuts: you are bound to find yourself hopelessly lost after a very short time.

Left: the Colosseum, Rome

Pescara

Pescara is the Abruzzo's biggest resort. It is also its most popular watering hole, partly because it has a very good jazz festival. Gabriele D'Annunzio, poet and dramatist, was born here in 1863, and you can visit his birthplace – Casa Natale. But apart from this and the very odd Fish Museum, Pescara's principle attractions are down on the beach and the promenades, beyond the 19th-century holiday villas and the pine trees.

L'Áquila

L'Áquila, capital of Abruzzo, was founded by the Hohenstaufen Emperor Frederick II, and the city took the name of the imperial symbol – the eagle. It is well endowed with fine buildings, and the more precious items from its history and from the region have been gathered together in the excellent Museo Nazionale d'Abruzzo (National Museum of Abruzzo), housed in the Castello. From L'Áquila you get the finest views of the Gran Sasso peak of the Apennines which is over 2,000m (6,560 feet) high.

The popular resort of Sorrento, on the dramatic Amalfi Coast

TOUR
14

The Apennines & the Adriatic

This tour takes in maritime Abruzzo, which consists of a coastal plain fringed by thick pinewoods and long sunny beaches. Pescara has 16km (10 miles) of sandy shoreline. Just inland, beyond the fertile valleys close to the sea, are the rugged mountains of the region – you can see the vast Gran Sasso range to the west.

4 DAYS • 373KM • 229 MILES

ITINERARY	
PESCARA	▶ **Pineto (21km-13m)**
PINETO	▶ **Teramo (41km-25m)**
TERAMO	▶ **Atri (39km-24m)**
ATRI	▶ **Penne (36km-22m)**
PENNE	▶ **Loreto Aprutino (8km-5m)**
LORETO APRUTINO	▶ **Ortona (65km-40m)**
ORTONA	▶ **Lanciano (20km-12m)**
LANCIANO	▶ **Vasto (44km-27m)**
VASTO	▶ **Chieti (78km-48m)**
CHIETI	▶ **Pescara (21km-13m)**

Via N Fabrizi 172, Pescara

▶ *From Pescara, take the coastal **SS16** for 21km (13 miles) to Pineto.*

1 Pineto, Abruzzo
Pineto is one of the prettiest resorts on the Abruzzo coast. Its wide, sandy beach is lined with pines about five trees deep, so that in the heat of summer you can be near the sea without boiling on the sand all day. Many people come here for the campsites, though if you cannot find places in these there are a great many others to choose from, lining the coastline practically all the way from Pescara to Martinsicuro, about 35km (22 miles) further north from Pineto. There are seafront hotels, some with swimming pools, nightclubs and restaurants where the speciality is *brodetto alla pescarese*, an extremely hot, peppery fish stew.

Otherwise, Pineto's chief attraction is the Torre di Cerrano, a tower built by the Emperor Charles V as defence against the threat of the Ottoman Turks in the 16th century.

▶ *From Pineto, continue along the **SS16** for 16km (10 miles) as far as Giulianova, at which branch inland on the **SS80** in the direction of Teramo, about 25km (15 miles).*

2 Teramo, Abruzzo
Teramo is the capital of the northern chunk of the Abruzzo. Its special attractions, apart from the amazing views to the Gran Sasso, are its two cathedrals. The earlier Duomo di Santa Maria Aprutiensis is full of assorted decorative bits and pieces – such as the ancient frescos of angels and some splendid Lombard carvings. The 'newer' (12th-century) cathedral has a lovely Romanesque entrance portal, which incorporates sculpture, a rose window and mosaics. Its chief interior attractions are the 15th-century altarpiece by Jacobello del Fiore and a silver altar frontal of the same date by a local artist Nicola da Guardiagrele, which depicts scenes from the New Testament. Guardiagrele was obviously very much in favour at the time: his work can also be seen on the façade of the building, in the statues of the Archangel Gabriel and the Virgin Annunziata that balance on the tops of columns borne by lions.

One for the connoisseur of hilltowns: Loreto Aprutino

Teramo was originally a Roman city and evidence of its ancient past can be seen everywhere. You might have noticed the remains of a Roman house (*domus*) incorporated within Santa Maria.

Near the 'new' cathedral are buildings from more recent times – a relative term, of course, in a town with such a long history. Look out for the Casa dei Melatini, a well-preserved 14th-century house, and the old Franciscan Church of the Madonna delle Grazie which houses a painted wooden *Madonna and Child* by Silvestro dal 'Aquila, one of the region's most important 15th-century sculptors. The Museo Archeologico explores the history of the town from Roman times. The Picture Gallery, reopened following restoration, is worth a vist.

Via del Castello 10

▶ *Take the* ***SS81*** *southeast for 14km (9 miles), turn east on to the* ***SS150*** *for 13km (8 miles) then take a right turn for Atri.*

FOR CHILDREN

About 29km (18 miles) south of Teramo, just off the motorway, is the village of Castelli, where the recently restored Institute of Ceramic Art has a 100-figure ceramic crib. Highly detailed, this is a remarkable example of the crib-maker's art, popular throughout southern Italy.

3 Atri, Abruzzo

Still in the shadow of the Gran Sasso massif, Atri is another ancient place that was once a Roman colony. You can survey relics of this era of its past among the excavations in the piazza and in the crypt of the Cattedrale dell'Assunta (Cathedral of the Assumption). In the gloom beneath this building are the remains of a Roman *piscina* (pool). The cathedral itself contains some excellent 15th-century frescos of the *Lives of the Virgin and Jesus* by Andrea Delitio, one of the most renowned local painters, and there is an interesting 16th-century tabernacle. But Atri's real treasures are in the cathedral museum – ivories, statues, majolicas and an interesting array of fragments from the ancient church that preceded the cathedral. A wander around Atri should also take in the churches of Sant'Agostino and Sant'Andrea and the courtyard of the Palazzo Acquaviva, which dates from the 14th century.

BACK TO NATURE

The Riserva Naturale Regionale Lago di Penne lies to the west of the town of Penne. A good place to start is the Museum of Natural History, which covers the flora, fauna and traditional crafts of the area.

▶ *The best way to Penne is across country. Leave Atri the way you came in, and after 1.5km (1 mile), follow signs left to Villa Bozza, then follow the signs to the* ***SS81*** *and Penne, 36km (22 miles) in all.*

RECOMMENDED WALKS

Near Atri, on the outskirts of the town, in fact, and within easy walking distance from it, are the strange *calanchi* rock formations – you cannot miss them. The odd geology of the area has also given rise to caves which were once inhabited by humans.

4 Penne, Abruzzo

Penne is a small town that sits on a low rise not far from the Lake of Penne. Surprisingly for its size it is full of miniature but majestic palaces and mansions. Just by the town's main gate is the Palazzo Castiglione with two tiers of wrought-iron balconies.

Further up among the old brick-paved streets and alleys is the Palazzo del Bono (in the Via Pansa), a lovely Renaissance palace. There is a homogeneity about Penne: churches, houses, palaces and streets are all built of the same reddish brick,

Pineto's beautiful beach is typical of the Abruzzo coast

The impressive campanile of Atri's Cathedral of the Assumption

which gives the town a warm glow. Penne's cathedral is perhaps the town's least interesting building. It was destroyed in World War II, then rebuilt, but it does have an interesting crypt which has survived from the earlier building.

Also, in the Piazza Duomo, is the town's museum which has Roman antiquities, medieval and Renaissance items and religious art. The 18th-century Church of the Annunziata is far more interesting; with its columned façade it is considered to be the most perfect church of its period anywhere in the region.

▶ *Loreto Aprutino is 8km (5 miles) to the southeast.*

5 Loreto Aprutino, Abruzzo

Everybody who comes to Loreto Aprutino comes to see the *Last Judgement* fresco in the Church of Santa Maria in Piano. Here the dead are seen heaving themselves out of their graves, some to end in Hell, the others in Paradise. A centre for the production of olive oil, this is one of the region's prettiest hilltowns; the cottages that make up the bulk of the town are squeezed among churches, whose bell towers can be seen from afar.

At the summit of the town is San Pietro Apostolo which has a good Renaissance portal. Nearby is the Palazzo Acerbo in which is a small museum housing a stunning collection of antique Abruzzesi ceramics with examples from the very early Middle Ages to the 18th century.

▶ *Take the* ***SS151*** *towards the coast, branch left on to the* ***SS16bis*** *at Cappelle sul Tavo, then join the* ***A14*** *north of Montesilvano (Pescara Nord junction). Follow the autostrada south to the exit for Ortona.*

SPECIAL TO...

Special to Loreto Aprutino, are the celebrations of the Feast of St Zopito. An elaborately dressed ox carrying a child dressed as an angel is led to the statue of the saint. The ox is made to kneel and receive the abbot's benediction.

6 Ortona, Abruzzo

Most of Ortona was reconstructed after two of the most horrific battles fought during World War II – the battles of the Sangro and Moro rivers in November–December 1943. The Duomo (cathedral) has been partially rebuilt since, but its lovely 14th-century portal was unscathed. The Palazzo Farnese, begun in 1584 for a visit to the town by Margaret of Parma, also survived. On its third floor is a gallery dedicated to the works of Michele and Basilio Cascella.

Ortona is now the region's largest port with the usual kind of raffish, tangy character to match, particularly in the Terravecchia quarter beside the remains of the Aragonese castle. While the restaurants here are good, you will probably find it more pleasant at the resort of Francavilla a Mare, just 6km (4 miles) to the north, a more popular place to stay and to relax.

▶ *Rejoin the* ***A14*** *travelling south to the next exit (Lanciano). Lanciano is 7km (4 miles) to the southwest along a minor road.*

7 Lanciano, Abruzzo

Lanciano was an important market town with international trade in the Middle Ages. Its medieval nucleus survives, known as Lanciano Vecchia, at the centre of which are the churches of Sant'Agostino and San Biagio. However, in the

Penne's main gate

Città Nuova, the 16th-century 'new town', the Church of Santa Maria Maggiore is far more interesting. Dating mostly from the early 14th century, it has two perfect rose windows and a huge Gothic portal lined with highly decorative columns. Its most spectacular interior fitting is a 15th-century crucifix. The Duomo (cathedral), with its 17th-century belfry, actually sits on the remains of a Roman bridge, dating from the time of the Emperor Diocletian and restored in the 11th century. The only town gate to survive from medieval times is the Porta San Biagio.

FOR HISTORY BUFFS

Just beyond Lanciano is Guardiagrele, whose most famous inhabitant, Nicola da Guardiagrele, produced some superb gold and silver work in the 15th century. The Cathedral Museum has fragments of a silver crucifix by this artist.

► *From Lanciano return to the **A14** and travel south to the Vasto Nord turn-off. Take the **SS16** and follow the signs to Vasto, a distance of 44km (27 miles).*

SCENIC ROUTES

Fine views can be seen on the route via Orsogna from Lanciano to Guardiagrele and the approach to Loreto Aprutino from the Penne side.

8 **Vasto,** Abruzzo

The fine old town of Vasto is dominated by a huge 13th-century fortress which looks on to the Piazza Rossetti, the centre of town and the site of a former Roman amphitheatre. It sits on the edge of the medieval town whose limits are still marked out in part by walls, punctured occasionally by old gates. The aspect of the town changes as you pass from the newer part to the old: whereas the streets are wider and more elegant outside the Porta Santa Maria or Porta Nuova, inside the walls, beyond these gates, they are narrow and tortuous, full of strange little squares and old doorways. The older precincts contain the more interesting churches, particularly San Giuseppe (the cathedral) and Santa Maria Maggiore. The 13th-century cathedral has a good Gothic portal.

The remains of another church, San Pietro, can be found not far from the Palazzo d'Avalos. In the lunette of the entrance portal – all that remains of the church – is an interesting sculpture of the crucified Christ wearing a regal crown rather than the usual crown of thorns.

Vasto has a Museo Civico (Civic Museum) whose section on the Roman antecedents of the town is the most interesting. One last fact about the town – in the Piazza Diomede is a statue of the English Pre-Raphaelite poet and painter Dante Gabriel Rossetti, whose family originated in Vasto.

► *Rejoin and travel north on the **A14** until the Pescara Ovest-Chieti turn-off, 78km (48 miles).*

9 Chieti, Abruzzo
Chieti has a number of star attractions which make it an indispensable part of the tour. You should set aside two hours to see the excellent Museo Archeologico degli Abruzzi (Archaeological Museum), where the chief exhibit, the peculiar-looking *Warrior of Capestrano*, is a larger-than-life-size figure that probably dates from the 6th century BC, accompanied by an as yet undeciphered inscription. Substantial parts of the town's Roman baths have survived, including a room which still has its mosaic pavement in situ.

The Roman theme continues throughout the town with the ruins of three small temples, a large rock-cut cistern (the former reservoir) and the intact original early town layout (of the Civitella district, the oldest section of Chieti). If you examine these then look at the Roman artefacts in the museum, you should be able to build up a good picture of ancient Chieti. Another important period of Chieti's history is represented by the Gothic Cathedral of San Giustino, which contains a silver statue of St Justin.

Art lovers should head for the Museo d'Arte Constantino Barbella in the Palazzo Martinetti-Bianchi, which houses a fine collection, spanning the Middle Ages to the present day.

Chieti's Good Friday Procession is one of Italy's oldest Easter ceremonies. Participants in the torchlight procession wear the black tunic and grey mantle of penitents.

RECOMMENDED WALKS

From Passo di Lanciano, a small resort in the Abruzzo massif between Chieti and Lanciano, there is mountain walking in the Maiella range, which reaches over 2,700m (9,000 feet).

BACK TO NATURE

From Chieti and Lanciano it is not far into the mountains of Abruzzo. The area is rich in woodlands, including the pinewoods of Piana delle Mele and Valle delle Monache. Look for birds of prey, including perhaps even a red kite or a golden eagle soaring overhead, and warblers, nightingales and other songbirds among the trees.

i Via B Spaventa 29

▶ *Return towards the **A14** and follow the signs to Pescara, about 21km (13 miles).*

The Aragonese castle at Ortona dates from the 15th century

TOUR
15

Abruzzo – the Remote Interior

Although geographically not very far from some of Italy's biggest cities, the Abruzzo is a largely untamed region. This tour introduces you to Italy's natural environment at its wildest. Centred on the area between southern Italy's highest mountain, the Gran Sasso, and the Abruzzo National Park, most of the smaller towns on this tour have managed to escape the march of progress.

3 DAYS • 362KM • 226 MILES

ITINERARY	
L'ÁQUILA	▶ **Cocullo (92km-57m)**
COCULLO	▶ **Scanno (20km-13m)**
SCANNO	▶ **Pescasseroli (43km-27m)**
PESCASSEROLI	▶ **Pescocostanzo (58km-36m)**
PESCOCOSTANZO	▶ **Sulmona (37km-23m)**
SULMONA	▶ **Pacentro (9km-6m)**
PACENTRO	▶ **Celano (55km-34m)**
CELANO	▶ **L'Áquila (48km-30m)**

i *Via XX Settembre 10, L'Áquila*

▶ *From L'Áquila, take the* ***SS17*** *for 34km (21 miles) until Navelli, at which bear left via the* ***SS153*** *to the* ***SS5****. Turn left and after 2km (1 mile) join the* ***A25*** *at the Bussi junction. Travel in the direction of Roma for 30km (18 miles) until Cocullo, just 3km (2 miles) off the autostrada.*

1 Cocullo, Abruzzo
Cocullo is a small rural town full of ancient mud-coloured houses clinging to the side of a hill beneath the spire of a church. It has one main street, a single piazza and an important sanctuary dedicated to San Domenico Abate. The town's patron saint and a hermit who, like St Francis, made 'friends' with animals, he used to live in a cave that still exists beneath the sanctuary. The sanctuary itself contained the painted wooden statue of the hermit which, in 1981, following an earthquake, was transferred further up the hill, to an ancient chapel whose miniature pilastered façade faces the main piazza.

Autostrada viaduct near Scanno gives access to the mountains

SPECIAL TO...

Cocullo holds the Processione dei Serpari which takes place in the town every year on the first Thursday in May. Snakes (non-poisonous) are collected from the surrounding countryside then flung at the statue of San Domenico Abate. Those that cling on are carried around the town entwined around the statue – the aim is to touch one. If you do, the villagers say you will have a longer life.

▶ *Cross over the* ***A25*** *and go south, following the little country road via Anversa degli Abruzzi to Scanno, 20km (13 miles).*

2 Scanno, Abruzzo
Scanno, which overlooks the attractive Lago (Lake) di Scanno, is one of the most popular places in the region, especially for summer holidays. At the same time, Scanno itself is a perfectly preserved medieval hilltown. The old town sits apart from the new, partly because it crowns the pinnacle of a low rise on the side of a hill. A map on a signboard as you enter the town suggests a route through its centre. This will take you past the medieval Santa Maria della Valle church, built on the remains of a pagan temple, the 16th-century Saracco Fountain and the little Church of Santa Maria di Constantinopoli, which contains a fresco of the *Madonna Enthroned*, signed 'De Ciollis AD 1478'.

There are other churches squeezed into oddly-shaped little squares, Renaissance and baroque houses and small palaces. There are also ancient mansions in whose windows you sometimes catch glimpses of old women in costume mending clothes or embroidering. Other characteristic features are the external staircases on to steep streets, arches and dark passages. Scanno has much else to offer: superb landscape views; folklore; local arts and handicrafts, such as lace-making and the production of gold and silver jewellery (beautiful filigree earrings for example); and a handful of delicatessens that cater for tourists, selling local wine, bottled peppers, sausages and local cheeses.

▶ *From Scanno, follow the* ***SS479*** *south for about 7km (4½ miles) to Villetta Barrea at which turn right on to the* ***SS83****, following the signs to Pescasseroli, 16km (10 miles).*

The hilltop above Celano is topped by a massive castle

SPECIAL TO...

In Scanno, the women's costumes are little different from medieval garb. They take the form of long patterned dresses and turban-like headdresses. The older women often still wear them for every-day work, but many younger ones bring them out of wraps only for special occasions.

3 Pescasseroli, Abruzzo
Pescasseroli lies within the confines of the Parco Nazionale d'Abruzzo (Abruzzo National Park), and its Natural History Museum gives an excellent overview of the habitats. It also has an enclosure of animals native to the area. Although the town's principal attraction is as the starting point for walks and expeditions into the mountains and valleys of the park, it does also have a handful of interesting buildings. The parish church has been added to over the years, having started life in the 8th century as part of a monastery. It has a simple Gothic entrance portal and inside, in the Cappella della Madonna Nera (Chapel of the Black Madonna), is a very early wooden statue of the Madonna carved from black wood. In the Strada Valle del Fiume is one of the town's earliest remaining houses and some slightly later characteristic baronial palaces.

In the Piazza Benedetto Croce is the Palazzo Sipari, birthplace of Pescasseroli's most famous inhabitant, the philosopher Benedetto Croce, who was born here in 1866. As you wander through the town, look out for old, carved stone doorways and windows – in particular notice the Gothic mullioned window in the Piazza Umberto I which is thought to have come from Pescasseroli's castle. For winter visitors there are ski runs in the nearby mountains – on Monte Ceraso and Monte Vitelle.

i *Viale Piave 2*

▶ *Go back via Villetta Barrea, continuing on the* ***SS83*** *to its junction with the* ***SS17****. Follow this road northwards for about 15km (9 miles), at which branch off on the* ***SS84*** *and follow the signs to Pescocostanzo, about 5km (3 miles).*

FOR CHILDREN

Organised riding lessons can be had at equitation centres in and around Pescasseroli in the Abruzzo National Park. Also available are guided rides on horseback through the countryside – for adults and children.

BACK TO NATURE

Accessible from Pescasseroli via the Sangro Valley, the Parco Nazionale d'Abruzzo is a region of wooded slopes and mountains offering a last refuge for the Italian race of the European brown bear and chamois as well as the European wolf.

The alpine meadows are a riot of colour in the spring and summer and golden eagles, goshawks and peregrines are regularly seen. Mountain birds are well represented at high altitudes.

FOR HISTORY BUFFS

At Alfedana, on the way to Pescocostanzo, are the ruins of the ancient Samnite town of *Aufidena*, with cyclopean walls (built with enormous stone blocks) above the river and the ancient necropolis. The Samnites flourished in the 4th century BC. They came into conflict with the Romans, who eventually crushed them in 82 BC. The Museo Civico in Alfedena has finds from the site.

4 Pescocostanzo, Abruzzo
The collegiate Church of Santa Maria del Colle (or Collegiata) in Pescocostanzo, is one of the most beautiful churches in the Abruzzo – even though it was badly damaged during World War II. Having been started in the 13th century, it was rebuilt after an earthquake 200 years later. Nowadays its most beautiful components are the late 17th-century wrought-iron gates to the Chapel of the Sacrament, and the gilded and painted wooden ceiling of the nave. Look out for the medieval wooden statue of Santa Maria del Colle incorporated in a niche of the high altar.

Pescocostanzo is an unusual place: it seems bland, even uninteresting at first, but it has a surprising number of worthwhile buildings. The principal piazza has a 16th-century Palazzo Comunale and there is an array of mansions in the Corso Roma – Palazzo Grilli and Palazzo Mansi in particular – and in the Via della Fontana are Palazzo Colecchi, Palazzo Ricciardelli and Palazzo Mosca. You sometimes see local women wearing the town's traditional costume – bright red skirts, lace aprons and dark bodices in brown, blue or black, decorated with gold thread. Local handicrafts here are the same as those in Scanno. Once a wealthy town, Pescocostanzo was at one time controlled by Vittoria Colonna, patroness of Michelangelo and a member of the great Roman Colonna family.

i *Vico delle Carceri 4*

▶ *Return to the **SS17**, then continue northwards via Pettorano to Sulmona.*

Corso Ovidio in Sulmona: the poet Ovid was born here

SCENIC ROUTES

Perhaps the most scenic parts of this tour are the following:
– the first 10km (6 miles) of the road by which you leave Scanno, going south. You might be forgiven for thinking yourself in Scotland;
– the famous Passo del Diavolo (the Devil's Pass), just north of Pescasseroli. Although this is not strictly part of the tour route, it is worth a detour to drive at least a section of it. The pass takes you through part of the Parco Nazionale d'Abruzzo (Abruzzo National Park).

5 Sulmona, Abruzzo
Sulmona is the biggest town (apart from L'Áquila) on the tour, with an attractive situation at the centre of a small plain surrounded by high mountains. It is also an ideal base for excursions into the Abruzzo National Park. As the birthplace of Ovid, the great Roman poet (43 BC–AD 17), however, and with its complement of old buildings, it has a decidedly antique air. The church and palace of Santa Maria Annunziata are perhaps the finest buildings. Originally a mixture of Gothic and Renaissance styles, the exteriors were rebuilt in baroque style early in the 18th century. The palace is the finer. Its façade has richly carved elements, statues and delicate tracery. Today the palace houses the town's

museum, with local paintings and goldsmiths' work, and the 'In Situ' Museum, with items from the Roman building discovered beneath the palazzo.

Running through the centre of town is the old aqueduct, constructed in the mid-13th century. Sulmona's best-known product is confetti, not coloured paper but sugared almonds which are handed out at weddings and christenings – there is even a museum dedicated to the confection, with old machinery, a reconstructed confetti-maker's workshop and a collection of tiny containers.

i Corso Ovidio 208

▶ *Take the **SS487**, going east to Pacentro, 9km (6 miles).*

6 Pacentro, Abruzzo

Pacentro is just one of a clutch of pretty hilltowns in the vicinity of Sulmona. Its ancient centre focuses on the Castello Cantelmo with its handful of surviving towers. Beneath these and the church steeple, the rustic houses, a collection of sandy-coloured blocks, sit crammed together, linked by tiny weaving passages and alleys.

Further north is Caramancio Terme, a hilltown resort with sulphur baths. It lies at the very heart of the Maiella mountains. Caramancio has a lovely parish church, Santa Maria Maggiore, with a fine late 15th-century portal and reliquary by local master Nicola da Guardiagrele.

▶ *From Pacentro, return to Sulmona, then take the **SS479** via Anversa degli Abruzzi in the direction of Roma for 20km (12½ miles), exiting at the Aielli-Celano turn-off, and follow the signs to Celano.*

7 Celano, Abruzzo

Celano is another lovely hilltown, this time overlooking the Fucino Basin, the most fertile piece of Abruzzo countryside, in antiquity a lake. The little town clusters beneath the Castello Piccolomini, which was begun in 1392. This imposing building was restored after an earthquake earlier this century and today has regained its appearance as a formidable example of a feudal power base, in this case of the Piccolomini family. It contains the Marsica National Museum, which has displays of gold, textiles, sculpture and paintings. Not far from Celano is the Gole di Celano, a spectacular, narrow and very deep gorge – or canyon – containing a torrent. It runs down from the direction of Monte Sirente towards the town.

▶ *From Celano, take the **SS5bis** back to L'Áquila, a distance of 48km (30 miles).*

RECOMMENDED WALKS

The best walks on this tour are to be had in the Parco Nazionale d'Abruzzo (Abruzzo National Park). Pick up trail maps at Pescasseroli – there are special trails as well as refuge huts should you want to stay overnight.

Market day in L' Áquila

Roman
Country Retreats

The upper echelons of Roman society have always relaxed in villas and secluded countryside retreats just outside Roma (Rome). There are all kinds of villas and castles from Emperor Hadrian's ruined country palace at Tivoli to Pope John Paul II's country house at Castel Gandolfo. But there are also more 20th-century forms of relaxation available on the beaches at Ostia, Gaeta and Sperlonga. Rome itself has a variety of palaces and villas that can be visited.

4 DAYS • 483KM • 300 MILES

ITINERARY

ROMA	▶ Tivoli (32km-20m)
TIVOLI	▶ Anticoli Corrado (28km-17m)
ANTICOLI CORRADO	▶ Subiaco (21km-13m)
SUBIACO	▶ Gaeta (201km-125m)
GAETA	▶ Sperlonga (16km-10m)
SPERLONGA	▶ Castel Gandolfo (98km-61m)
CASTEL GANDOLFO	▶ Frascati (19km-12m)
FRASCATI	▶ Ostia (40km-25m)
OSTIA	▶ Roma (28km-17m)

i *Via Parigi II, Roma*

▶ *From the centre of Roma, the* ***SS5*** *goes east for 32km (20 miles) to Tivoli.*

BACK TO NATURE

The Parco Nazionale del Circeo is well worth a visit. This area lies less than 100km (60 miles) south of Rome on the Italian coast. It is a calcareous promontory with unspoilt beaches and dunes. The evergreen oak forests and *macchia* are good for flowers, insects and birds.

1 Tivoli, Lazio

Tivoli sits on a wide spur of Monte Ripoli just before Lazio becomes really mountainous. The town grew up as a strategic point on an ancient route from the east to Rome. Today it is largely associated with the Villa Adriana (Hadrian's Villa), built by the Emperor Hadrian. Construction began at his accession to the imperial throne and continued until AD 134. Here the Emperor set about reconstructing buildings he had seen on his foreign travels, such as the Canopic Temple at Alexandria and Plato's Academy in Athens. But this huge villa, the biggest ever in Italy, also contained libraries, baths, temples and theatres, and there was even a little private palace built on an island in a huge pool and surrounded by a colonnade. The richness of the complex is demonstrated by the enormous quantity and excellent quality of the sculpture which has been found on this site over the centuries. Most of it has ended up in the Vatican Museum in Rome.

During the Renaissance other villas were built at Tivoli by rich cardinals. The most sumptuous is the Villa d'Este, built by Ippolito d'Este. The gardens here are more elaborate than the actual buildings; a river was diverted to provide water for countless fountains and a huge variety of cascades and pools. The Villa Gregoriana (closed for restoration) is another place worth a visit, with a fine waterfall by the great architect and sculptor Bernini, formed by the diversion of the River Aniene.

Ceiling fresco from St Benedict's monastery church at Subiaco

i *Largo Garibaldi*

▶ *Continue along the* ***SS5*** *from Tivoli for 23km (14 miles) until the turning on the right to Anticoli Corrado.*

2 Anticoli Corrado, Lazio

This is a lovely hilltown poised dramatically on an eminence dominating the countryside all around. It has remained completely unspoilt by the passage of time and has for years been the destination of painters in search of sublime landscape scenes. Anticoli Corrado's houses are mostly medieval with small windows and outside staircases. The Church of San Pietro preserves fragments of its early mosaic floor.

▶ *From Anticoli Corrado return to the* ***SS5*** *and turn right. Shortly after, branch right and follow the winding country road* ***(SS411)*** *southeast, past the hamlet of Agosta to Subiaco, a total of 21km (13 miles).*

The impressive Roman ruins of Ostia Antica

> **SCENIC ROUTES**
>
> The road from Anticoli to Subiaco goes through one of the most mountainous parts of Lazio. Look at the views, up to the left, to Monte Simbruini. Particularly fine is the approach to, and views from, Anticoli Corrado. From here you can see over the artists' landscape to the village of Saracinesco and Marano Equo.

3 Subiaco, Lazio

One of an isolated group of interesting little places on the edge of the Simbruini mountains, Subiaco has some very ancient buildings, most of which have something to do with St Benedict. This saint retired here late in the 5th century to write his *Rule* which was to heavily influence Christian monasticism. Subiaco originally had 12 monasteries organised by Benedict. Much later, in the atmosphere of piety and learning that these engendered, the first printed books in Italy were made (1464). While not much remains of the early illustrious period of St Benedict himself, there is the Monastery of Santa Scolastica (Benedict's sister) which has three cloisters. Of St Benedict's own monastery, San Benedetto, high upon a rocky site, all that remains are two churches, one carved out of the rock, with frescos of varying ages.

Near by is the gorge of the River Aniene, where there is a lake with a waterfall that might have been the work of the Emperor Nero who once had a villa here.

► *Retrace the route via the **SS411** to the **SS5**. Head for Roma, but after 9km (6 miles) join the **A24** at the Vicovaro-Mandela junction continuing towards Roma. About 22km (14 miles) along the autostrada, turn on to the **A1** heading towards Naples. Continue on the **A1** for 106km (66 miles) until the Cassino turning. Follow the signs to Gaeta via the **SS630**.*

4 Gaeta, Lazio

The old town of Gaeta sits at the end of a promontory jutting into the Tyrrhenian Sea. This ancient centre still stands behind its old walls and remains largely medieval. There is plenty to see here, and with its beaches, restaurants and lively scene, it makes a good base. Apart from the Duomo (Sant'Erasmo), there is a 13th-century fortress and a maze of little ancient alleys and streets harbouring churches, old doorways and quirky little squares full of cats. There is also an excellent museum, with some notable highlights, including the Banner of the Battle of Lepanto (1571) and frescos by Giovanni da Gaeta.

A great rock known as Torre

Fountain in Tivoli's Villa d'Este

d'Orlando (the Tower of Orlando) dominates Gaeta and on it is the circular mausoleum of the Roman consul Lucius Munatius Plancus, who died at Gaeta in 22 BC. Mount Orlando divides ancient Gaeta, called *Sezione Erasmo*, from the newer part of town. This is the Porto Salvo, consisting of a series of narrow, straight streets of brightly painted houses and lots of wrought-iron balconies.

Along the coast to the east, Formia is a departure point for ferries to the islands of Ponza and Ventotene, popular with holidaying Italians, and with a long and interesting history – Homer mentioned Ponza in the *Odyssey*.

FOR HISTORY BUFFS

Near Gaeta (20km/12 miles going south on the SS213) are the remains of *Minturnae*, a Roman town founded in 295 BC. You can visit the excavations which include an aqueduct, theatre and forum, and the Antiquarium which contains memorable sculptures. Closer to Gaeta, just before Formia, is the so-called Tomb of Cicero. The great orator and writer was killed in 43 BC near his villa at Formia.

[i] *Piazza Traniello 19*

▶ *Take the **SS213** from Gaeta to Sperlonga, 16km (10 miles).*

5 Sperlonga, Lazio

The coastline from Gaeta to Sperlonga is beautiful, with many coves and promontories. Like Gaeta, Sperlonga sits on a spur of land that juts out into the Tyrrhenian Sea. Its centre is consistently medieval. Near by is the Grotta di Tiberio (Tiberius' Cave), where the emperor is said to have made merry in his own particular way. There is also the emperor's villa, and some good classical sculpture in the Museo Archeologico Nazionale di Sperlonga.

▶ *From Sperlonga, continue along the **SS213** to Terracina, then take the **SS7** for 80km (50 miles) to Castel Gandolfo, leaving the **SS7** and following the signs from Albano Laziale.*

6 Castel Gandolfo, Lazio

Castel Gandolfo is where the Pope has his summer residence. Both town and papal palace are poised on a ridge above Lago (Lake) Albano and both come alive each year from July to September when the papal court transfers itself there from the Vatican City. All year round, however, the Swiss Guards are pacing up and down at the palace entrance, which faces a large square full of cafés and little shops. Entry to Castel Gandolfo, which takes its name from the castle built on the site of the present papal palace by the Gandolfi dukes in the 12th century, is via a magnificent 16th-century doorway. After resting in the square by the palace, visit the Church of San Tommaso di Villanova by Bernini, inside which are frescos by Pietro da Cortona. Both Bernini and da Cortona were among the founders of the Roman high baroque style.

From any number of points around the town you can look down over Lago Albano, a lake of volcanic origin that was chosen in the 1960s as the venue for the Olympic Games'

rowing competitions. The installations built at the time are still in use and it is a lovely place to swim. All around are thick woodlands of oaks and chestnuts and there are also some ancient remains in the form of the Bagni di Diana (Baths of Diana) and the Villa dell'Imperatore Domiziano (Villa of the Emperor Domitian) – follow the yellow signs from the centre of town to find these.

i Piazza Libertà 5

▶ *From Castel Gandolfo, rejoin and continue along the* ***SS7*** *to Frattocchie, then branch right across country for about 9km (5½ miles), past the* ***SS511*** *to the* ***SS215****, turning right for Frascati.*

SPECIAL TO...

The area around Frascati and Castel Gandolfo has a favourite snack often consumed out in the piazza. This is *porchetta*, pig roast on a spit and eaten in huge chunks. It is very salty and delicious, especially the crackling. Wash this down with ice-cold, white Frascati wine.

7 Frascati, Lazio

This little country town is famous not for the buildings in its centre, but for the country retreats in the hills surrounding it. Although Frascati itself is medieval, the existing villas are much later. However, villa retreats have been a part of Frascati's landscape since ancient Republican times when wealthy Romans settled at nearby *Tusculum*, an even more ancient city, now ruined, some distance up the slope behind modern Frascati.

The villas at Frascati date mostly from the 16th and 17th centuries. Most are still private and are not normally accessible.

The Villa Aldobrandini is the most spectacular here. Around 1,600 plans were made to bring water to the villa and a large cascade and water theatre were constructed. You can see the villa from the road and at odd times it is open to the public. The town has a pretty cathedral (San Pietro) built in 1598.

The former Aldobrandini Stables, dating from the 17th century, have recently been restored and converted into a prestigious cultural complex, including the Museum of Tuscolo, an exhibition space and an auditorium.

Frascati is also famous for its crisp white wine, which has a touch of almond flavour in its aftertaste.

i Piazza G Marconi 1

RECOMMENDED WALKS

Take the boat from Formia to the Pontine Islands of which Ponza and Ventotene are the most interesting. Ponza has some lovely beaches. You could walk along these, visiting the little isolated coves on the way, and lunching perhaps in the main town there. Ventotene is much smaller. It has only a small beach but you can walk to the remains of the villa built by Augustus' daughter, Giulia, in the 1st century AD.

▶ *From Frascati, return on the* ***SS215*** *to the GRA encircling Roma and continue clockwise on it for 18km (11 miles)* *until the turning left to the* ***SS8****, bound for Ostia and the sea.*

8 Ostia, Lazio

Ostia, the port of Rome, offers two contrasting attractions: the archaeological site of Ostia Antica and Lido di Ostia.

The old port of Ostia Antica, now Italy's best preserved Roman town after Pompeii, was established in about 338 BC when Rome needed to establish a settlement to supervise naval traffic and protect the mouth of the Tevere (Tiber) from raids by Tyrrhenian pirates. But old Ostia saw further construction right up to the 4th century AD, when it was abandoned.

A visit should start perhaps at the Porta Romana (the Roman Gate), past the statue of Minerva Victoria and the forum. There are some re-erected columns of temples in the forum and a little further on are the Terme di Nettuno (Baths of Neptune) with their installations for heating. There is also a small restored theatre capable of holding 3,000 spectators.

View over the quiet, medieval town of Subiaco

Some of the houses have lovely mosaic floors – see the Casa di Apuleio (House of Apuleius) – and there is one, the Casa di Diana (House of Diana), which still has its first floor intact, which is very unusual.

You could spend hours in Ostia Antica, so much is there to see, but make sure you pick up a map before you go and plan a route. The Museo Ostiense, reopened following restoration, contains the portable artefacts from the site.

The Lido di Ostia is the closest seaside resort to Rome and is very popular, but over the years it has become immensely crowded and commercialised, and the water and sand are often dangerously polluted. A safer bet for swimming in the area are the beaches around Sperlonga, to the southeast.

Gaeta's popular beach on the Tyrrhenian Sea

▶ *From Ostia, the* ***SS8*** *goes directly back to the centre of Roma.*

The Roman Countryside

North of Roma (Rome) the countryside is contorted into weird shapes by the prehistoric upheavals that took place beneath the earth's surface. It has a dour brooding aspect, heightened by the fact that the ancient towns in this area are built of local purple-black volcanic rock.

ITINERARY

ROMA	▶ **Cerveteri (45km-28m)**
CERVETERI	▶ **Santa Marinella (24km-15m)**
SANTA MARINELLA	▶ **Tarquinia (30km-19m)**
TARQUINIA	▶ **Tuscania (76km-47m)**
TUSCANIA	▶ **Caprarola (46km-29m)**
CAPRAROLA	▶ **Viterbo (19km-12m)**
VITERBO	▶ **Bagnaia (5km-3m)**
BAGNAIA	▶ **Vitorchiano (7km-4m)**
VITORCHIANO	▶ **Bomarzo (15km-9m)**
BOMARZO	▶ **Roma (95km-60m)**

3 DAYS • 362KM • 226 MILES

TOUR
17

[i] *Via Parigi II, Roma*

▶ *From Roma, take the **SS1** going west towards the coast for 28km (17 miles) until the turning inland for Cerveteri.*

1 Cerveteri, Lazio
Under the name of *Caere*, Cerveteri was one of the richest Etruscan towns as long ago as the 7th century BC. Today, however, what you see is largely medieval. Its old walls still exist as does the Rocca (castle) of the Orsini, later altered for the Ruspoli family. But it is for the Etruscan remains that Cerveteri is important. A great deal survives here from the period including an extensive necropolis, the Banditaccia Necropolis, that has yielded important treasures – jewellery and other elegant gold objects. It was laid out like a town and if you get a map on entering the site, you can walk down its principal streets and visit a great number of old family burial chambers including the Tomba dei Rilievi (Tomb of the Reliefs) which is covered in painted bas-reliefs of cooking utensils and other household objects. Another, called the Tomba degli Scudi e delle Sedie (Tomb of the Shields and Chairs) reflects the appearance of an Etruscan house. This is a rare find. You will never see the actual remains of an Etruscan house anywhere because they were built of wood, plaster or terracotta, and they never survived. Many of the finds from the tombs have found their way into Rome museums, but there are good displays in the National Etruscan Museum of Archaeology (Muzeo Nazionale di Ceveteri) in the Palazzo Ruspoli in Piazza Santa Maria.

▶ *From Cerveteri, return to, and turn right on to the **SS1** which hugs the coast for 20km (12½ miles) until Santa Marinella.*

2 Santa Marinella, Lazio
Santa Marinella is a pleasant beach resort that provides a very welcome diversion off the exhausting trail of the area's history. But even this place is located on Roman foundations, though there is a big castle here which was built by the Odescalchi family during the late Renaissance period.

Formal beauty in the garden of the Villa Lante, Bagnaia

▶ *Continue along the **SS1** for 30km (19 miles) to Tarquinia.*

3 Tarquinia, Lazio
Modern Tarquinia stands on a hill not far from Etruscan *Tarquinii*, which was built on another hill to the east. There is a lot to see in both places. Perhaps you could visit the newer town first: there are some pretty churches and picturesque medieval streets, particularly around the Church of San Pancrazio. The Romanesque Church of Santa Maria Castello (begun in 1121) has a lovely façade by Pietro di Ranuccio. The Museo Nazionale Tarquiniese, in the 15th-century Gothic Palazzo Vitelleschi, contains an extraordinary collection of objects, including sarcophagi from the Etruscan and Roman periods and the celebrated terracotta winged horses from a temple frieze dating from the end of the 4th century BC. The best of the 5th-century BC tomb paintings from the Etruscan period are kept here, including 'the Chariots', 'the Ship' and 'the Sofa'.

No visit would be complete, however, without seeing at least some of the old tombs themselves. The necropolis is all that has survived from the old city, and on the walls of the tombs you will see some of the best art ever produced by these mysterious people. If time is short, make for the tombs of 'the Lionesses', 'the Augurs' and 'the Leopards'.

[i] Piazza Cavour 1

FOR HISTORY BUFFS

On the way from Tarquinia to Tuscania, drop in on the tombs and catacombs cut out of the rock at Blera, about 12km (7½ miles) south of Vertralla. Nearby San Giuliano has one of the most important rock necropolises in the area; one tomb has a chamber decorated with reproductions of the wooden beams of a genuine habitation. Some of the tombs date back to the 8th century BC. The town to which the necropolis belonged was connected to Blera in Etruscan times by roads, cut into the soft rock. Magnificent rock-cut tombs can also be seen at Norchia, north of Blera, characterised by great façades with false entrances.

▶ *It is 5km (3 miles) southeast to the **SS1 bis**. Follow this to Vetralla, 32km (20 miles), then change to the **SS2** for 13km (8 miles) to Viterbo. Follow the signs to Tuscania, 26km (16 miles) westwards.*

SCENIC ROUTES

On the approach to Tuscania, the landscape is unusual – flat and with bamboo – quite unlike any other part of Lazio. The views from the ramparts of Bomarzo are spectacular. Look for Vitorchiano to the southwest. On the stretch of the A1 from Orte to Rome, look back and see the characteristic Lazio hilltowns littering the landscape.

4 Tuscania, Lazio

Tuscania is another town of great antiquity, though the visible remains of its past are confined, for the most part, to the medieval period. Here you can view the Etruscan past in the National Museum of Etruscan Archaeology. You can also see a section of the ancient road, the Via Clodia, that once connected Rome with the Etruscan cities further north, in Tuscany.

But the real treasures of the town are the fascinating little churches of San Pietro and Santa Maria Maggiore. Both are very ancient foundations (8th century), added to in the 11th, 12th and 13th centuries.

Romanesque San Pietro is one of the most important churches of its age in Italy and is especially noteworthy for its unusual sculpted façade – look at the shallow relief figures and plants around the rose window above the central door. There are early sculpted panels on the interior and an ancient crypt constructed using columns, some of which are Roman.

Santa Maria Maggiore also has some excellent, early sculpture, including the work on its entrance portal, a lovely rose window and an old pulpit.

▶ *Go back to Viterbo, then follow the signs south, in the direction of Lago di Vico (Lake Vico), to Caprarola – from Viterbo a distance of 19km (12 miles).*

5 Caprarola, Lazio

The main reason for coming to Caprarola is to visit the vast 16th-century Villa Farnese, built for the Farnese family (Pope Paul II, who was a member of this important family, was for a while Michelangelo's patron). It dominates the little town spread out beneath it as well as the countryside for miles around. The palace, more like a vast pentagonal fortress, was built by Giacomo Barozzi da Vignola, the influential 16th-century architect, on the foundations of an

BACK TO NATURE

Lying to the north of Lago di Vico, the Riserva Naturale Lago di Vico comprises wooded hills and mountains. In this region to the west of Caprarola, birds of prey soar overhead and wild boar and other forest animals haunt the slopes. Most of the reserve's creatures are rather shy of people, and patience and luck are needed to get good views.

Villa Farnese, status symbol of Cardinal Alessandro Farnese

earlier fortress. Inside there is a massive circular staircase that spirals up to the centre of the building, and all around it are frescos glorifying aspects of the Farnese family's sudden rise to power. The sheer vulgarity of these is the early equivalent of a modern billionaire's tendency to display his new-found wealth.

Grotesquerie in the extraordinary Monster Park at Bomarzo

The main rooms are no longer furnished, decoration being provided by the frescos. The gardens behind the palace are still well kept (by the state – the family is now extinct), and they make much use of water, with fountains and a 'water chain'. There is also an elegant little summer house, the Palazzina. If you stand in the forecourt of the palace and look to the right you can see the 17th-century Church of Santa Teresa, designed by the important baroque architect Girolamo Rainaldi.

▶ *From Caprarola, return to Viterbo by the same route.*

6 Viterbo, Lazio

The biggest town in this northern corner of Lazio, Viterbo is an impressive walled city, full of medieval buildings and fountains and with a lovely Romanesque cathedral with Gothic campanile. Viterbo once rivalled Rome as the place of residence of the popes. The 13th-century Palazzo dei Papi (Papal Palace), a battlemented pile more like a city hall than a palace, was where the Viterbo popes were elected. These elections were never easy and on one occasion, after the death of Clement IV, the cardinals were locked into the building and not allowed out until they had done their duty and elected a new pope. It took two years, during which the people of Viterbo tried to hurry the unfortunate cardinals by starving them out and then taking the roof off the building.

The pleasant beach resort of Santa Marinella

There is a variety of churches, including the rebuilt Santa Rosa, where you can see the remains of Viterbo's patron saint. Santa Rosa's preaching is supposed to have helped the people of Viterbo defeat Emperor Frederick II in 1243 when he laid siege to the town. Santa Maria Nuova, the cathedral, is a good example of the local Romanesque style, altered during the Renaissance. The Church of San Sisto dates in part from the 9th century. Throughout the old centre of Viterbo, there are little medieval alleys, flights of steps and carved balconies hanging on to the ancient buildings. Some of the houses have little stone towers.

RECOMMENDED TRIPS

Instead of driving or walking, why not take a boat trip? On the lake of Bolsena, in the crater of a volcano just north of Viterbo, boat trips are organised from the towns of Bolsena or Capodimonte. Trips are to Martana, a rocky island covered in woodland, and to Bisentina, another island which has a lovely church, SS Giacomo e Cristoforo. There is also the Chapel of Santa Caterina with, below it, an artificial grotto and gardens created by the Farnese family. This island is a must.

i Piazza San Carluccio 5

Bagnaia lies on the eastern outskirts of Viterbo, about 5km (3 miles) from the centre.

7 Bagnaia, Lazio

This hill village juts out on a spur overlooking the surrounding countryside. It is part medieval and part Renaissance. In the older section, crammed behind the old walls and overlooked by a watch-tower, the houses line dark stone alleys and there are splendid views out to the surrounding countryside. In the newer part of town, built around the square that faces the watch-tower and the old town gate, the streets are more regular. In this quarter is one of the most beautiful gardens to have emerged from the Italian Renaissance, and what is more, it is mostly still intact.

The Villa Lante was built by Giacomo Barozzi da Vignola, in the late 1560s, for Cardinal Gambera, whose family emblem, the crayfish (in Italian *gambero*), is scattered around the garden carved in stone. The gardens are more important than the buildings: there are fountains linked by an underground stream, a water chain, formal parterres and a series of

Etruscan tombs in Cerveteri's 'city of the dead'

Tarquinia's Roman aqueduct

giocchi d'acqua, water jokes. The Cardinal enjoyed entertaining his guests (and himself) with these mechanical practical jokes. A servant would trigger a secret mechanism somewhere behind the fountain, and the guests would be sprayed with water from some hidden source. The keeper of the garden might be persuaded to show you these – some of them still work.

▶ *Take the cross-country route that leaves the main square in the centre of Bagnaia. Vitorchiano is only 7km (4 miles) away.*

> **SPECIAL TO...**
>
> The menus of this area include great plates of wild boar, dishes using offal, and lamb scented with rosemary. Try *Saltimbocca alla Romana*, which is slices of veal cooked with *prosciutto*, *mozzarella* cheese and sage. The whole lot is dunked in Marsala. Its name means 'jump in the mouth'. Most of the wines from this region are white, and by far the most common is one called *Est Est Est* from Montefiascone.

8 Vitorchiano, Lazio
Vitorchiano is very similar to Bagnaia. Both are built of *peperino*, the local volcanic stone, purplish in colour. They also have the same medieval aspect. Vitorchiano is fortified only on one side. The rest of the town sits on a huge impregnable rock that provided a natural defence. Walking through the little dark streets, look out for the SPQR ('Senatus Populusque Romanus') symbol of Vitorchiano's allegiance to Rome. Traditionally this goes back to when an ancient Roman is said to have run from Vitorchiano to Rome to warn the city that it was about to be attacked by the Etruscans. The man died soon afterwards but the City of Rome rewarded the people of Vitorchiano calling it the 'faithful city', and giving it special powers. This relationship persisted, hence the little medieval wall plaques showing the wolf suckling Romulus and Remus, symbol of Rome.

Have lunch at Vitorchiano and wander slowly around the town. It has no special art treasures or monuments. Quite simply it is an enchanting, if strange, place, full of young people restoring their old family houses.

▶ *From Vitorchiano, follow the signs to Bomarzo via the* ***SS204****.*

9 Bomarzo, Lazio
Bomarzo is another town built out of *peperino* stone. Very small, it has a forbidding military look about it. Most of its houses are crammed around a large fortress traditionally belonging to the Orsini family, though now partially divided into flats. After wandering through the slightly damp streets, and paying a quick visit to the brightly painted but tiny main church, you should spend some time at the Parco dei Mostri (Monster Park) on the edge of town.

> **FOR CHILDREN**
>
> The Parco dei Mostri (Monster Park) at Bomarzo is an extraordinary park filled with enormous fantastical creatures, beasts, grotesques and monsters hewn from the local rock by Turkish prisoners of war in the 16th century. Among these is a huge elephant squeezing a helpless Roman soldier in its trunk and a figure tearing its adversary in half. The sheer madness exhibited could frighten children and can only be fully appreciated by adults. Children would enjoy another grotesquerie – a little house with a steeply inclined floor, which gives the impression of walking across the deck of a ship at very rough sea. There is a small park adjacent offering tamer delights – swings and a herd of deer, as well as a café and shop.

▶ *Return to the* ***SS204****. Turn left and take this road to the* ***A1*** *autostrada which leads to Roma (from the nearby Orte junction). Follow the signs.*

In the Shadow of Vesuvius

Campania divides neatly into two areas – a coastal region and an inland landscape of mountains and valleys. This tour covers the coast which, after Liguria, is one of the most popular in Italy. The difference between the two rivieras is that, in addition to the idyllic seaside resorts, Campania's coast also has a series of rich historical sites to be visited, such as Pompeii and Ercolano.

5 DAYS • 323KM • 199 MILES

ITINERARY

NAPOLI	▶ **Pozzuoli (12km-7m)**
POZZUOLI	▶ **Ercolano (20km-12m)**
ERCOLANO	▶ **Pompeii (15km-9m)**
POMPEII	▶ **Napoli (Capri ferry) (23km-14m)**
POMPEII	▶ **Sorrento (Capri ferry) (28km-17m)**
SORRENTO	▶ **Positano (23km-14m)**
POSITANO	▶ **Amalfi (16km-10m)**
AMALFI	▶ **Ravello (6km-4m)**
RAVELLO	▶ **Salerno (28km-17m)**
SALERNO	▶ **Paestum (36km-22m)**
PAESTUM	▶ **Agropoli (Cilento coast) (9km-6m)**
AGROPOLI	▶ **Napoli (107km-67m)**

In the Shadow of Vesuvius

i Piazza del Gesù Nuovo

► *From Napoli, take the autostrada or the coastal road to Pozzuoli – it is only 12km (7 miles) from the centre of Naples going in the direction of Gaeta.*

FOR HISTORY BUFFS

Near Pozzuoli are the ancient sites of Cumae (about 5km/3 miles) and Baia (about 4km/2½ miles). At Cumae, thought to be the oldest Greek colony in Italy, visit the Antro della Sibilla (Cave of the Cumaean Sibyl) just below the summit of the Acropolis. The hero Aeneas consults the Sybil in Virgil's great poem the *Aeneid*. At Baia, there are the remains of an imperial villa and at Capo (Cape) Miseno, 5km (3 miles) further on, are the tumble-down remains of what was the greatest naval base of the Roman Empire.

1 Pozzuoli, Campania
Pozzuoli was once a city in its own right, though nowadays it seems more like an extension of Napoli itself. Its claim to fame is that from among its aged villas and the clutter of houses around the Roman ruins, emerged the sultry film actress Sophia Loren. This, her birthplace, was once a Roman city, named Puteoli. It has the remains of the third largest amphitheatre in Italy – the Anfiteatro Flavio. You can see the well-preserved dens for wild animals beneath it, but earthquakes as well as intermittent eruptions of Mount Vesuvius have otherwise destroyed much of its ancient character. What was once thought to be a Serapeum (Temple of Serapis – an Egyptian god), survives from the 1st century AD, though it is partially submerged beneath the water near the harbour. It is now believed to be the remains of a market building. You can visit other parts of the archaeological park in which it is situated. Back in the centre of town is the Duomo (cathedral) dedicated to St Procolo. Nowadays it is a rather tumbledown building, most of it destroyed in 1964 in a fire; after the fire, its baroque additions were removed revealing a Roman structure in marble beneath.

i Piazza Matteotti

► *Go back through the centre of Naples and follow the signs to Ercolano (Herculaneum) which lies on the other side of the city beyond Portici.*

2 Ercolano, Campania
Ercolano is an important Roman site. Not as big or important as Pompeii, the city was once a residential enclave for wealthy Romans. A great many villas have survived, some with their furnishings, the whole lot having been buried beneath the mud and lava from the eruption of Vesuvius in AD 79. You can see the excavations in just a couple of hours, time enough to appreciate this fossil of everyday Roman life, eerily

Amalfi's striking Duomo – an exotic blend of styles

preserved by the catastrophe of nearly 2,000 years ago. The Casa del Tramezzo Carbonizzato (House of the Carbonised Wooden Partition) gives some idea of an early double-storeyed house, while in the Casa del Mobilio Carbonizzato (House of the Carbonised Furniture) you can see ancient furniture in its original position. In the Casa dell'Atrio a Mosaico (House of the Mosaic Atrium) are some splendid mosaic floors, while the House of the Gem still has an ancient kettle in its kitchen. Places such as the *palaestra* (the gym) and the baths survive, reached on streets paved with original limestone slabs.

▶ *From Ercolano, the* ***SS18*** *continues to Pompeii.*

3 Pompeii, Campania

Pompeii was a large commercial city also destroyed by the eruption of Vesuvius in AD 79, but, in this case, covered by layers of volcanic ash rather than mud. The site is huge and would take at least a morning to complete successfully. Buy a map or a guide before you enter: villas, shops, temples – there is much to see and the extent of it is confusing without some kind of guide. There are human ones only too willing to offer their services; agree a price in advance. One of the most sumptuous villas is the Casa dei Vettii (House of the Vettii), a large house with a decorated interior. Much of it has been reconstructed and in addition to the lavish frescos there are fountains and statues.

In the Via di Nola is a tavern in which were found three trumpets dumped by gladiators as they fled from the nearby amphitheatre and in the shop of Verus the Blacksmith you will see a lamp and other objects either under repair or being made at the time of the eruption. Of the public buildings, the basilica (law courts) was the most monumental; in the Antiquarium you will see casts taken from the impressions left by original bodies found among the ruins. Pompeii is an extraordinary and evocative place. To see many of the movable treasures found here you will have to visit the museum in Naples, but there are some replicas in Pompei's Vesuvian Museum, which is mostly devoted to the volcano and its eruptions.

Pompeii's amphitheatre could accommodate 12,000 spectators

i *Via Sacra 1*

▶ *To get to the island of Capri, either go back to the port of Naples or go to Sorrento via the* ***SS145,*** *28km (17 miles) further along the coast. If you choose the latter it will add about 5km (3 miles) to the total road mileage of the tour. Either way, both ports have regular island ferry services. From Naples the trip takes one hour and 10 minutes; from Sorrento 35 minutes.*

4 Capri, Campania

Capri is a good place to avoid in the middle of the summer when it is absolutely packed with tourists. Just before or just after the season you will have the benefit of pleasant rocky coves in which to swim and tan unmolested by the hordes. There is plenty to see and do on the island. Capri town is bursting with designer shops but if you are not interested in these, you can visit the Duomo built in the 17th century and the Giardini di Augusto (Gardens of Augustus), founded by Augustus himself. The Villa Jovis, a 45-minute walk from the town, was the home of the Emperor Tiberius towards the end of his reign. Combine a visit to the ruins with the grim Salto di Tiberio, the cliffs from which the emperor was supposed to have flung his enemies.

The little town of Anacapri is known for the Villa San Michele, immortalised by Axel Munthe in *The Story of San Michele*. Near by are the remains of the Villa Imperiale, Augustus' villa (not as well preserved as the Villa Jovis). You could walk to here as well as to the ruined Castello di Barbarossa, but buses do the rounds. A chair-lift runs from the town up to the summit of Monte Solare, from where there are wonderful views. Of great natural beauty are the Grotta Azzurra (Blue Grotto) – take a boat from Capri port – and the Grotta Verde (Green Grotto), reached from Anacapri.

i *Piazza Umberto I*

▶ *From Capri, the quickest way to Positano is to take the boat back to Sorrento. From Sorrento take the **SS145** (which joins and becomes the **SS163**) to Positano, about 23km (14 miles).*

SPECIAL TO...

Capri celebrates New Year festivities. Performing musicians play the *putipù*, a characteristic folk instrument, in the piazzas of Capri and Anacapri. If you are here over Christmas and New Year, then try Campania's traditional Christmas Eve dish – *capitone marinato* – eel cooked in vinegar with bay leaves and garlic, then left to marinate in its own sauce for a few days. You should also try the more usual *insalata caprese* – a salad of *mozzarella* cheese, tomatoes, basil and olive oil. It originated here.

RECOMMENDED WALKS

It is possible to see the whole of Capri on foot. The walks from Capri town itself are most enjoyable. One, from the Via Tragara, leads to Faraglioni – the three enormous rocks that stick up out of the sea off the southeast coast of the island. You could have a swim a little way beyond, off the Punta di Tragara.

5 **Positano,** Campania

The town of Positano sits almost vertically above the sea. From the high cliff road above, it seems as though the characteristic whitewashed houses have been tipped over the edge to the water. There are no great monuments to be seen in Positano; the little town is simply a picturesque coastal resort, full of restaurants and cafés in which to while away the days.

Within easy reach of Positano are a number of other tiny ports. One of these, Praiano, has a fine beach while at Conca dei Marini are the remains of a Norman watch-tower. Just before Conca dei Marini is the Grotta dello Smeraldo (Emerald Cave), a large cavern to which you can descend in a lift from the roadside. It gets its name from the colour of the light filling its interior. If you look carefully, you can see, now under water, stalagmites formed when the cave was above sea-level.

i *Via del Saracino 4*

▶ *The **SS163** continues to Amalfi, 16km (10 miles).*

6 **Amalfi,** Campania

In the early Middle Ages, Amalfi was a powerful maritime republic, possibly the most important in Italy. This seems

Ancient Pompeii started life in the 6th century BC as a Greek trading post

surprising at first glance, because the town today is so small. But its monuments reveal the truth, notably the restored Arsenale. The Duomo di Sant'Andrea (cathedral) is one of the loveliest south of Naples. The approach is up a long, steep flight of steps and you enter through bronze doors made in Constantinople in 1066.

Next door to the cathedral is the 13th-century Chiostro del Paradiso (Cloisters of Paradise), with beautiful double columns, the pair intertwining voluptuously.

Climbing up the steep hillside outside Amalfi are villas and small hotels. One of the latter – the biggest – was at one time a Capuchin convent. Access is via a lift that rushes up the side of the mountain; the views from its terrace are spectacular. The town also has a small civic museum and a historic paper mill, with displays on paper-making.

i Corso delle Repubbliche Marinare 19–21

▶ *From Amalfi, branch off the* ***SS163*** *on to a minor road which winds up the hillside to Ravello, about 6km (4 miles).*

7 Ravello, Campania
The beautiful village of Ravello is isolated at the top of the hill directly above Amalfi at about 350m (1,150 feet) above sea-level. It has two historic villas, Villa Cimbrone and Villa Rufolo, both of which have splendid gardens.

The Villa Rufolo was begun in the 11th century and its remarkable Saracenic-Norman character has survived. The composer Richard Wagner was its most illustrious guest; in fact its gardens were the inspiration for the magic garden of Klingsor in

There is a Moorish look to Positano, clinging to the cliffs

The enchanting town of Ravello is set high above the Amalfi Coast

the opera *Parsifal*. The villa, once the residence of popes, has a fine view of the coastline from its terrace. But the gardens of the Villa Cimbrone are more spectacular. These rather wild and surprisingly lush gardens with their arbours and old lichen-covered terraces, end in a long terrace from which you have an unrivalled view of the Amalfi coastline. Ravello's Duomo (cathedral) contains some very early art: 12th- and 13th-century pulpits, with inlaid marble and mosaic, and fine bronze doors, dating from 1179 and modelled on the more famous Amalfi cathedral doors. There is a small museum in the cathedral.

i *Piazza Duomo 10*

RECOMMENDED WALKS

A good walk to take is from Ravello to the little village of Scala, about 1.5km (1 mile) away. It has a pretty miniature cathedral.

▶ *From Ravello, go back to the* ***SS163****, then continue eastwards along it for 24km (15 miles) to Salerno.*

8 Salerno, Campania

The name of Salerno is renowned as the place where the Allies began their invasion of Italy in September 1943. Today it is a town that people tend to ignore on a tour of Campania. It is a working town with a busy port and industries. Its treasures are eclipsed by those of the other more popular towns along the coast, but it has a Duomo (Cathedral of St Matthew), consecrated in 1085, but much altered. This cathedral follows the local fashion in having a pair of bronze doors (from Constantinople) and another set of 12th-century mosaic-inlaid pulpits of the kind found in Ravello. In the former seminary, the Diocesan Museum contains various fragments from the cathedral building.

Try to get to the Provincial Museum, which contains finds from archaeological excavations from all over the province of Salerno, including a bronze head of Apollo from the 1st century.

i *Piazza Ferrovia*

SCENIC ROUTES

The most scenic route on this tour is the journey from Positano to Salerno on the SS163. On the way look out for the ceramic-covered domes of the churches in the midst of the hamlets that cling to the side of the steep hillsides just above the sea.

▶ *From Salerno, follow the long straight coastal road for about 36km (22 miles) to Paestum.*

9 Paestum, Campania

There was once a great city at Paestum. All that remains is a handful of ancient buildings in a remarkable state of preservation – the Basilica (dedicated to the queen goddess Hera), the Tempio di Nettuno (the Temple of Neptune), the Tempio di Cerere (Temple of Ceres) and about 4km (2½ miles) of walls that once surrounded the old city.

Paestum was abandoned around the 9th century because of the threat of malaria from surrounding marshes and attacks by invading Saracens, and the temples lay hidden for centuries in a kind of subtropical forest, now converted, into a dry plain.

The Temple of Neptune, dating from about 450 BC, is the best preserved building here. Huge and solid, it is in the unadorned, Doric style. The museum contains some of the sculptural fragments from the temples here as well as finds from the Sanctuary of Hera, about 10km (6 miles) to the north of Paestum.

But the prize exhibits in the museum are the tomb paintings – in particular those from the Tomba del Tuffatore (Tomb of the Diver), thought to be the only surviving examples of Greek funerary mural painting anywhere.

i Via Magna Grecia 887

From Paestum, it is only a short run to the beginning of the Cilento Coast. Go south for about 9km (6 miles) and begin at Agropoli.

10 **Agropoli,** Campania

The coastline changes completely after Paestum; if you follow the sea all the way to Pioppi you encounter miniature bays, long white beaches and a series of small ports with nothing more than a fine position to recommend them. Agropoli is perhaps the most popular. Its core is medieval and you can visit the Convent of San Francesco.

Further along at San Marco there are ancient Roman remains including the breakwater carved out of the rock. From here the road leads to Agnone, bypassing Monte Licosa which rises almost vertically from the sea. You should not miss this part of the coast so take the smaller road – or track – to Ogliastro Marina, park the car, then walk around to the Punta Licosa (Licosa Point). It is named after the siren Leucosia, who is said to have jumped into the sea from the promontory after failing to enchant Odysseus as he sailed past on his epic voyage.

*From Agropoli, make for the **SS18** going north across the Sele Plain to Battipaglia, at which join the **A3** going back to Naples, a further 76km (47 miles).*

The superb Temple of Neptune at Paestum

BACK TO NATURE

Because it is effectively land-locked, the Mediterranean has a small tidal range and so relatively few marine creatures can be seen on its shores. However, the coastal vegetation is impressive in unspoilt areas. For bird-watchers, colourful *macchia* vegetation may grow almost to the shoreline and this harbours a wide variety of warblers. Blue rock thrushes sing from exposed rocky outcrops.

FOR CHILDREN

If you are here towards the end of the year, the children will be fascinated by the *presepi* (Christmas cribs). Churches and private homes begin preparing to display their *presepi* in November. You find the best ones in Naples itself, but all over Campania – even in little country churches – you will find the tradition adhered to. They usually have miniature Roman ruins, animals, beggars, musicians and many other figures, quite apart from the Holy Family.

TOUR
19

Small Cities
of Campania

Away from the coastal resort, Campania is a quiet rural region. Great tracts of countryside are empty but even the loneliest parts are within reach of Napoli (Naples). Here you will find good restaurants representative of the great variety of cooking from the provinces. Napoli is Campania's melting pot. As in the provincial towns surrounding it you will find Roman and Greek remains as well as buildings with Byzantine or Spanish influences.

4 DAYS • 176KM • 110 MILES

ITINERARY	
NAPOLI	▶ **Aversa (17km-11m)**
AVERSA	▶ **Capua (16km-10m)**
CAPUA	▶ **Caserta (11km-7m)**
CASERTA	▶ **Benevento (50km-31m)**
BENEVENTO	▶ **Avellino (33km-21m)**
AVELLINO	▶ **Napoli (49km-30m)**

BACK TO NATURE

Although built up to a large extent, the outskirts of Naples still support areas of woodland, with associated wildlife. Look and listen for firecrest, golden orioles and spotted flycatchers in the trees. It can also be rewarding to look down, as orchids often grow in the leaf litter on the ground below in early spring.

i Piazza del Gesù Nuovo, Naples

► *From Naples, take the **SS7bis** north to Aversa for 17km (11 miles).*

1 Aversa, Campania
This small town was founded by the Normans in 1029 – in fact it was their very first settlement in this part of Italy. Although the castle was originally their work, it was rebuilt in the 18th century and later turned into a hospital. King Andrew of Hungary was murdered here in 1345 and here, too, his death was avenged by his brother Louis of Hungary. The Duomo (cathedral of San Paolo) was also founded by the Normans. Though it was altered later, you can see some original Norman work inside. If you are not reeling from the effects of the potent local brew, a white wine called *Asprinio* which is generally considered a 'thirst-quenching' wine for hot summer days, then be sure to visit the Church of San Lorenzo which has a beautiful cloister.

Galleria Umberto I, Naples' elegant glass and iron arcade

Caserta is famous for its 18th-century palace and gardens

▶ *The SS7bis continues for 16km (10 miles) to Capua.*

> **SCENIC ROUTES**
>
> The most scenic parts of this particular tour are the following: the last 20km (12½ miles) on the SS88 from Benevento to Avellino, which wind through the mountains past Altavilla Irpina and a scattering of small hilltowns. There is nothing in particular to look out for; it is simply a lovely scenic route; the trip to the Sanctuary of Monte Vergine from Avellino looks back over the valley to Altavilla Irpina.

2 Capua, Campania

Capua was the greatest town in Campania during the Roman period. Its small size today makes this hard to believe, but enough survives from its heyday to give some idea of its early importance. At Santa Maria di Capua Vetere, the old city that was utterly destroyed in about AD 830 by the Arabs, and about 2km (1 mile) from newer Capua, are the remains of a large amphitheatre, second in size only to the Colosseum in Rome. Great blocks of stone and a hefty arched construction survive among the cypresses. Here, too, is the Arco di Adriano (Hadrian's Arch – also called the Arch of Capua) built in honour of the emperor who restored the amphitheatre in AD 119. One of the best preserved ancient monuments here is the Mithraeum, an underground hall dedicated to the worship of the Persian Sun-god Mithras – a cult very popular with Roman soldiers. It dates from about the 2nd century AD and is probably the best example of a rectangular underground area with a vault painted with stars. The rites of the cult included the slaying of a bull and here there is a fresco of Mithras killing a large white bull – a very rare survival.

New Capua contains the most interesting finds from these ancient sites in the Museo Campano, including an array of ancient sculpture. The Duomo (cathedral), founded in AD 835, was destroyed in 1942 and completely rebuilt, though its beautiful campanile (bell tower) dates from 861.

▶ *From Capua, follow the signs to Caserta, only 11km (7 miles) away.*

3 Caserta, Campania

The only reason to come to Caserta is to see the biggest palace in Italy, started in 1752 by Vanvitelli for the Bourbon King of Naples, Charles III, and intended to rival Versailles. Known as La Reggia, or the Palazzo Reale, its interior, in which there are some 1,200 rooms, is extremely richly decorated (in particular the State Apartments) with gilding, different types of marble, tapestries, paintings and frescos. Bringing the attractions at the palace right up to date is the Mostra Terrea Motus exhibit (additional charge) which recalls the devastation of the 1980 earthquake that rocked the area. The park and the gardens, famous for their water gardens, cascades and fountains, are as elaborate as the interior is extravagant. They are also huge. One of the focal points, the statue group of *Diana and Actaeon*, is about 3km (2 miles) from the palace itself. If, for some reason, you cannot get into the building, there is plenty to see and do in the garden. Look out for the 18th-century English Garden.

King Vittorio Emanuele III presented the palace to the State in 1921.

Not far from the palace, which is situated in the newer town, is Caserta Vecchia, a medieval town which was all but abandoned when the newer one was built along with the palace. There is an interesting Norman and Sicilian-style cathedral. Its interior is a hotch-potch of fascinating details: particularly noteworthy are the 18 antique columns and the early mosaic details.

> **RECOMMENDED WALKS**
>
> The best walks on this tour would, perhaps surprisingly, be in the vast grounds of La Reggia, the royal palace at Caserta. They are amazingly big and full of little surprises, such as hidden fountains among the undergrowth.

i *Piazza del Dante 35*

▶ *The SS7 leads to Benevento, 50km (31 miles).*

4 **Benevento,** Campania

Benevento is possibly the most interesting town on the tour of Campania's hinterland. The old streets in its centre preserve monuments ranging from a Roman theatre to an early medieval gate, the Port'Arsa. Benevento was badly bombed in World War II, with the near total loss of its cathedral, a 13th-century Romanesque building of which only the richly sculpted façade and bell tower are original. The rest has been rebuilt. The Roman theatre was begun in the 2nd century AD, in the reign of Hadrian; its most remarkable features are three monumental gates.

The *triggio* quarter of town contains more visible remains of Benevento's Roman past. You will see bits of ancient stonework built into the walls of the houses, and on the outskirts of town is the Ponte Leproso (Leproso Bridge), a Roman construction carrying the Via Appia (Appian Way) over the Sabato river. A particularly fine Roman monument is the Porta Aurea (Arch of Trajan), a marble triumphal arch 15m (50 feet) high, excellently preserved, with bas-reliefs of the life of Trajan and a variety of mythological subjects.

i *Via N Sala 31*

▶ *From Benevento, take the **SS88** to Avellino, a cross-country route.*

5 **Avellino,** Campania

Like many of the cities in this region, 'modern' Avellino occupies a site just a few kilometres from its original position. In this case, ancient Abellinum was situated near to the present-day village of Atripalda, just 4km (2½ miles) to the east of Avellino. The Museum of Irpinia in Avellino (Corso Europa) houses the finds from the old town as well as archaeological collections from the necropolises of Mirabella Eclano (take the A16 going north from Avellino for 40km/25 miles) and Ariano Irpino (about 12km/7½ miles further on, just off the A16 on the SS90). The modern section of the museum includes ceramics, paintings and a magnificent 18th-century crib (*presepio*), a very popular element of southern Italian religious culture. Also in the town are a medieval castle and a 17th-century customs house, the Palazzo della Dogana, with a sculpted façade.

> **FOR CHILDREN**
>
> Just outside Benevento (about 16km/10 miles to the east) is the town of Foglianise where every year, on 16 August, the villagers celebrate with a wheat festival.
>
> Children would probably like to see this: tractors decorated with straw are paraded through the streets followed by young girls in traditional costume with baskets of wheat on their heads. In the evening there is a display of coloured lights.

i *Via Due Principanti 5*

▶ *From Avellino, take the **A16** west for 41km (25 miles) then the **A1** south for 8km (5 miles) back to Naples.*

> **SPECIAL TO...**
>
> The province of Avellino has a wide variety of arts and crafts including inlaid and carved woodwork. In Avellino you will also find lots of shops selling the local brands of *mozzarella*, *pecorino* and *treccia* cheeses – *mozzarella* is made from buffalo's milk, *pecorino* from the local ewe's milk, while *treccia* (which means 'plait') is a mixture of cheese from cow's milk and *mozzarella*.

> **FOR HISTORY BUFFS**
>
> About 22km (15 miles) from Avellino up in the heart of the Partenio massif is the Santuario di Monte Vergine (Sanctuary of Monte Vergine), a church dedicated to the Mother of God, founded in the 12th century. Preserved here, in this very beautiful spot on the mountainside, is a painting of a head of the Virgin, supposed to have been done by St Luke. Visit the museum and the basilica.
>
> If this is not enough, further down the hill is the Convent of Loreto which was built on the site of a pagan laurel grove. Here you will find an 13th-century pharmacy with a collection of majolica apothecary's jars, important 16th-century Flemish tapestries and a vast archive.

CALABRIA, BASILICATA, PUGLIA

The lovely hilltop town of Rivello, Basilicata

The far south is perhaps the most intriguing and dramatic part of Italy. Wild, uncontrollable territory alternates with dense woodland and gentle, cultivated plains. For many people, Italy stops at Rome or, at a push, Naples. Beyond, there is nothing but an unfamiliar mountainous land mass, full of strange rustics with peculiar customs and leading backward lives. Nothing could be further from the truth; the attractions of the south are merely less obvious and altogether extraordinary. Who would have thought that some of the strangest customs and dialects in Calabria had their origins in 15th-century Albania; or that some of the inhabitants of Matera in Basilicata are quite happy to live underground; or even stranger – that people in parts of Puglia live in prehistoric-type houses that look like beehives?

Most of Calabria and Basilicata is mountainous, with craggy outcrops of rock blanketed with thick forests. Shut away in the hinterland of both regions are remote whitewashed hill villages, cities and castles. Ancient buildings, medieval city centres, and traditional customs, dress and dialect have survived in Calabria and Basilicata as a result of the lie of the land and its inaccessibility.

But these areas are fascinating, especially to anyone interested in archaeology and history. Much of the south was once a part of Magna Graecia – the name given to the ancient Greek colonies founded in southern Italy and Sicily from the 8th century BC – and the archaeological sites of the region have yielded important finds from that period, the time of their greatest prosperity. In these areas, and in Puglia too, there are Roman remains as well as Byzantine and Norman architecture and a variety of other evidence of the trail left behind by the conquerors of the south over the centuries.

In Puglia, which forms the spur and heel of the boot of Italy, the terrain is mostly gentler – flatter, with greater areas of cultivation. Some of the region's ports are the busiest in Italy, with regular ferries to Greece and Croatia. It bustles with life, where Calabria and Basilicata seem to brood on their past.

Catanzaro
Catanzaro is a lively town. It sits on a stony peak with deep gorges on either side, surrounded by a wonderful panorama. Just a few kilometres away is the sea. Although it might not be obvious behind the results of Catanzaro's rapid modern development, the city has ancient Byzantine origins and a rich cultural tradition, some traces of which can be seen in the fine Museo Provinciale (Provincial Museum).

Cosenza
Cosenza had an eventful history giving it a varied cultural background – at different times it fell under the sway of the Romans, Normans, Swabians, Angevins and Aragonese. All these have left their mark, though the old city has a predominantly medieval aspect, dominated by a huge Norman castle. Cosenza is a thriving market town, and can boast some of Calabria's best restaurants.

Matera
The different periods of Matera's history are clearly defined as you walk through the city centre and around its outskirts. The town's main attraction is the fascinating Sassi, with rockcut dwellings gouged from the city's foundations along with tunnels and labyrinthine grottoes; there are also rock chapels, some of whose walls are covered with frescos. Just outside town there are many more small churches cut into the hills. But more normal buildings are in plentiful supply – the Duomo is 13th-century Romanesque, with much of interest to be seen both inside and out.

Bari
Bari, Puglia's capital, consists of an old quarter – the Città Vecchia – which lies nearest the sea and has medieval buildings in its streets; the newer Città Nuova, with a neat grid-plan of streets; and the industrial area further inland. The city contains some of the most magnificent buildings in the region: the Romanesque cathedral, the castle and the great Basilica of San Nicola, founded in the 11th century by the Normans – their first major church in Puglia. The Museo Archeologico, with its fine ceramics, and the Pinacoteca Provinciale, full of southern Italian art from the 11th to the 18th centuries, are also worth seeing.

Brindisi
Both Bari and Brindisi are important Adriatic ports. The latter sits on a peninsula between two arms of land, at the head of a wide inlet, forming a natural harbour. Strangely, for a city whose claim to fame is as the major point of embarkation for Greece, the centre of Brindisi has the air of a small provincial town. Cafés line the main street and there is a pretty promenade at the town centre overlooking the water. Brindisi's archaeological museum (Museo Archeologico Provinciale) preserves the best of the finds from nearby Roman sites. Be sure to visit the colourful Church of Santa Maria del Casale with its impressive Byzantine *Last Judgement*, a few kilometres north, near the airport.

Foggia
Foggia, once known as 'Capitanata', is Puglia's third city. Not much of its ancient aspect survives. Today it is a city of wide avenues and mostly low-rise, modern buildings. However, the cathedral survives, a strange mixture of Romanesque and baroque. The Museo Civico (Civic Museum) contains archaeological finds from the area as well as an exhibition of Puglian traditional crafts.

Green and rolling Apulian countryside near Bovino

TOUR **20**

The Toe of the Boot

Southern Calabria consists mostly of the Aspromonte mountain range. While its coastline is largely built up, the interior, being more difficult to access, has been left relatively untouched. Catanzaro is the exception. Big, lively and modern, it engulfs the outcrop on which it stands.

5 DAYS • 478KM • 296 MILES

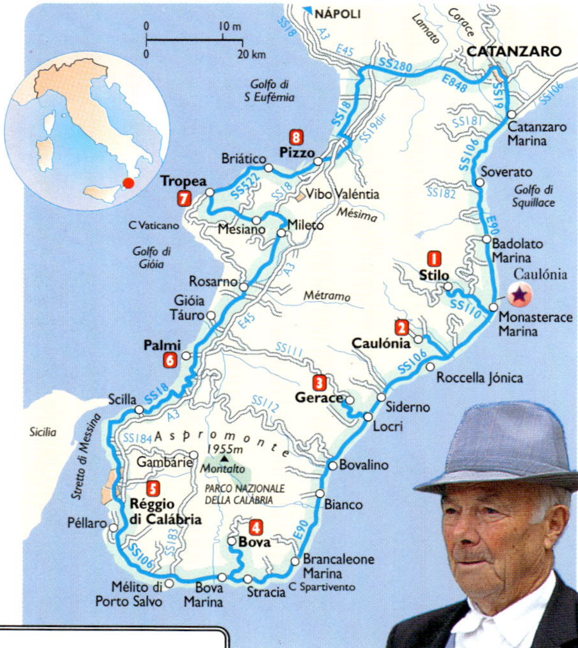

ITINERARY	
CATANZARO	▶ **Stilo (66km-41m)**
STILO	▶ **Caulonia (37km-23m)**
CAULONIA	▶ **Gerace (39km–24m)**
GERACE	▶ **Bova (76km-47m)**
BOVA	▶ **Reggio di Calabria (57km-35m)**
REGGIO DI CALABRIA	▶ **Palmi (49km-30m)**
PALMI	▶ **Tropea (67km-42m)**
TROPEA	▶ **Pizzo (27km-17m)**
PIZZO	▶ **Catanzaro (60km-37m)**

i Via Spasari 3, Catanzaro

SCENIC ROUTES

To get to the sea at Copanello, about 6km (3½ miles) on the SS106 south of Catanzaro, you drive through the flat lands between the sea and the mountains, an area characterised by clumps of umbrella pines and 2m (6-foot) high reeds. From here, right down the coast of Calabria, the scenery is the same.

The whole of the SS18 going north is a panoramic route: to one side are the famous white Palmi sands and the beautiful beaches right up to Nicotera (22km/13 miles from Tropea), and on the other, high mountains that drop sharply down to sea-level.

▶ *Take the **SS19** south to the coast, then branch southwest on the coastal **SS106** for 48km (30 miles) until Monasterace Marina. Follow the **SS110** to Stilo.*

1 Stilo, Calabria

Stilo, halfway down the Monte Consolino, contains one of the most exquisite buildings in Calabria. Called La Cattolica, it is a terracotta-coloured Byzantine chapel. Inside, one of its antique columns has been placed upside down as a symbol of the defeat of paganism by Christianity. On a ledge above the town, La Cattolica looks out over the rocky valley at the head of which Stilo stands. The best time to come to Stilo would be at Easter, when Holy Week is celebrated with religious processions that meander through the town from church to church. In one of these the inhabitants start at the parish church, the Chiesa Madre, following the statue of the Madonna Addolorata, weaving through the ancient and narrow stone-walled streets, on their way to the Church of San Giovanni Jeresti where, before a large cross they pray, listen to music and sing hymns in dialect. Special cakes with names like *nzulle* and *cuzzepe* are prepared for the occasion. Shaped like hearts and fishes, they are made of nuts, eggs, dried figs and sugar. In addition to this all the town's churches (there are five) are open for the event. Try to see the Church of San Francesco, founded in 1400, with its ornately carved wooden altar. On the edge of town the Porta Stefanina, one of Stilo's ancient gateways, still has an intact defensive tower.

▶ *Go back to Monasterace Marina and continue south on the **SS106** for 14km (9 miles) until the turning west for Caulonia, 8km (5 miles).*

2 Caulonia, Calabria

This little clay-coloured town, situated between the rivers Assi and Amusa, was founded by refugees from the ancient city of Caulonia which was destroyed by Dionysius I of Syracuse in 389 BC. There is little to be seen here except for a notable tomb in the Chiesa Madre (parish church). By a Tuscan sculptor, it belongs to one of the members of the Carafa family and is dated 1488. There is also the Chiesetta Zaccaria, a little church filled with Byzantine frescos. None the less, Caulonia is interesting as a country town where not much has changed for centuries.

The little Church of Santa Maria dell'Isola in Tropea

▶ *Returning to the **SS106**, continue south as far as Locri at which follow the signs west to Gerace on the **SS111**.*

FOR HISTORY BUFFS

For those interested in clambering over the ruins of ancient Calabria, Locri (near Gerace) has the most visible remains – temples, a theatre, and both Greek and Roman tombs. Though most of the artefacts from the site are now in the museum at Reggio di Calabria, on site is a museum with a small collection of vases, votive statues and sculpture as well as a diagram of the site which, for the uninitiated, is a must. The ruins of old Caulonia (on the coast near Stilo) are more fragmentary. If you haven't time for both, go to Locri.

3 Gerace, Calabria

You could spend hours in Gerace simply sitting in the sun in the piazza in front of the cathedral. Wild flowers poke up between the old battered cobbles; goats wander by; widows in black and old men in grey peaked hats slowly pass; while the odd tiny Fiat might squeeze into sight from some narrow adjacent alley. Gerace,

The market in Scilla, between Reggio di Calabria and Palmi

sitting on an impregnable crag above the Gerace river on one side and the great dried-up bed of the Novita river on the other, is an ancient place, originally founded by refugees from Locri who fled there in the 10th century to escape the continual stream of Saracen attacks. It is full of little churches and houses ranging from the Norman period to the baroque. The Cattedrale, the largest cathedral in Calabria, dominates the town. It is a strange building containing additions from a variety of centuries. Consecrated in 1045, it was rebuilt in the 13th century and restored in the 18th. Worth studying are the columns supporting the vault of the crypt – which you will not want to leave in summer because it is cool and dark – and those dividing the nave from the aisle in the upper church. Some of red and white marble, others of granite, they are believed to have come from ancient Locri down on the coast where they would have adorned an antique temple. Do not miss the cathedral treasury with its exquisite Renaissance ivory crucifix.

Picking your way over the cobbles to the right of the cathedral, through the elaborate baroque archway you come to the Church of San Giovanello, part Byzantine and part Norman in style. At the back of the town is the old ruined fortress of Gerace, which still bears traces of its Roman origins. Before leaving Gerace you should consider buying some of the local ceramic vases and jugs. The origins of their decoration can often be traced back to the period when southern Italy was part of Magna Graecia (ancient Greek colonies in the west) – long before the Romans. You will see the ceramics spilling out of shops in the piazza by the cathedral.

SPECIAL TO...

The district around Gerace is noted for *Kalipea*, another local red wine, best drunk with piquant dishes and with roast meat, and for the locally produced ceramics.

▶ *Returning once again to the coastal **SS106**, continue still further south for 53km (33 miles) until Bova Marina at which branch inland to Bova.*

4 Bova, Calabria

The most extraordinary thing about Bova is that the dialect spoken by its inhabitants is a version of ancient Greek. The little mountain town is of great antiquity, shut away at a height of 820m (2,690 feet) on a remote peak of the Aspromonte. But the oldest visible remains – part of the cathedral and the ruins of the castle – date only from the Norman period, and the cathedral was rebuilt in 1783 after a tremendous earthquake. Also worthy of a visit is the Church of San Leo which, along with the cathedral, is the town's most prominent building. It dates from the 17th century, and is a later reconstruction of a much earlier church.

The countryside around Bova, which you can observe from the ramparts of the town, gives a wild, rugged and desolate impression. However, it is also full of gnarled old olive trees and in spring glows with masses of wild flowers. The Agro-Pastoral Museum has objects relating to farming and crafts of the area.

▶ *Back to the coast, the **SS106** continues to Reggio di Calabria.*

5 Reggio di Calabria, Calabria

From Reggio di Calabria, the regional capital, you can see across the Straits of Messina to Sicily – one of the most stunning views in southern Italy. This city is a big, lively town, straddling the coastline beneath the great peaks of the Aspromonte. It was shattered by an earthquake in 1908 and subsequently rebuilt, mostly of concrete. However, older fragments of its past have survived and, apart from viewing them in the important National Museum of Archaeology (see below), you can see one or two of them still *in situ* in the town. Apart from the mid-15th-century Castello Aragonese (Aragonese fortress), of which two massive circular bastions remain, there are the remains of the old Greek city walls and the Roman baths – both near the cathedral.

But not to be missed is the National Museum of Archaeology. It contains a fascinating array of treasures – statuary, jewellery, sarcophagi, vases, glassware and mosaics – from classical sites like Locri and ancient Caulonia, but its most celebrated exhibits are the Bronzi di Riace (the Riace Warriors), two sculptures dredged from the sea in 1972. Of ancient Greek origin, one dates from about 460 BC, the other from about 430 BC. The later figure is thought to be by the greatest of ancient Greek sculptors, Phidias, and to have come from the temple at Delphi in Greece. What they were doing at the bottom of the sea off the coast of Italy is anyone's guess.

RECOMMENDED WALKS

Above Reggio di Calabria is the little town of Gambarie, on the side of the Aspromonte mountain. Here you can walk among the pinewoods and admire the views out over the Straits of Messina to Sicily.

i Via D Tripepi 72

▶ *The route continues out the other side of Reggio di Calabria and is now called the **SS18**. After 49km (30 miles) it comes to Palmi.*

BACK TO NATURE

Nature-lovers should not miss the Parco Nazionale della Calabria. To the east of Reggio di Calabria lies the southernmost of the 10 zones of this fragmented national park, an area of granite mountains with forests, rivers and meadows. The wildlife includes birds of prey, wild cats and deer.

6 Palmi, Calabria

Palmi is the best place in which to examine the minutiae of rural Calabrian life. Its Museo Calabrese di Etnografia e Folclore (Ethnographic and Folklore Museum) in the Casa della Cultura displays all kinds of everyday tools and household items that went out of use long ago in the region. It also has an exhibition of ritual sweets handed out on religious occasions (some still observed in the remoter areas), allegorical masks relating to popular superstitions and legends, fascinating in an area noted in the past for Saracen raids and brigands, and traditional costumes. There are three other museums in the building, one of them devoted to locally born composers, F Cilea and N A Manfroce and an art gallery with nearly 200 paintings. Palmi is also the first place after Reggio di Calabria where the coastline is pleasant enough to swim.

Palmi was first developed in the 10th century by the inhabitants of ancient Taurianum, of which there are only the barest remains 4km (2½ miles) further up the coast. Palmi was devastated in the 18th century and again in 1908 by violent earthquakes. Today, while its wide streets are pleasant enough, the attractions of the coastline are greater. Just off the coast there is an odd clump of rock with a single olive tree, known as Isola d'Olive (Isle of the Olive), to which you can swim (if you have the energy on a scorching Calabrian summer's day).

▶ *From Palmi continue north on the **SS18** to Mileto. After 6km (4 miles) branch left and take the small country road towards the sea to Tropea.*

7 Tropea, Calabria

Tropea is a fishing town with the prettiest stretch of beach on Calabria's western coastline. The town, clamped to the cliff above the sea, is faced by a great lump of rock out in the sea, joined to the mainland by a stretch of sand. The islet is known as Santa Maria dell'Isola, after the old Benedictine sanctuary there. Since everything closes in the afternoon in Italy – churches, shops and most museums – you should spend the morning in the old town, whose most impressive monument, the Duomo (cathedral), is of pre-Norman origin. Try not to miss the *Madonna of Romania*, in a silver frame, supposed to have been painted by St Luke himself, and the even stranger 15th-century black crucifix with wood inlay.

There are numerous little old palaces scattered about the town: Casa Trampo, in Vicolo Manco has an elaborate doorway; and further down the same alley you will find the Palazzo Cesareo, whose balcony has lovely carved corbels. Further on there are others – some with carved doorways, others sporting a defence against the evil eye. Most often this takes the form of a grotesque face but sometimes it is a single eye in a circle. Other sights include the 18th-century Church of San Giuseppe and, of course, the startling views out over the sea that suddenly meet you as you turn a corner in one of the town's alleys. You can sometimes see as far as the Lipari Islands, out over the bright roofs of the fishermen's cottages.

▶ *Continue northwards along the **SS522** to Pizzo.*

8 Pizzo, Calabria

While Tropea has generous expanses of white sandy beaches, the country around Pizzo plunges dramatically into the sea. The medieval origins of this little fishing town are obvious when you wander through its narrow streets full of ancient houses crammed into the confined space. Ferdinand of Aragon's stout, impregnable Castello di Pizzo greets your arrival at one side of the town. Built in 1486, and since restored, it is famous for having been the scene of the execution in 1815 of Joachim Murat (or Il Re Gioacchino, as locals called him) ex-king of Naples.

▶ *Take the **SS18** north until it joins the **SS280** and follow to Catanzaro.*

FOR CHILDREN

You can wash away the dust of the endless historical sites at the Zambrone Aquapark, on the SS522 between Tropea and Pizzo. There are pools, channels, lagoons and water slides, including the Flow Rider, where you can descend on surfboards or bodyboards, and the 'sliding hill', which rocks gently on soft mounds of water. The Hawaiian Lagoon has a waterfall concealing a secret passage, and lots of games and entertainment for children.

TOUR
21

The Highlands of Calabria

Little-known, unexplored towns where some of the inhabitants speak ancient Albanian are common in this more northerly part of Calabria. Known as La Sila, it is only slightly less mountainous than its southern counterpart.

4 DAYS • 556KM • 345 MILES

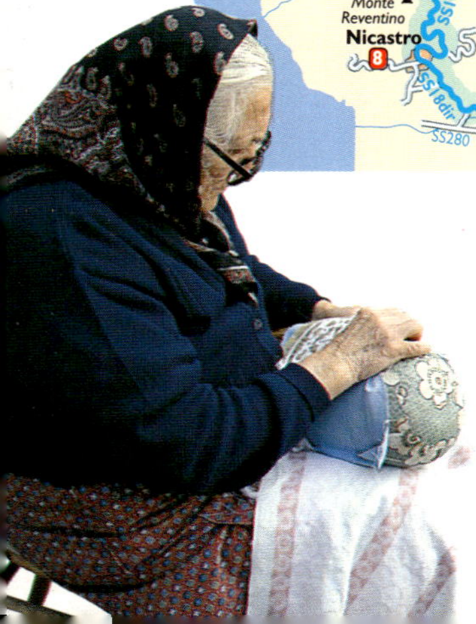

ITINERARY

COSENZA	▶ **Morano Calabro (81km-50m)**
MORANO CALABRO	▶ **Spezzano Albanese (42km-26m)**
SPEZZANO ALBANESE	▶ **San Demetrio Corone (37km-23m)**
SAN DEMETRIO CORONE	▶ **Rossano (41km-25m)**
ROSSANO	▶ **Santa Severina (120km-75m)**
SANTA SEVERINA	▶ **San Giovanni in Fiore (34km-21m)**
SAN GIOVANNI IN FIORE	▶ **Tiriolo (96km-60m)**
TIRIOLO	▶ **Nicastro (28km-17m)**
NICASTRO	▶ **Rogliano (59km-37m)**
ROGLIANO	▶ **Cosenza (18km-11m)**

i *Corso Mazzini 92, Cosenza*

▶ *Take the Autostrada **A3** north from Cosenza to the Morano Calabro turning. Then follow the signposted country road.*

1 Morano Calabro, Calabria
From afar Morano Calabro looks like a part of the rock on which it was built. Although it sits on the pinnacle of a conical mountain 694m (2,277 feet) above sea-level, it is dwarfed by the huge Pollino mountain range all around it. The approach from the autostrada is enchanting: as you wind through the valleys at its feet, the town appears and vanishes with equal consistency as the car dips and turns. At dawn it is shrouded in mist, only the tips of the highest buildings visible from below. At dusk it is a murky silhouette enlivened by flickering lights. Close inspection reveals little square houses piled one on top of the other beneath the gaze of the Church of Santi Pietro e Paolo and the derelict remains of a Norman castle, partly rebuilt in the 16th century. The town was once an important centre of the local rural economy and some of the houses lining the steep streets have a prosperous air about them. Some have carved doorways. Many still have barns for livestock in use on the ground floors; while cattle were taken to the fields during the day to graze, they were brought home for the night for their own protection against thieves.

The area's agricultural heritage is displayed in the Historical Museum of Agriculture and Sheep Breeding, which has reconstructed rural interiors, spinning and weaving exhibits and a collection of tools and photographs. The museum is due to relocate to the 15th-century Monastero di San Bernardino.

A steep walk to the top of the town's hill will be rewarded in Santi Pietro e Paolo by statues of Santa Caterina and Santa Lucia thought to be by Pietro Bernini, father of the more famous Gianlorenzo Bernini, architect of St Peter's in Rome. Others in the church are by Bernini Senior's followers. The little town is an excellent base for excursions into the Pollino massif, in particular the Serra del Prete and the Serra Dolcedorme, 2,271m (7,451 feet) above sea-level.

▶ *Back to the **A3**, return southwards for 23km (14 miles) until the Spezzano Albanese turning. Follow the **SS534** eastwards for about 4km (2½ miles), then branch right along the **SS19** until Spezzano Albanese.*

SCENIC ROUTES

Stretches of this tour that are particularly scenic are the countryside around Morano Calabro, excellent for walks and drives, and the views from Tiriolo to the sea on either side of the Calabrian peninsula. The approach roads to the town (SS109 and SS19) are spectacular.

A quiet corner of Cosenza, flourishing provincial capital

Vineyard in the Santa Severina region – home of fine wines

2 Spezzano Albanese, Calabria

This little town has a very un-Italian aspect. In the height of summer, as the bleached, whitewashed walls of the buildings hurt your eyes in the glare of sunlight, visions of Greece are never far from the mind's eye. The flat-roofed houses in the old quarter, with their small, square windows and their outside staircases, abut a warren of old passages and alleyways stacked with firewood. Adding to the strangely foreign character is the fact that most of the inhabitants of Spezzano speak Albanian – not the modern version but a dialect going back to the 15th century when their ancestors fled here from the Turks. You hear it in the bars, in the market, in the pastry shops, in the streets – everywhere. Some older women wear antique-looking costume; the everyday version is simple and rustic with floral-printed long skirts and wide lace collars. A more elaborate outfit is kept for festive occasions such as the Easter celebrations during Holy Week. For these events the women often wear costumes of great antiquity and deck themselves with gold jewellery.

The Sanctuary of the Madonna delle Grazie on the outskirts of town is the focal point of the Easter celebrations during which its resident Madonna is covered in jewellery matching that of the local girls. Perhaps this is the best time to come to Spezzano Albanese. Everyone flocks here from the surrounding countryside; cakes and drinks are sold and most people make an effort to wear their traditional costumes. Spezzano is also a spa town, its installations dating from the 1920s and 1930s.

▶ *Leave by the **SS19** travelling south, branching left within 2km (1 mile) on to the **SS106bis**, passing through Terranova da Sibari, and continue until you join the **SS106**, turning right. One kilometre (½ mile) further is the turning for San Demetrio Corone, just by the River Mizofato. Continue along this small country road for 15km (9 miles) until San Demetrio Corone.*

3 San Demetrio Corone, Calabria

While Spezzano Albanese is sometimes called the capital of 'Little Albania', as this district is known, San Demetrio Corone is perhaps its most picturesque town – and its most uncompromisingly Albanian one. Here the street signs are in two languages and there is an Italo-Albanian college which trains young men as priests for the Orthodox church. The college stands next to the 12th-century Church of Sant'Adriano where you will see antique columns incorporated into the building work and a Byzantine tesselated pavement decorated with pictures of leopards, birds and snakes.

In the main square is a statue of Skanderbeg, the Albanian hero who died in the fight against the Turks in the 15th century.

▶ *Return to the **SS106**. Turn right and continue along it for 7km (4 miles), then turn left at Corigliano station. After 2km (1 mile) you reach the **SS106r**. Join this and continue south for 10km (6 miles) until the turning for Rossano, 7km (4 miles) further.*

4 Rossano, Calabria

This is one of the most important and picturesque hilltowns in the Sila Greca (so called because the Albanians were formerly thought of as Greeks by the locals). It has had a colourful history and was an important settlement during the Roman period and again during the 9th and 10th centuries. The single most important monument to its great past is the *Codex Purpureus*, the 6th-century Greek 'Rossano Gospels', in the cathedral's treasury, the Museo Diocesano. This early Christian illuminated manuscript is extremely rare. Scenes from the New Testament are jewel-like with brilliant colour and fine

detailed drawing. There is more to see in the town. A walk around the upper part will take in the Church of San Bernardino and the cathedral, which contains early sculpture. Perhaps more worthwhile are the small Byzantine churches of Santa Maria del Pilerio and the Panaghia, the latter with pretty frescos, while San Marco is not to be missed. Standing on high above the Celati river, this Byzantine church is not unlike the Cattolica at Stilo, with five little domes covered in terracotta tiles.

RECOMMENDED WALKS

Continue from Rossano to Longobucco (take the SS177 via Cropalati – 23km/14 miles to Longobucco – 18km/11 miles) at the edge of a section of Parco Nazionale della Calabria. In the national park there are walks, wonderful scenery, rivers and places for picnics.

► *Return to and continue along the coastal* ***SS106r*** *(which becomes the* ***SS106****) for 84km (52 miles) until the junction with the* ***SS107****, approximately 5km (3 miles) before Crotone. Take the* ***SS107*** *to Santa Severina, about 28km (17 miles) further on.*

FOR HISTORY BUFFS

The site of the ancient Greek city of Sybaris, once with a population of nearly 300,000 people, lies on the plain about 20km (12½ miles) along the SS106 northwest of Rossano. Destroyed in 510 BC, it disappeared for millennia under the swamps of the Crati river and its ruins have been excavated only in the past 30 years. There are the remains of houses, some of which have surviving mosaic floors. Some of the artefacts found here have been deposited in a museum on the site. Otherwise you have to go to Crotone (on the way to Santa Severina) to see items from Sybaris in the museum there. It was once the richest city in Magna Graecia, and its luxury and decadence – as well as its corruption – were legendary (giving rise to the word 'sybaritic').

Don't miss the site of the Tempio (Sanctuary) di Hera Lacinia at Capo Colonna, 11km (7 miles) south of Crotone. It has a single huge remaining column near the beach.

Cascading down the hillside, the town of Morana Calabro

Santa Severina now dreams peacefully of its days of glory

5 Santa Severina, Calabria
From its much eroded rocky pinnacle, Santa Severina dominates a now deforested, hot, dry landscape. It was denuded of its trees by the ancient Greeks and the Normans, who needed wood for their ships. This area is characterised by strange otherworldly rock formations scattered about among the huge old, gnarled olive trees. Santa Severina's situation means that it has always been provided with natural defences, utilised first by the Byzantines then by the Normans.

Part of the town was abandoned after an earthquake in 1783 and you can see the remains of buildings which cannot have changed much since the first Byzantine settlement of the town. Do not miss the adjacent Iudea (Jewish) quarter – this is still inhabited. As so often, it is the churches that are full of the more interesting items of the town's history, in particular the Addolorata, the Norman cathedral with its 13th-century entrance portal. While the cathedral has largely been rebuilt, the adjacent Battistero (Baptistry) is still very largely Byzantine, dating mostly from the 8th century. Its construction is reminiscent of the buildings of Ravenna. The Diocesan Museum, in the former residence of the Archbishops, has furnishings, vestments and some remarkable historic documents.

The little 11th-century Church of Santa Filomena, with the Church of the Pozzolio underneath, looks like something from Armenia or Anatolia, its construction very un-Italian. It is a remarkable survivor in this part of the world. The old Castello may have been rebuilt by Robert Guiscard on top of an earlier Byzantine one. In its present form it dates from the Norman period; from here there are incredible views out over the Neto valley. The castle houses a museum of finds from the immediate area, dating from Iron Age and classical times.

▶ *Continue on the **SS107** in a northwesterly direction for about 34km (21 miles) until you reach the turning for the town of San Giovanni in Fiore.*

SPECIAL TO...

In certain areas of this region are individual wines which you will not find outside Italy. *Val di Neto Bianco* (best with antipasti and fish), *Rosso* (good with local cheese) and *Rosato* (drunk with any local dishes), are wines from the Santa Severina district.

Melissa Bianco (best with antipasti and fish) and *Rosato* (best with soups, dishes using offal and light sweet cheese), originate from around Santa Severina and Crotone.

Ciro Bianco DOC (best with antipasti and fish) and *Rosso DOC* (best with any sort of local dish) are both excellent and well known wines from Ciro, just off the SS106 about 32km (20 miles) from Crotone.

6 San Giovanni in Fiore, Calabria

From San Giovanni in Fiore, 1,049m (3,442 feet) above sea-level, there are fine views of the surrounding countryside. This hilltown, in the heart of the Sila, grew up around the old Badia Florense; in fact, the town's community land today corresponds to the former territories of the *Badia* (abbey), which was founded in 1189. The abbey itself was suppressed at the beginning of the 19th century and its buildings now include the Sila Folk Museum, with reconstructed rural interiors and items relating to local art, agriculture and trades.

The older townswomen still wear the traditional costume (the *rituartu*) of black velvet skirt, bodice, white lacy blouse and jewellery. All the town's traditional crafts continue to flourish, including its wrought-iron workshops. It is also an important textile centre, as well as one of the few places where you will find craftsmen working with inlaid wood.

Go directly south from San Giovanni in Fiore for about 15km (9 miles) until you reach the ***SS179****. Turn right and follow this west for a further 15km (9 miles) at which point turn left on to the* ***SS179dir*** *heading south. On reaching the* ***SS109*** *after a further 27km (16½ miles) turn right and follow this road through Taverna and (remaining on the* ***SS109*** *where the* ***SS109bis*** *branches off to Catanzaro) follow the signs to Gimigliano to Tiriolo.*

FOR CHILDREN

One way to add extra excitement to exploring the Sila Highlands is to do it on horseback. In the nature parks qualified guides lead organised riding excursions, and there are treks through secluded areas with spectacular views. Mountain-biking is another option, with many paths winding up the hills and mountains.

7 Tiriolo, Calabria

The views of the surrounding countryside from Tiriolo are legendary. It stands high above the narrow ridge of mountains that divides the Tyrrhenian Sea from the Ionian Sea. If you venture about 200m (650 feet) further up the mountain from Tiriolo, you can see both seas – one of the great views of Calabria. In summer it is far cooler up in Tiriolo than at the bottom of the valleys – a good place to stop for lunch. The Museum of Antiquities is worth a visit, if you can tear yourself away from the views.

Take the ***SS19*** *from Tiriolo going south but almost immediately turn right on to the* ***SS19dir*** *for 17km (11 miles) until the* ***SS18dir*** *turning for Nicastro.*

8 Nicastro, Calabria

Nicastro is another Calabrian town of Byzantine origin.

Red-roofed Rogliano in its green setting is largely 17th century

Hanging precariously from the side of Monte Reventino, it is dominated by what remains of the Norman castle, mostly demolished in an earthquake in 1638. Emperor Frederick II rebuilt the fortress and imprisoned his son Henry there. Scattered up and down the precipitous streets of this little town are a number of churches worth looking at.

Apart from the 18th-century cathedral and Church of San Domenico, there is the Church of Santa Caterina and the even more interesting Church of the Cappuccini dedicated to Sant'Antonio.

► *The* ***SS109*** *wends its way north to Rogliano, becoming the* ***SS19*** *at Soveria Mannelli after 27km (16½ miles).*

9 Rogliano, Calabria

A town has existed on this site since before the Romans ever came here. An earthquake destroyed the medieval town in 1638 so that much of what survives today dates from the later 17th century.

The Church of Santa Maria Maggiore (also called San Giuseppe) houses a Museum of Religious Art, with works from many churches in the area (may be closed for restoration). Other churches include the Cappuccini with a good wooden altar, and the Church of Santa Maria delle Grazie with a wonderful inlaid and gilded wooden ceiling. Woodcrafts in the churches are a speciality of this town, with more in the little Chiesetta dell'Annunziata.

► *Continue north on the* ***SS19*** *to Cosenza, a distance of 18km (11 miles).*

SPECIAL TO...

Savuto DOC, a robust red wine best with more piquant dishes and with roast meat, comes from the province of Cosenza, in particular from the countryside near Rogliano.

BACK TO NATURE

In the northern part of the Sila, in the Sila Greca, is another part of the Parco Nazionale della Calabria. Easy to reach from either Cosenza, Rossano or San Giovanni in Fiore, the national park comprises mostly forest of ancient larch, beech, chestnut and Hungarian oak. In the spring there are clearings of asphodels and wild violets. The greatest wild population of wolves left in Italy survives in this park and in another just south of San Giovanni in Fiore. There are also wild cats and fallow deer, kept in enclosures which can be visited. Walks in the parks are recommended – the best way to see the goshawks, buzzards and eagle owls of the region.

The delightful town of Cosenza, set on the River Crati

TOUR
22

Forgotten Basilicata

The towns of this region are the least discovered in southern Italy. The countryside is possibly also the most unspoilt in the south. From the troglodytic old city of Matera to the great castle of Melfi, the Norman tombs at Venosa and the Greek-looking, white-washed town of Pisticci, Basilicata is a world all on its own.

4/5 DAYS • 710KM • 442 MILES

ITINERARY

MATERA	▶ **Metaponto (50km-31m)**
METAPONTO	▶ **Pisticci (31km-19m)**
PISTICCI	▶ **Maratea (169km-105m)**
MARATEA	▶ **Rivello (24km-15m)**
RIVELLO	▶ **Melfi (192km-120m)**
MELFI	▶ **Venosa (25km-16m)**
VENOSA	▶ **Pietrapertosa (110km-68m)**
PIETRAPERTOSA	▶ **Tricarico (45km-28m)**
TRICARICO	▶ **Miglionico (42km-26m)**
MIGLIONICO	▶ **Matera (22km-14m)**

TOUR

22 **Forgotten** Basilicata

SPECIAL TO...

Matera holds its Festa della Bruna on 2 July, an event linked to the fertility of the earth and an abundant harvest. It involves a procession in which a large wagon containing the Madonna is dragged around the town by eight mules. Although the wagon, constructed by the same family each year, takes a laborious four months to complete, it is destroyed during the procession each year (as a part of the rite and not the work of vandals), everybody hoping to grab a piece of it as a relic. This is a strange festival in which the whole town takes part.

[i] *Via De Viti de Marco 9, Matera*

► *Leave Matera going south on the main road to Ferrandina, the **SS7**, and after 12km (7½ miles) branch left on the **SS380** (which, after about 12km/7½ miles becomes the **SS175**) and continue for 38km (23½ miles) to Metaponto.*

1 Metaponto, Basilicata
The countryside on the way to Metaponto has a North African look. The eucalyptus and the maritime pines lining the route are strangely out of place. The ancient city of Metapontum was founded in the 7th century BC by Greek colonists and today is one of the better known sites of Magna Graecia (the Greek colonies in southern Italy). By contrast, the modern town is no more than a small resort by the sea. Beaches, hotels and restaurants make it a good place to stay and a convenient base from which to explore the ruins of the old city. Much of the latter survives including the remains of four large temples, a theatre, a forum and a Roman camp. Metapontum is famous for having been the town in which the mathematician and philosopher Pythagoras chose to live (at the end of the 6th century BC). He taught here and you can still see the 15 surviving columns (out of a total of 30 plus) of the Tavole Palatine, once his home and school, later transformed into the Temple of Hera. The antiquarium on the

The glory that was Greece: the Temple of Hera at *Metapontum*

site provides welcome relief in its cool dark rooms from the hot sun. Look out for the ancient fertility statues.

FOR HISTORY BUFFS

At Policoro, 19km (12 miles) south of Metaponto on the SS106, are the remains of the ancient colony of Siris-Heradeia. It has the remains of living quarters and a Temple of Demeter. An outstanding museum of antiquities from the area – Museo Nazionale della Siritide – contains sculpture, metalware and some fine Greek painted pottery.

▶ *From Metaponto, take the **SS407** west, turning left on to the **SS176** after 22km (14 miles). A further 2km (1 mile) along this road, a minor road leads to Pisticci.*

2 Pisticci, Basilicata

The country town of Pisticci, built on an incline, has a colourful daily market. Go in the morning, because that is when you will see the women of the town shopping in their traditional costumes, with huge wide skirts and strange headgear. The streets are lined with houses, linked together with white-washed walls and dusty brown terracotta roofs. The Chiesa Madre, the parish church (1542), was built on the ruins of a 13th-century building and there is also a ruined medieval castle.

BACK TO NATURE

Basilicata is predominantly a mountainous region. The most peculiar rock formations found in the area are the *calanchi* around Pisticci, strange dry hillocks of rock.

▶ *From Pisticci, return to and take the **SS176** going south. Turn left at the junction with the **SS103** and continue for 19km (12 miles) until you hit the **SS598**. Go east along this for 16km (10 miles) until you reach the coastal **SS106**. Follow this for about 9km (6 miles), going south, until you reach the **SS653**. This latter goes inland again – follow it for 85km (53 miles) until you reach the autostrada **A3**. Go under this and turn left on to the **SS19**. After 5km (3 miles), turn right and follow the country road through Lauria to the **SS585**. Turn right on to this and very shortly left on to the minor road which leads, via Trecchina, to Maratea.*

3 Maratea, Basilicata

This is perhaps the best known part of Basilicata. The coastline is unspoilt and is studded with little rocky coves where you can swim in complete privacy. The Marina di Maratea and the old port have a number of restaurants and little hotels. The old town, climbing up a hill, is still mostly intact. You can visit the picturesque medieval quarter with its loggias and small doorways. Maratea is the kind of place to explore on your own, discovering the odd café for a quick drink or *cappuccino*. You can also visit the 17th-century former Convento di San Francesco with its two-storeyed cloister of pointed arches. On a peak just above Maratea you cannot fail to notice the huge

Fine local cheeses for sale near Rivello

statue of the Redeemer – 22m (72 feet) high.

[i] Piazza del Gesù 40

> **SCENIC ROUTES**
>
> Monte Biagio, way above Maratea, affords magnificent views of the Gulf of Policastro. The drive to the top of the mountain is worth every crippling hairpin bend. Bagni, on the western slopes of Monte Vúlture, gives you some stunning views of the extinct volcano.

▶ *From Maratea, retrace the route of the **SS585**. Turn left and after a short distance you come to the minor road off to Rivello.*

4 Rivello, Basilicata

This must be one of the prettiest towns in southern Italy. It straddles the spine of two hills and, because of its shape, is thought to look like a dragon. Rivello coils itself around the top of the hill, each little street thick with outside staircases and small galleries and overhung with wrought-iron balconies. At each end of the town is a – mainly Byzantine – church. Santa Barbara has a very pretty apse decorated with tiny hanging arches, while San Nicola dei Greci seems more like a fortress than anything else. The lovely, frescoed 15th-century Convento dei Minori has a wooden choir carved by local monks, and depicting various trades and guilds.

▶ *Take the **SS585** to its junction with the autostrada **A3**, then follow the latter for 70km (44 miles) until you hit the autostrada going east to Potenza from the Sicignano junction. At Potenza, go north on the **SS93** for 50km (31 miles) towards Melfi before branching off on the **SS303** for the final 6km (4 miles) of the journey.*

> **BACK TO NATURE**
>
> Sirino Range, the highest peak of which is Monte del Papa (Mount Papa) 2,005m (6,578 feet), is visible as you leave Rivello and join the A3. It is densely wooded with hazelnut, oak, chestnut, alder and beech and it harbours forest birds, foxes and wolves.

5 Melfi, Basilicata

Dark and medieval Melfi is crammed with the remains of its illustrious past, in particular those from the Norman and

Hohenstaufen periods. You can see part of the old perimeter wall, the Norman castle with its eight towers, each one different, and the cathedral of 1155, with its Norman Sicilian bell tower. The castle contains a museum of antiquities whose prize exhibit is a 1st-century Roman sarcophagus, the *Sarcofago di Rapallo*. The old city gate, the Porta Venosina, is Norman, though Frederick II (Hohenstaufen) tampered with it. A walk around the town would include a handful of little churches including the very much restored 17th-century San Lorenzo.

▶ *Return via the **SS303** to the **SS93** at Rapolla. Turn left and proceed for 8km (5 miles) before turning right on to the **SS168** for Venosa, a total of 25km (16 miles).*

6 Venosa, Basilicata

Venosa belongs, visually, more to the nearby region of Puglia than to Basilicata. As in Melfi, you can trace the town's history in the streets, but here the various periods are more easily distinguishable. It was particularly favoured by the Romans, whose Via Appia passed through it, and it was the birthplace of Quintus Horatius Flaccus, the poet Horace (65–8 BC). Others who came here include Byzantines, Saracens, Normans, Hohenstaufens, Angevins and the Spanish. The formidable castle, dominating Piazza Umberto, dates from 1470, while the cathedral, which shows Catalan influence, is early 16th-century.

Wander around the medieval centre with its huge old paving slabs and carved doorways. Behind the Church of San Rocco you can see the even older remains of Roman houses and baths, while further on appear some fragments of an early Christian baptistery and a Roman amphitheatre. Perhaps the most interesting of all is the Abbey of La Trinità. Begun around 1050, it is in three parts, having an old church, an abbey and a later (1135), but unfinished, 'new' church. It became the final resting place of the five De Hauteville brothers who were responsible for conquering southern Italy for the Normans (while William the Conqueror was doing the same to England).

RECOMMENDED WALKS

Just south of Melfi, around the base of the extinct volcano, Monte Vúlture, are some good walks that follow the paths used by brigands in the past. However, there is nothing to fear today: the paths are quite safe, and the only thing that will cross your path will be wild game and maybe shepherds and their flocks. Walks in this area take you around the beautiful Laghi (Lakes) di Monticchio. You can also use horses on the longer routes and local people sometimes act as guides.

The pretty hilltown of Rivello

▶ *Return to the **SS93** and then to Potenza. Then take the **SS407** going east for 30km (19 miles), branching inland for about 11km (7 miles) to Pietrapertosa.*

Ancient Puglia

SPECIAL TO...

Bari holds its Festa di San Nicola (Feast of St Nicholas) on 7 May. Recalling the arrival in Bari of the bones of the saint, brought from the Far East by sailors in 1087, an antique icon of the saint is carried in procession to the Basilica of St Nicholas. The following day the saint's statue is mounted on a boat which leads a water-borne procession.

The district around Bari has a particularly fine brand of olive oil. If the label says it comes from Bitonto in particular, then buy it.

i Piazza Moro 33, Bari

▶ *Take the **SS96** from the city centre, then branch along the **SS98**.*

1 Bitonto, Puglia

Right in the centre of Bitonto is the fine Puglian Romanesque 13th-century cathedral. Its best features are the women's gallery, the carvings of animals on the entrance portals, and the pulpit with its primitive bas-reliefs. Other interesting churches are San Francesco with its late 13th-century façade, and the Church of the Purgatorio which has a sculptured relief of human skeletons just above the main entrance portal. Most of the centre of town is either Renaissance or baroque. The Palazzo Rogadeo has a museum on its first floor.

▶ *Travel north to the **A14**. Take the autostrada northwest until the Molfetta exit.*

2 Molfetta, Puglia

Molfetta is an active fishing port. Predominantly medieval, it has a lovely 12th- to 13th-century cathedral, the Duomo Vecchio, dominated by three domes. There is also the Duomo Nuovo (new cathedral), though in this case 'new' means late 18th-century. This building has a baroque façade. There are three museums. The

Archaeological Museum and A Salvucci Museum and Gallery (may be closed for restoration) contain the finds, including Hellenistic ceramics, from local digs. The Museum of Popular Devotion is in the Sanctuary of the basilica. A gallery of contemporary art in the town hall has works by old masters.

▶ *Take the coastal **SS16** north-west via Bisceglie to Trani.*

3 Trani, Puglia
Trani has always been an important port. Trade with the Orient in the 11th century drew into its orbit merchants from Genoa, Pisa and Amalfi and attracted a large Jewish community. Still a large and thriving port, it is full of little seafood restaurants.

The cathedral, in an open-ended piazza facing the sea, is a fine Romanesque building, containing the remains of two earlier structures. The oldest is an early Christian catacomb, with marble columns and frescos: above that, and below the existing nave, are the remains of the earlier Byzantine cathedral. Most noteworthy in the present building is the pair of 12th-century bronze doors by a local master.

Two other buildings that should not be missed are the Church of the Ognissanti, built by the Knights Templar as a hospice and the Palazzo Caccetta, a 15th-century Gothic palace – unusual in Puglia.

Until fairly recently, the great 13th-century castle served as a prison. It's an atmospheric structure, and well worth a visit.

i *Piazza Trieste 10*

▶ *Continue up the coast on the **SS16** to Barletta.*

4 Barletta, Puglia
In Barletta is the largest known bronze statue in existence, on a pedestal at the end of the Corso Vittorio Emanuele. Called the Colosso, it is 5m (15 feet) high and represents a Roman emperor, possibly Valentinian, who died in AD 375. In the Middle Ages Barletta was an important and prosperous port. Like Trani it retains much of its prosperity and has a pretty, if somewhat dilapidated medieval centre. The 12th-century cathedral is the town's most interesting building. It has a lovely rose window, and an inscription above the left entrance portal records how Richard Coeur de Lion was involved in its construction. Visit the 13th-century Church of San Sepolcro, the design of which recalls the Church of the Holy Sepulchre in Jerusalem, and the former convent building of San Domenico. The castle, which now houses the Museo Civico (Civic Museum) and picture gallery, is a massive structure, originally built by Emperor Frederick II and enlarged by Charles of Anjou.

i *Corso Garibaldi 208*

Castel del Monte is one of the great medieval buildings of Europe

Ruvo di Puglia's fine cathedral

SPECIAL TO...

One of the best-known medieval pageants in Italy takes place annually in Barletta (check dates with tourist office). The Disfidia, also celebrated in a novel by Massimo d'Azeglio, recalls a tournament that took place here on 13 February, 1503, in which a group of Italian knights confronted and defeated a band of French knights. The colourful costumed re-enactment is accompanied by various other revelries.

BACK TO NATURE

The Saline di Margherita is a large area of salt-pans and wetlands just along the coast from Margherita (west of Barletta). Birds such as black-winged stilts, Kentish plovers, pratincoles and short-toed larks breed in the area, and migrant waders, including curlew sandpipers, spotted redshanks and wood sandpipers, pass through on passage.

Trani's cathedral is considered one of the best in Puglia

▶ *The **SS93** branches inland from Barletta and goes to Canosa di Puglia.*

5 Canosa di Puglia, Puglia
Standing in the Tavoliere Plain, this town was an important Roman centre, called Canusium. Remains of Roman baths, amphitheatres and basilicas can be seen, and there is a Roman bridge over the Ofanto river which only survives because its arches were rebuilt in the Middle Ages. There are two later items of interest in the town's Romanesque cathedral: the marble 11th-century bishop's throne, which rests on the backs of two elephants; and the Tomb of Bohemund, Prince of Antioch, who was the son of Robert Guiscard and who died in 1111. The tomb's doors were made from a single slab of bronze. Other relics of the town's past are kept in the Museo Civico (Civic Museum).

FOR HISTORY BUFFS

The site of Cannae, where Hannibal gained his last great victory over the Romans, lies between Barletta and Canosa di Puglia on the Ofanto river. The remains of a huge necropolis can be seen and traces of the former city of Cannae. An Antiquarium houses finds from the site. On a hill above is the citadel which has yielded mainly medieval remains.

▶ *From Canosa di Puglia, take the **SS98** towards Andria, turning off right after 7km (4 miles) on the **SS97** to Minervino Murge.*

6 Minervino Murge, Puglia
Minervino Murge is known as the 'Balcony of Puglia' because of its wonderful position at the edge of the Murgia Alta, the rolling hills on Puglia's southern border. 'Minervino' derives from an ancient temple dedicated to the worship of Minerva on whose remains rises the present-day Church of the

SCENIC ROUTES

The views from Minervino Murge to the surrounding countryside show a landscape that is most typically Puglian – gently rolling, almost flat.

RECOMMENDED WALKS

On a visit to the Castel del Monte, walk some way from the castle to appreciate the full impact of this extraordinary building.
All around is a pretty, agricultural and virtually empty landscape, called the Tavoliere, splendid for walks and also for picnics.

Madonna del Crocifisso. Apart from the church and the panoramas of the countryside, this little town has a 12th-century castle, a Palazzo Comunale built in local style and a Norman cathedral, re-embellished in the Renaissance.

▶ *Take the* ***SS170*** *eastwards for 22km (13½ miles) until the* ***SS170dir*** *branches off to the left. Follow the latter for 1km (½ mile) to the turning for Castel del Monte on the left.*

7 Castel del Monte, Puglia
This huge isolated castle is one of the most impressive monuments surviving from the reign of Emperor Frederick II and is worth a visit. With its eight Gothic corner towers, you can see it from miles away, crowning an isolated peak way above the surrounding countryside. It was built around 1240 and in plan is a perfect octagon – the number eight being the symbol of the crown. You can wander through huge rooms, eight on each floor, that were once decorated with reliefs in Greek marble, porphyry and precious stones, now mostly disappeared. The castle may have been used originally as a centre for astronomy as its proportions are said to relate to the movements of the planets. But it was also the grim prison of Frederick II's grandsons, who were incarcerated here for 30 years. Notice the beautiful carved entrance portal and, among what is left of its decoration, the signs of classical, Gothic, Persian and Arabic influences.

▶ *Return to the* ***SS170*** *and follow it eastwards. It joins the* ***SS98*** *2km (1 mile) before Ruvo di Puglia.*

8 Ruvo di Puglia, Puglia
Ruvo di Puglia was a town celebrated in ancient times for its pottery. As long ago as the 5th century BC, its terracotta vases were highly sought after and some of these can be seen in the Jatta National Museum of Archaeology. Here, too, is the magnificent red-figured Greek vase known as the 'Crater of Talos'. It is a collection that you should not miss. Ruvo's cathedral is an important Puglian Romanesque building – one of the best in Puglia. Built in the 13th century, it has a richly decorated façade and a superb 16th-century rose window. In particular, notice the griffins surmounting the columns on either side of the main entrance. Around the sides of the building are little sculpted figures of ancient, pagan gods, which it is thought may have been copied from classical pottery.

▶ *Return to Bari via the* ***SS98****. Skirt round the southern edge of the city on the* ***SS16*** *and turn right on to the* ***SS100****. Take the latter as far as Casamassima, 15km (9 miles), then branch left along the* ***SS172*** *to Alberobello, 35km (22 miles).*

9 Alberobello, Puglia
Alberobello is a very curious town. Clustered together in its centre is a collection of the prehistoric-looking local buildings called *trulli*. These small, circular, single-storey, stone buildings with cone-shaped tiled roofs look a bit like upside-down ice-cream cornets. There is nothing quite like them in any other part of Italy. Once such houses were common in Mediterranean countries – the prehistoric Sardinian *nuraghi* are not dissimilar – but in Puglia, for some reason, they are a living tradition. Wander through the narrow streets of the Rione Monti and Aia Piccola quarters of Alberobello, where most of the *trulli* (there are over 1,000) are whitewashed and still inhabited. Even the style of the Church of Sant'Antonio seems to have derived its looks from the *trulli*. Most of Alberobello is a national monument, so that what has survived of its strange appearance is in very good condition. One or two of the

Conical-roofed *trulli*, the traditional houses of Puglia

TOUR

23

Molfetta's domed 'old cathedral' gazes benignly over the harbour

trulli are open to the public or have been turned into shops and restaurants.

FOR CHILDREN

Puglia is really not an area to bring children. However, they might enjoy looking into the *trulli* – built, it seems, more for hobbits than for humans. Everything in these igloo-like structures is in miniature. In both Alberobello and Locorotondo, one or two of them are open to the public. At Fasano, a developing holiday centre about 10km (6 miles) from both Alberobello and Locorotondo, there is a zoo/safari park, where animals of the African plains, such as giraffes, can be seen in the rough, dry terrain not far removed from their natural habitat.

▶ *The SS172 leads straight to Locorotondo.*

10 Locorotondo, Puglia

Locorotondo was laid out in concentric circles around the pinnacle of a low hill, and takes its name ('round place') from this plan. From the town there are wonderful views out over the Itria Valley in which you can see clumps of *trulli* scattered about – generally farmhouses and barns. In Locorotondo everything is covered with whitewash and gleams in the scorching Puglian summer sun. Small Greek-looking houses cluster around secret courtyards. There are geraniums in pots on the balconies, and the cobbled alleys and passages make this one of the more picturesque towns of Puglia. If you want to get out of the sun for a while, visit the churches of San Giorgio and San Marco della Greca, the former neo-classical, the latter a much earlier, possibly late Gothic, building.

▶ *The **SS172dir** leads via Fasano to the **SS16**. From Fasano, take the **SS16** to Monopoli, about 12km (7½ miles).*

SCENIC ROUTES

The views from Locorotondo across the Trulli Zone of the Itria Valley make it is easy to imagine yourself in a prehistoric landscape: the strange, *trulli* (beehive-like buildings) which dot the countryside are the kind of houses that the long-ago ancestors of present-day Puglians might have lived in. Nobody knows the real age or origins of these dwellings which are found solely in a small region round Alberobello and nowhere else in Europe.

11 Monopoli, Puglia

Monopoli is the most beautiful port on this strip of the Adriatic coastline. In the older quarter, tall medieval houses are built right up to the quay, overlooking the port and the little brightly painted fishing boats. The old centre is full of churches and other buildings which bear the traces of Byzantine and Venetian invaders. There is a castle, a Romanesque cathedral of 1107, with an impressive baroque façade and bell tower, and the Church of San Domenico, perhaps the most magnificent building in the town. The Renaissance façade of San Domenico is split into three parts by columns and decorated with statues, and there is a fine rose window. At various points beneath Monopoli, there are underground chambers and places of worship. One such is the Chiesa-Grotta, a natural cave, decorated in Byzantine times.

▶ *From Monopoli, take the coast road northwest to Polignano a Mare, about 8km (5 miles).*

12 Polignano a Mare, Puglia

Polignano a Mare is a delightful old city with little alleyways and flights of steps. In the old quarter is the parish church dedicated to Our Lady of the Assumption. Although it is Romanesque in style, it was added to during the Renaissance period. Ask to see the painting by the 15th-century Venetian artists Vivarini, in the sacristy. Just outside town are the Grotte Palazzese (Palazzese Caves), set into the cliffsides. These are two huge sea caves, reached by climbing down precarious steps set into the rock just below the town.

▶ *The **SS16** leads back to Bari, 34km (21 miles).*

SCENIC ROUTES

The coastline from Polignano a Mare to Mola di Bari, going along the SS16, is lovely unspoilt coastal scenery (though not suitable for swimming except from the rocks).

The Heel of Italy

Scattered all over southern Puglia are monuments that seem more Greek than Italian, while others look as though they should be in northern Europe rather than in the hot sunny Puglian countryside. Greeks, Arabs, Normans – these were just some of the inhabitants of Puglia in the past.

3 DAYS • 352KM • 219 MILES

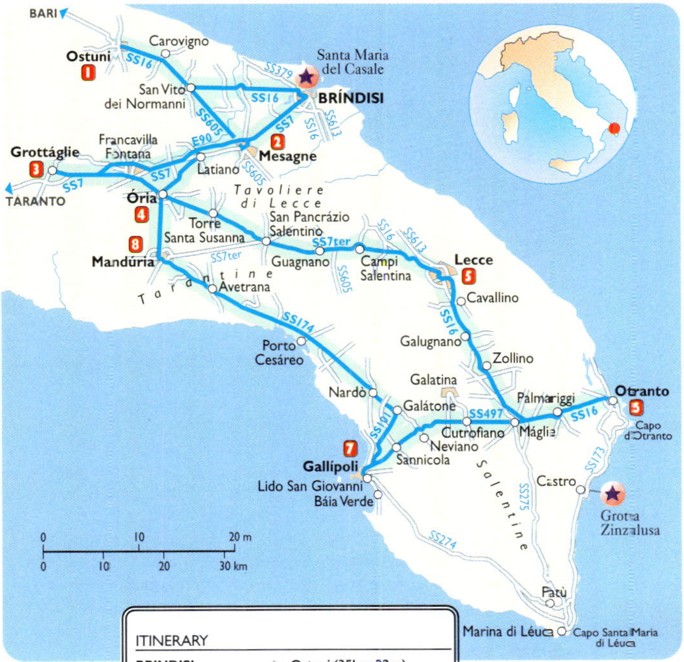

ITINERARY

BRINDISI	▶ **Ostuni (35km-22m)**
OSTUNI	▶ **Mesagne (28km-17m)**
MESAGNE	▶ **Grottaglie (38km-24m)**
GROTTAGLIE	▶ **Oria (20km-12m)**
ORIA	▶ **Lecce (50km-31m)**
LECCE	▶ **Otranto (48km-30m)**
OTRANTO	▶ **Gallipoli (30km-19m)**
GALLIPOLI	▶ **Manduria (60km-37m)**
MANDURIA	▶ **Brindisi (43km-27m)**

The Heel of Italy

SCENIC ROUTES

The approach road (either the SS605, the SS16 or the narrow country road that leads from the coast) to Ostuni is scenically outstanding, principally for the stunning views to the town itself. Rising on to a little hill and bleached white in the sun, it looks more Greek than Italian.

i Via C Colombo 88, Brindisi

▶ *From Brindisi, the **SS16** leads via San Vito dei Normanni to Ostuni, 35km (22 miles).*

1 Ostuni, Puglia

Ostuni is built on three hills about 200m (600 feet) above sea-level. The oldest part of the town, also the highest, is the most interesting, dominated by the huge Gothic cathedral. This building, which seems more Spanish than anything else, has three lovely rose windows in its façade. Near by is the Palazzo Vescovile (Bishop's Palace), the two parts of which, on two sides of the square in which it stands, are connected by a little honey-coloured stone bridge. Also near by is the Southern Murgia Museum of Pre-Classical Civilizations, its star exhibit being 'Delia', a paleolithic woman (with foetus) who lived 25,000 year ago. All around these three buildings, and leading down to the huge dusty Piazza Libertà in the 19th-century part of the town, are little alleys burrowing through the gleaming whitewashed buildings of the old quarter.

i Corso Mazzini 6

▶ *Take the **SS16** back to San Vito, where you should turn on to the **SS605** to Mesagne.*

FOR CHILDREN

If you can make it to Ostuni for La Cavalcata di Sant'Oronzo (St Oronzo's Cavalcade) – check with the local tourist office for dates – the children will be good for the rest of the trip. Horses and riders trundle through the streets colourfully dressed in Saracen attire – both animals and riders decked out in embroidered cloth and plumes.

Ostuni's whitewashed houses climb steeply up its winding streets

2 Mesagne, Puglia

Mesagne sits in the middle of the Tavoliere di Lecce, a large, flat plain heavily cultivated with figs, olives and vineyards. Nowadays, Mesagne prospers from the fertility of the surrounding landscape and its market should be one of the stopping points on this itinerary. The castle is worth taking an hour or two to look at. Built originally in 1062 by the Norman adventurer Robert Guiscard, various attackers destroyed it over the years and the last time it was rebuilt was in the 17th century. It is a spectacular construction with a rather lovely Renaissance loggia which runs along its north and east sides. The parish church, the Chiesa Madre, is baroque and the Church of Sant'Anna is rococo; both are worth a visit – in fact the latter is the best example of its style in the area.

▶ *Join the **SS7** on the north edge of town which leads west to Grottaglie, about 38km (24 miles).*

3 Grottaglie, Puglia

This town is one of the most renowned centres for ceramics in southern Italy. Many of the items for sale are traditional designs, long abandoned elsewhere. The ceramicists' quarters lie behind the massive castle. Here you can still see people working in the traditional ways and their wares line practically every flat surface in sight – including roofs. In the Episcopal Castle is a ceramics museum, with historic and contemporary examples of the craft. You can visit the Church of the Carmine which has a traditional Presepio (Christmas crib) of 1530. The early 12th-century Chiesa Matrice is a very decorative building. Its Chapel of the Rosary is topped by a cupola decorated with local tiles.

▶ *Return along the* ***SS7*** *branching off to Francavilla Fontana, 14km (8½ miles), at which head towards Oria, only 6km (3½ miles) – follow the signs in the south of the town.*

4 Oria, Puglia

Oria is yet another Puglian town dominated by a castle built by Emperor Frederick II. Although over the years it has been altered and enlarged, it still retains its basic triangular shape. In its vaulted hall is a small museum. Not far away is the Cripta dei Santi Crisante e Daria, a small subterranean basilica dating from the 9th century topped by a series of shallow domes and decorated with frescos. Oria's cathedral was rebuilt in the 18th century following an earthquake; its most noteworthy element is its ceramic-covered dome. In the old town, with its winding streets and whitewashed houses, search out the Jewish quarter – the Giudecca – which is still very much as it was in the Middle Ages.

▶ *From Oria, continue along the country road for 20km (12 miles), via Torre Santa Susanna, to the* ***SS7ter*** *which runs to Lecce, 50km (31 miles), joining and becoming the* ***SS16*** *shortly before the town.*

5 Lecce, Puglia

Lecce is to southern Italy what Florence is to central Italy. The city is an architectural gem and is filled with magnificently decorated, ebullient, baroque (mostly late 16th- and early 17th-century) buildings built from a soft, golden sandstone called 'Pietra di Lecce'. The most notable architects were Antonio and Giuseppe Zimbalo who, between them, were responsible for most of the Basilica di Santa Croce, begun in 1549. In particular, notice the more florid parts of the façade and the rose window. Next door, the Palazzo del Governo was also designed by Giuseppe Zimbalo ('Zingarello'), as was the Duomo (cathedral).

Not everything is baroque in Lecce. In Piazza Sant'Oronzio are the remains of a Roman amphitheatre which at one time could probably seat about 25,000 people, and a Roman column topped by a statue of St Oronsius. There is also a lovely example of Puglian Romanesque architecture in the Church of Santi Nicolò e Cataldo. The Museo Provinciale S Castromediano, occupying three floors of a modern building, has good archaeological displays, a fine collection of ceramics and the town's art gallery. Lecce is a busy, thriving town with good ceramic shops selling the more expensive end of Grottaglie's range of wares. There are antique shops, restaurants and an indoor market selling local produce.

i Via Vittorio Emanuele 23

▶ *Take the* ***SS16*** *south as far as Maglie, 29km (18 miles). From the road bypassing Maglie, branch to the left along the* ***SS16*** *to Otranto.*

6 Otranto, Puglia

In the 11th century this little town was one of the leading Crusader ports. Nowadays it is better known as a port for ferries going to Greece. However, Otranto does have a good cathedral with one of the most stunning rose windows in Puglia. Founded by the Normans in 1080, it was added to and embellished over the years. This is the only medieval building in southern Italy to have preserved its entire original mosaic floor. There are scenes from the scriptures, depictions of animals and mythological subjects. In the oldest part of Otranto is the small Church of San Pietro, a delightful Byzantine building which may have been the town's old cathedral. There is

You can enjoy fresh seafood in the little port of Gallipoli

also a castle here, built by Ferdinand of Aragon at the end of the 15th century. Inside you can see the remains of Roman brickwork and some very early medieval masonry.

i *Piazza Castello*

▶ *Retrace the route to Maglie, then continue on the* ***SS497*** *as far as Neviano, about 17km (11 miles), then follow the signs for Gallipoli.*

7 Gallipoli, Puglia

Gallipoli is a remote place, on an island just off the west coast of the Salentine Peninsula. The oldest part of the town, with its narrow little streets, is joined to the mainland by a causeway. Dominating it is the Castello, the oldest part of which is Byzantine. There is also an elaborate baroque cathedral of 1630, sprinkled with works by local artists – see in particular the *Madonna with Sant'Orontius* by Giovanni Coppola. If it is open, go into the Church of the Purità and see the richly decorated ceramic paving tiles of 18th-century majolica.

FOR HISTORY BUFFS

Right down on the very tip of the Salentine Peninsula, at Patu, near Leuca (reach it from Otranto or Gallipoli), is the so-called Centopietre (Hundred Stones). This is a mysterious small building made of flat stone slabs with a pitched roof. It has two aisles divided by columns, and may be a Messapian (local pre-Greek civilisation) temple ... or some think it is medieval.

▶ *From Gallipoli, take the* ***SS101*** *to Galatone, turning left on to the* ***SS174*** *proceeding northwards via Nardo to Manduria, a further 47km (29 miles).*

RECOMMENDED WALKS

The Salentine Peninsula – the southernmost part of the Italian mainland – is good for walks, in particular just to the south of Otranto (Capo d'Otranto). The coastline leading to Otranto is fairly rugged but beautiful, with caves and places to swim.

8 Manduria, Puglia

Manduria was an important centre of the local Messapian civilisation which long predated

The town of Grottaglie is noted for its fine pottery

the coming of the Greek colonists to the area. The Messapians here fiercely opposed the Greeks, and the ruins of their ancient settlement can be seen to the north of the 'new' town.

There is a necropolis and a stretch of ancient city walls. The oldest of the latter (there are three sets of walls concentrically sited around what was the old city) date from the 5th century BC and the latest from about the 3rd century BC. Carefully cut blocks of stone, a strange triple gate and 2,000 rock-cut tombs survive. In the middle of the excavations is the famous Pozzo di Plinio (Well of Pliny – so called because Pliny himself mentions it), in which the water remains at a constant level however much you draw out of it. The most interesting part of the town itself is the Jewish quarter, the confines of which are marked by three large tufa arches. The houses here have no windows. See also the impressive 1719 Palazzo Imperiale, in Piazza Garibaldi.

▶ *From Manduria, go across country to Oria, 11km (7 miles), then from there to the **SS7** via Latiano, also about 11km (7 miles), then follow the **SS7** to Brindisi, 21km (13 miles).*

BACK TO NATURE

Wooded and shrub-covered hillsides in southern Italy are favoured by several species of birds of prey. They nest in the trees and use thermals generated off the land to gain lift. Species such as short-toed eagle, buzzard, sparrowhawk and goshawk are widespread and there is always a chance of seeing a golden eagle or Bonelli's eagle. Regrettably, birds of prey are much persecuted by Italian 'sportsmen'.

Puglia's harsh, dry landscape changes dramatically in spring

One of Puglia's many delightful hilltop towns

SPECIAL TO...

The western coast of the Salentine Peninsula, that is, between Gallipoli and Capo Santa Maria di Leuca, has some of Italy's best beaches. Gallipoli itself has good places for bathing, and there are other places at nearby Lido San Giovanni and Baia Verde, both within 10km (6 miles) of Gallipoli.

The Gargano Peninsula

While most of Puglia is relatively flat, the Gargano Peninsula, a rocky, partially wooded outcrop, constitutes what is possibly the only really scenic stretch of Adriatic coastline since Venice. It is the spur of Italy's boot which rises unexpectedly from the sea, an area of saints and mystic legends.

3 DAYS • 366KM • 228 MILES

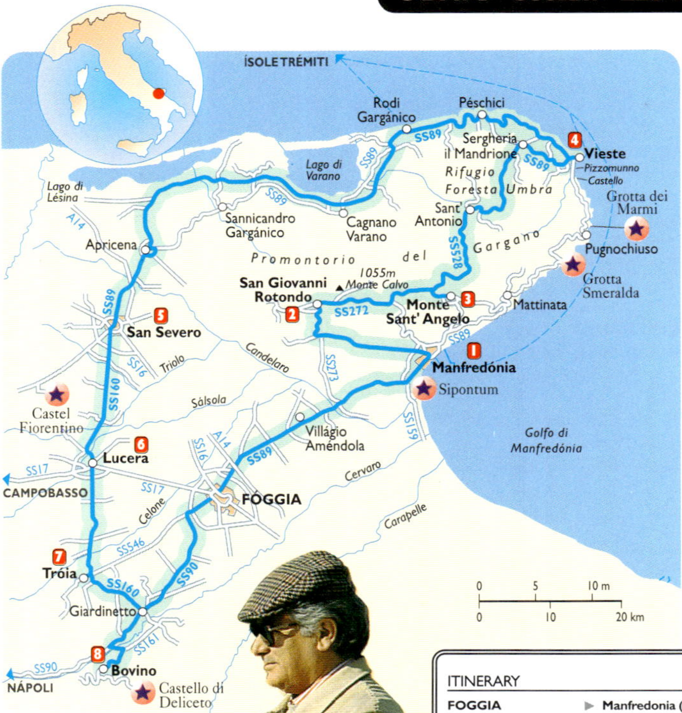

ITINERARY	
FOGGIA	▶ **Manfredonia (39km-24m)**
MANFREDONIA	▶ **San Giovanni Rotondo (23km-14m)**
SAN GIOVANNI ROTONDO	▶ **Monte Sant'Angelo (24km-15m)**
MONTE SANT'ANGELO	▶ **Vieste (59km-37m)**
VIESTE	▶ **San Severo (109km-68m)**
SAN SEVERO	▶ **Lucera (22km-14m)**
LUCERA	▶ **Troia (19km-12m)**
TROIA	▶ **Bovino (28km-17m)**
BOVINO	▶ **Foggia (43km-27m)**

Rocky coves and azure sea typify the Gargano Peninsula

i Via Senatore E Perrone 17, Foggia

▶ *From Foggia, take the SS89 to Manfredonia.*

1 Manfredonia, Puglia
This lively port takes its name from Manfred, the son of Emperor Frederick II and King of Sicily and Naples. Not much is left from that period in the 13th century, apart from the hefty remains of Manfred's castle, which now houses the Museo Archeologico del Gargano (National Archaeological Museum of Gargano), displaying artefacts from the remains of nearby ancient Sipontum. There is an undistinguished cathedral, built in 1680. More interesting is the Church of San Domenico with its Gothic doorway flanked by two stone lions and, inside, 14th-century frescos. Manfredonia is a base for ferries to the Tremiti Islands on the other side of the Gargano Peninsula. These tiny resorts are wonderful places to swim and sunbathe and consequently are extremely popular.

i Piazza del Popolo 11

▶ *From Manfredonia, follow the signs inland to San Giovanni Rotondo, about 23km (14 miles).*

FOR HISTORY BUFFS

To the south of Manfredonia are the remains of ancient Sipontum, abandoned in the Middle Ages because of malaria. Hannibal conquered it in the 3rd century BC, only to lose it to the Romans. There is a museum here as well as the lovely Santa Maria Siponto, an 11th-century church that survives from the very last period of the town. Near the museum is a recently discovered Christian catacomb (for details of access, ask at the museum).

SPECIAL TO...

Manfredonia is noted for its delicious red wine called Orta Nova. If you can stand up after a lunch including this, then good luck to you.

2 San Giovanni Rotondo, Puglia
The little town of San Giovanni Rotondo drifts down the side of Monte Calvo (Mount Calvo) and is one of the principal pilgrimage centres of Italy. Here lived Padre Pio da Pietralcina, a 20th-century miracle-worker who, like St Francis, received the *stigmata* – the wounds of Christ on his hands and feet and in his side. This modern saint (1887–1968) is buried in the newish church near the 16th-century Convent of Santa Maria delle Grazie and his tomb is the object of much veneration today. The town takes its name from a round temple, possibly dedicated to Jupiter, which became the Rotonda di San Giovanni, a baptistery of uncertain date. There are plenty of hotels and restaurants, and souvenir shops by the dozen.

SPECIAL TO...

In San Giovanni Rotondo, is the Festa dell'Ospite (the Guest's Festival). For a week there are lively folklore celebrations, exhibitions and displays, local gastronomic treats and a great deal of local – and very potent – wine is consumed (usually 11–20 August, but check for any changes to these dates).

i *Piazza Europa 104*

▶ *From San Giovanni Rotondo, the **SS272** winds eastwards to Monte Sant'Angelo.*

3 Monte Sant'Angelo, Puglia

This is another of Italy's important pilgrimage sites. St Michael is supposed to have appeared, in the 5th century, in a cave set deep within the ground – the same Santuario di San Michele (Sanctuary of St Michael) that you can visit today. A church was built in front of the grotto in 1273 and its contemporary bell-tower copies the plan, though in miniature, of the Castel del Monte (see page 147). On your way down to the dark, damp cave, you will pass a set of beautiful bronze doors dating from 1076. Reputedly made in Constantinople, they depict scenes from the Old Testament. In the grotto itself is a statue of St Michael by Andrea Sansovino, a Renaissance Florentine sculptor much under the influence of Raphael. The oldest quarter of Monte Sant'Angelo is the medieval Junno district, which would have been known by illustrious visitors of the past, such as St Thomas Aquinas and St Francis.

The Franciscan Monastery in the town centre is home to an interesting museum of folk arts and traditions.

The town is overlooked by its massive medieval castle, and there's a belvedere with magnificent coastal views.

▶ *Retrace the route for 6km (4 miles) before turning right on the **SS528** through the centre of the Gargano for 24km (15 miles) to Sant'Antonio. Here branch right, following the signs to Segheria il Mandrione, at which take the **SS89** to Vieste.*

4 Vieste, Puglia

Vieste, beautifully situated on a tip of the Gargano Peninsula, surrounded by coves, cliffs and beaches, is a popular resort, an appropriate location for the Museo Malacologico (Museum of Sea Shells), with thousands of examples from around the world.

The town is dominated by a castle and a cathedral. There are no saints here, and fewer monuments, but there are plenty of other attractions to keep visitors amused. Apart from shops and restaurants, there are all sorts of caves within reach of the town, accessible either on foot or by boat (tours) – just to the south are the Grotta Smeralda (Emerald Cave) and the Grotta dei Marmi (Cave of the Marbles).

South of the town are the beaches of Pizzomunno and Castello – both long. From Vieste ferries run to the Tremiti Islands.

i *Piazza Kennedy*

▶ *Take the coastal road going north to join the **SS89** at Peschici. Continue along the coast on the **SS89** to Rodi Garganico before striking inland. Follow the main road to the turning for Apricena and San Severo.*

5 San Severo, Puglia

Much of San Severo has a baroque overlay. For example, the town's main landmark, the medieval cathedral, looks anything but ancient, having been revamped in a baroque style.

The important Romanesque Church of San Severo did not escape. It retains its rose window, but manages to combine it rather cleverly with some baroque details. Other churches include San Giovanni Battista, also Romanesque but with a baroque bell tower and Santa Maria degli Angeli. About 13km (8 miles) from San Severo, you can visit the ruins of Castel Fiorentino, where the Emperor Frederick II died in 1250.

▶ *Take the **SS160** to Lucera, a distance of about 22km (14 miles).*

One of the Gargano Peninsula's delightful stretches of beach

FOR CHILDREN

If the children deserve a treat for sitting still and not complaining, then give them *cassata di ricotta*, a richer version of ice-cream made from fresh, light *ricotta* cheese.

6 Lucera, Puglia

The windy hilltop site of Lucera was once the town in which the Emperor Frederick II preferred to live. It contains the remains of the biggest castle he ever built (1233), one of the most magnificent in Puglia. The turreted walls survive, extending for about 900m (½ mile) and dominating the town and the great Tavoliere plain beyond. Charles I of Anjou transformed the castle (1269–83), and today there are only ruins of Frederick II's palace inside the walls. Lucera has a strange history. Cosmopolitan Frederick lured here from Sicily about 20,000 Saracen subjects who transformed Lucera into an Arab city. In 1300 most of these were massacred by Charles II, but there are traces of their existence around the town.

The 14th-century Duomo (cathedral), the second largest in southern Italy, is an impressive building and thought to be one of the least altered of its date anywhere. More French Gothic than anything else (people from Provence replaced the Saracens after 1300), its high altar is made from a slab of marble that was once Frederick II's dining table in his Castel Fiorentino (see page 156). In Lucera's Museo Civico (Civic Museum), you can see ceramics from the doomed Saracen period as well as some fine remains from the old Roman settlement of Luceria Augusta, in particular, a marble statue of Venus.

► *Take the **SS160** south for 18km (11 miles) to the turn-off for Troia, a further kilometre (½ mile).*

7 Troia, Puglia

Troia is one of the loveliest towns on this tour. It owes its fame to a splendid Romanesque cathedral, of which the rose window is its most noteworthy adornment. There are also two 12th-century bronze doors. They show classical and oriental influences. Inside, you should look at the 12th-century carved pulpit as well as the illuminated manuscripts in the cathedral treasury. A museum in the Convent of San Benedetto contains part of the treasure from the cathedral, church paintings and some baroque furnishings.

The restored 16th-century Palazzo d'Avalos houses the Municipal Museum, which spans the pre-classical to medieval eras.

► *Take the **SS160** to the junction with the **SS90**. Branch slowly for 7km (4 miles) then turn left on to the **SS161** for 1km (½ mile) before taking the winding country road on the right for 9km (5½ miles) to Bovino.*

BACK TO NATURE

The Rifugio Foresta Umbra (Umbra Forest Nature Reserve) on the Gargano promontory, is an area of woodland comprising mainly beech interspersed with field maple, yew and hornbeam. *Macchia* (scrub) vegetation flourishes in the forest clearings and includes species such as mastic, tree heather, cistuses and laurel. These are visited by numerous insects – look out for chafer beetles and hairstreak butterflies. Birds of prey and many woodland species such as woodpeckers and flycatchers inhabit the woods.

8 Bovino, Puglia

Bovino was once a Roman settlement called Vibinum. Its claim to fame, until about 80 years ago, was that it was an infamous centre of brigandage. Up on its hill, its remoteness protected its reputation. Bovino is a good centre for excursions into the surrounding countryside. At Giardinetto, about 17km (10½ miles) on the return to Foggia, is a wonderful 11th-century cathedral – examine its bronze doors. Then, closer to Bovino, is the Castello di Delceto (about 8km/5 miles).

Its ruined 15th-century castle dominates Monte Sant'Angelo

► *Retrace your route to the **SS90** which leads to Foggia, 43km (27 miles).*

SCENIC ROUTES

The eastern extremity of the Gargano Peninsula, as it thrusts into the Adriatic, is the region's most scenic area, with fine coastal views. Although the tour takes you from Monte Sant'Angelo to Vieste along an inland road, a very much longer alternative would be the coastal route. Apart from its great natural beauty, it is studded with beaches and tourist villages and is the kind of stretch you might like to complete very slowly, staying overnight where you can.

ACCIDENTS

If you have an accident, place a warning triangle 50m (55 yards) behind the car and call the police (tel: 112 or 113). Do not admit liability or make statements which might later incriminate you. Ask any witness(es) to remain, make a statement to the police and exchange names, addresses, car details and insurance companies' names and addresses with other driver(s) involved. A report must be made to the insurance company. If the accident involves personal injury, medical assistance must be sought for the injured party. On some *autostrada* there are emergency telephones as well as emergency push-button call boxes.

BREAKDOWNS

If your car breaks down, put on hazard warning lights and place a warning triangle not less than 50m (55 yards) to the rear of the vehicle. Call the Automobile Club d'Italia (ACI) 24-hour emergency number (tel: 116) and give your location, car registration and make. Roadside assistance will not be given. The car will be towed to the nearest ACI affiliated garage. The service is free to any visiting motorist driving a foreign registered vehicle.

CARAVANS

Brakes

Check that the caravan braking mechanism is correctly adjusted. If it has a breakaway safety mechanism, the cable between the car and caravan must be firmly anchored so that the trailer brakes act immediately if the two part company.

Caravans and trailers

Take a list of contents, especially if any valuable or

MOTORING IN ITALY

unusual equipment is being carried, as this may be required on arrival. A towed vehicle should be readily identifiable by a plate in an accessible position showing the name of the make of the vehicle and the production and serial number.

Lights

Make sure that all the lights are working (check that the flasher rate is correct: 60–120 times a minute).

Tyres

Both tyres on the caravan should be of the same size and type. Inspect them carefully: if you think they are likely to be more than three-quarters worn before you get back, replace them before you leave. If you notice uneven wear, scuffed treads, or damaged walls, get expert advice on whether the tyres are suitable for further use.

Find out the recommended tyre pressures from the caravan manufacturer.

CAR HIRE AND FLY/DRIVE

Car hire is available in most cities and resorts. Many international firms operate this service. Rates generally include breakdown service, maintenance and oil, but not petrol.

Some firms restrict hire to drivers over 21 years of age. Generally you must have had a valid licence for at least one year before applying for car hire.

People travelling by air or rail should be able to take advantage of special inclusive arrangements.

CHILDREN

Children under four must not travel in the front or rear seats unless using a suitable restraint system. Children between 3 and 12 may only travel in the front seat if using such equipment.

Note: under no circumstances should a rear-facing restraint be used in a seat with an airbag.

CRASH HELMETS

Visiting motorcyclists and their passengers must wear crash or safety helmets.

DIMENSIONS AND WEIGHT RESTRICTIONS

Private cars and towed trailers or caravans are restricted to the following dimensions: height – 4m; width – 2.5m; length – 12m.

DOCUMENTS

Visitors bringing their own (foreign registered) car to Italy must be at least 18 years of age (also for motorcycles over 125cc or with a passenger) and carry the vehicle's registration documents (logbook) and a full, valid driving licence (*patente* in Italian).

Third party insurance is compulsory; an international green card, though not compulsory, is recommended. A green UK, red Eire or other foreign licence is acceptable accompanied by a translation, available free from the ACI or the Italian State Tourist Office in the country of origin. The translation is not required for the new, pink EU, UK or Republic of Ireland licence.

DRINKING AND DRIVING

The permitted blood-alcohol level is 0.05%. Laws regarding drinking and driving are strict and the penalties severe, so if you drink don't drive.

DRIVING CONDITIONS

Italian traffic rules follow the Geneva Convention and Italy uses international road signs. Driving is on the right and you should give way at intersections to vehicles coming from your right.

You should keep close to the nearside kerb, even when the road is clear.

Vehicles travelling in opposite directions and wishing to turn left must pass in front of each other.

Motorcycles under 150cc are not allowed on motorways.

See also **speed limits.**

FUEL

Petrol (*benzina*) in Italy is some of the most expensive in Europe. Diesel (*gasolio*) is cheaper. Carrying fuel in cans is prohibited.

Petrol stations are open 7–12.30 and 3–7.30 (mornings only at weekends), but 24-hour service is guaranteed on motorways.

Self-service and 24-hour pumps are increasingly common.

INSURANCE

Fully comprehensive insurance, which covers you for some of the expenses incurred after a breakdown or an accident, is advisable.

LIGHTS

Full-beam headlights can be used only outside cities and towns. Dipped headlights are compulsory in tunnels, even if well-lit. It is recommended that visiting motorists equip their vehicles with a spare set of vehicle bulbs.

MOTORING CLUBS

The Touring Club Italiano (TCI) has its headquarters at 10 Corso Italia, 20122 Milano. Tel: (02) 85261. The Automobile Club d'Italia (ACI) has its headquarters at 8 Via Marsala, 00185 Roma. Tel: (06) 49981 (116 for foreign language assistance). The ACI provides towage from a breakdown to the nearest affiliated garage. Call from telephone columns placed every 2km along the motorway.

ROADS

Main and secondary roads are generally good, and there are an exceptional number of by-passes.

Mountain roads are usually well engineered. Italy has some 4,000 miles of motorway (*autostrada*) with tolls payable on most sections (see also **tolls**).

ROUTE DIRECTIONS

Throughout the book the following abbreviations are used for Italian roads:

A – Autostrada (motorway)
SS – Strada Statale (state road)
dir, ter, bis, q, qu – suffixes to state roads (**SS**) relating to links and extensions of major roads
minor roads – unnumbered roads

SPEED LIMITS

The speed limit in built-up areas is 50kph (31mph); outside built-up areas – 90kph (55mph) on ordinary roads, 110kph (68mph) on main roads and 130kph (80mph) on motorways. For cars towing a caravan or trailer the speed limits are 70kph (44mph) outside built-up areas and 80kph (50mph) on motorways.

Note: a maximum authorised speed sticker must be displayed at the rear by all vehicles, including caravans and trailers, whose maximum permitted speed is less than 130kph (80mph). The stickers are on sale at Italian petrol stations: fines are levied for failure to display.

A new regulation stipulates that you must not drive so slowly that you hinder the flow of traffic.

TOLLS

Tolls are payable on many motorways in Italy. Visiting motorists may purchase a motorway toll card (Via card) from ACI offices and motorway toll booths.

WARNING TRIANGLE/HAZARD WARNING LIGHTS

The use of a warning triangle is compulsory in the event of an accident or breakdown. It should also be used to give advance warning of any stationary vehicle which is parked on a road in fog, near a bend or on a hill at night when the rear lights have failed. The triangle must be placed on the road not less than 50m (55 yards) behind the vehicle.

Motorists who fail to do this are liable to an administrative fine.

ACCOMMODATION & RESTAURANTS

Following is a selection of hotels (🏨) which can be found along the routes of each tour, as well as suggestions for restaurants (🍴) where you can take a break.

Prices

Hotel charges are divided into three price brackets based on a double room per night.

€€€ – over €132
€€ – €78–132
€ – under €78

Restaurant prices are based on a meal for two without wine.

€€€ – over €30
€€ – €15–30
€ – under €15

TOUR 1
TORINO

🏨 **Alexandra €€**
Lungo Dora Napoli 14. Tel: 011/858 327; fax: 011/248 3805. *Closed 31 Jul–30 Aug.*

🏨 **President €€**
Via Cecchi 67. Tel: 011/859 553; fax: 011/248 0465.

ASTI

🍴 **Falcon Vecchio €€**
9 Via Mamelli. Tel: 0141/593 106. *Rustic dishes. Closed Sun eve, Mon & 9–31 Aug.*

ALESSANDRIA
Domus €€
Via Castellani 12. Tel: 0131/43 305; fax: 0131/232 019.

BAROLO
Barolo €
Via Lomondo 2. Tel: 0173/56 354; fax: 0173/56 354.
Locanda nel Borgo Antico €€
2 Piazza Municipio. Tel: 0173/56 355. *Dishes steeped in excellent local wine. Closed 20 Dec–mid-Jan & Jul, Wed & Thu (except Oct & Nov).*

LA MORRA
Belvedere €€
5 Piazza Castello. Tel: 0173/850 190. *Typical local cuisine. Closed Jan, 23 Feb–31 Jul, Sun eve & Mon.*

ACQUI TERME
Ristorante Cappello
Strada Visone 62. Tel: 0144 325114. *Regional cuisine; also offers cookery courses.*

TOUR 2
MILANO
Mirage €€€
Via Casella 61/Viale Certosa. Tel: 02/3921 0471; fax: 02/3921 0589.
Don Lisander €€€
12a Via Manzoni. Tel: 02/7602 0130. *Contemporary Italian cuisine. Closed Sun & 24 Dec–10 Jan & 12–22 Aug.*

COMO
Como €€
Via Mentana 28. Tel: 031/266 173; fax: 031/266 020. *Closed Dec–Jan.*
Tre Re €€
Via Boldoni 20.
Tel: 031/265374; fax: 031/ 241349.

BERGAMO
Arli €€
Largo Porta Nuova 12. Tel: 035/222 014; fax: 035/239 732.
Trattoria Sant'Ambroeus €€
2 Piazza Vecchia. Tel: 035/237 494. *Regional gastronomic experience. Closed 5–20 Jan & Wed.*

CREMONA
Continental €€
Piazza della Libertà 26. Tel: 0372/434 141; fax: 0372/454 873.

TOUR 3
BOLOGNA
Il Guercino €€
Via Luigi Serra 7. Tel: 051/369 893; fax: 051/369 893.
Residence Executive €€€
Via Ferrarese 161. Tel: 051/372 960; fax: 051/372 127.
Pappagallo €€€
3 Piazza della Mercanzia. Tel: 051/232 807. *The best, richest food experience in the city. Closed Sun.*

TOUR 4
RIMINI
Rondinella €
Via Neri 3. Tel/fax: 0541/380567.
Villa Lalla €€
Viale Vittorio Veneto 22. Tel: 0541/55 155; fax: 0541/23 570.
Giorgini €
18 Via Dante. Tel: 0541/24 322. *Restaurant & pizzeria. Closed Mon.*

RAVENNA
Astoria €
Via Circonvallazione alla Rotonda 26. Tel: 0544/453 960; fax: 0544/455 419.
La Madra
Via Faentina. Tel: 0544/463 750. *Seafood, pizzas. Closed Mon.*

FAENZA
Vittoria €€
Corso Garibaldi 23. Tel: 0546/21 508; fax: 0546/29 136.

TOUR 5
FELTRE
Nuovo €
Vicolo Fornere Pazze 52. Tel: 0439/2110-81345; fax: 0439/89 241.

VENEZIA
La Residenza €€
Campo Bandiera e Moro 3608, Castello. Tel: 041/528 5315; fax: 041/523 8859.
Osteria da Fiore €€
Calle del Scalater 220a, San Polo. Tel: 041/721 308. *Seafood. Closed Sun, Mon, 24 Dec–12 Jan & Aug.*
La Colomba €€€
1665 Piscina di Prezzeria. Tel: 041/522 1175. *Fish, pasta. Closed Wed May–Jun, & Sep–Nov.*

TOUR 6
VERONA
Aurora €€
Piazza delle Erbe 2. Tel: 045/594 717; fax: 045/801 0860.
Giulietta e Romeo €€€
Vicolo Tre Marchetti 3. Tel: 045/800 3554; fax: 045/801 0862.
El Cantinon €€
11 Via San Rocchetto. Tel: 045/595 291. *Regional food. Closed Mon Jul–Aug, Wed rest of year.*

PADOVA
Al Fagiano €
Via Locatelli 45.
Tel/fax: 049/875 3396.
Igea €
Via Ospedale Civile 87. Tel: 049/875 0577; fax: 049/660 0865.
Bastioni del Moro €€
18 Via Bronzetti. Tel: 049/871 0006. *Regional cuisine. Closed Sun & 10–23 Aug.*

MONSELICE
Ceffri €€
Via Orti 7/b. Tel: 0429/783 111; fax: 0429/783 100.
La Torre €€
14 Piazza Mazzini. Tel: 0429/ 737 52. *Robust regional cooking. Closed Sun eve, Mon & Aug.*

TOUR 7
SAN REMO
Nyala Suite Hotel
Via Solara. Tel: 0184/667 668; fax: 0184/666 059.
Grand Hotel de Londres €
Corso Matuzia 51.
Tel: 0184/65511; fax: 0184/ 668 073.
Da Giannino €€€
23 Lungomare Trento e Trieste. Tel: 0184/504 014. *Seafood; bruschetta with marinated fish a speciality. Closed Sun eve, Mon & 1–15 Oct.*
La Lanterna €
16 Via Molo di Ponente. Tel: 0184/506 855. *Seafood. Closed Thu & 15 Nov–15 Jan.*

TRIORA

🏨 **Colomba d'Oro €**
Corso Italia 66. Tel: 0184/94 051; fax: 0184/94 089.

TOUR 8
GENOVA

🏨 **La Capannina €€**
Via Tito Speri 7. Tel: 010/317 131; fax: 010/362 2692.

LEVANTO

🏨 **Villa Margherita €–€€**
Via Trento e Trieste 31. Tel: 0187/807 212.

PORTOVENERE

🏨 **Paradiso €€**
Via Garibaldi 34/40. Tel: 0187/ 790 612; fax: 0187/792 582

AMEGLIA

🍴 **Locanda dell'Angelo**
Viale XXV Aprile 60. Tel: 0187/64391. *Also cookery courses.*

TOUR 9
PISA

🏨 **Amalfitana €**
Via Roma 44. Tel: 050/29 000; fax: 050/25 218.

🏨 **Verdi €€**
Piazza Repubblica 5/6. Tel: 050/598 947; fax: 050/598 944.

LUCCA

🏨 **Palazzo Alexander €€€**
Via Santa Giustina 48. Tel: 0583/583 571; fax: 0583/583 610.

SAN GIMIGNANO

🏨 **Bel Soggiorno €€**
Via San Giovanni 91. Tel: 0577/940 375.

🍴 **Dorando €€**
2 Vicolo dell'Oro. Tel: 0577/941 862. *Tuscan specialities. Closed Mon from Easter–Oct & 10 Jan–Feb.*

TOUR 10
FIRENZE

🏨 **Jane €€**
Via Orcagna 56. Tel: 055/677 382; fax: 055/677 383.

🏨 **Orcagna €€**
Via Orcagna 57. Tel: 055/669 959; fax: 055/670 500.

🍴 **Osteria n l €€**
20 Via del Moro. Tel: 055/284 897. *Pasta, local dishes. Closed Sun, Mon & lunch 3–26 Aug.*

MONTALCINO

🏨 **Il Giglio €**
Via Soccorso Saloni 5. Tel/fax: 0577/848 167.

SIENA

🏨 **Santa Caterina**
Via E.S. Piccolomini. Tel: 0577/221 105; fax: 0577/271 087.

TOUR 11
PERUGIA

🏨 **Priori €**
Via dei Priori. Tel: 075/572 3378; fax: 075/572 9155.

🍴 **Osetria del Bartolo €€**
30 Via Bartolo. Tel: 075/573 561. *Local cuisine. Closed Sun.*

TODI

🏨 **Villaluisa €€**
Via Cortesi 147. Tel: 075/894 8571; fax: 075/894 8472.

TOUR 12
PORTONOVO

🏨 **Internazionale €€**
Via Poggio. Tel: 071/801 001; fax: 071/801 082.

ASCOLI PICENO

🏨 **Gioli €**
Viale De Gasperi 14. Tel: 0736/ 255 550; fax: 0736/255 550.

🍴 **Kursaal €**
66 Via Luigi Mercantini. Tel: 0736/253 140. *Local family-style cooking. Closed Sun.*

CAMERINO

🏨 **I Duchi €**
Via Favorino 72. Tel: 0737/630 440; fax: 0737/630 455.

TOUR 13
URBINO

🏨 **Dei Duchi €**
Via G Dini 12. Tel: 0722/328 226; fax: 0722/328 009.

🏨 **Raffaello €€**
Via Santa Margherita 40. Tel: 0722/4896; fax: 0722/328 540.

🍴 **Nene €**
Via Crocicchia. Tel: 0722/350 161. *Country-style cuisine. Closed 7–26 Jan.*

PESARO

🏨 **Atlantic €€**
Viale Trieste 365. Tel: 0721/370 333; fax: 0721/370 373.

JESI

🏨 **Mariani €**
Via Orfanotrofio 10. Tel: 0731/207 286; fax: 0731/200 011.

🍴 **Tana Libera Tutti €**
1 Piazza Baccio Pontelli. Tel: 0731/59 237. *Seafood. Closed Sun.*

TOUR 14
PESCARA

🏨 **Maja €€**
Viale della Riviera 201. Tel: 085/471 1545; fax: 085/ 77 930.

🍴 **Brigantino €€**
9 Viale Pepe. Tel: 085/691 945. *Seafood. Closed Mon.*

ATRI

🏨 **Du Parc €**
Viale Umberto 1. Tel: 085/879 324; fax: 085/879 8326.

ORTONA

🏨 **Ideale €**
Corso Garibaldi 65. Tel: 085/906 3735; fax: 085/906 6153.

🍴 **Miramare €**
15 Largo Farnese. Tel: 085/906 6556. *Local specialities. Closed 10–30 Nov.*

VASTO

🏨 **Excelsior €€**
Strada Statale 16 Sud. Tel: 0873/802 588; fax: 0873/802 222.

TOUR 15
L'AQUILA

🏨 **Grand Hotel e del Parco €€**
Corso Federico II 74. Tel: 0862/413 240; fax: 0862/65 938

🍴 **Tre Marie €€**
3 Via Tre Marie. Tel: 0862/413 191. *Typical regional dishes. Closed 24 & 31 Dec, Sun eve, & Mon except Aug.*

SCANNO

🏨 **Miramonti €**
Via D di Rienzo 32. Tel: 0864/74 369.

🍴 **Lo Sgabello €**
45 Via Pescatori. Tel: 0864/747 476. *Local-style cuisine. Closed Wed Jun & Sep.*

PESCOCOSTANZO
Le Torri €€€
Via del Vallone 4. Tel: 0864/642 040; fax: 0864/641 573.

TOUR 16
ROMA
Hotel la Giocca €€
Via Salaria 1223. Tel: 06/880 4411; fax: 06/880 4495.
Hotel Imperiale €€€
Via Veneto. Tel: 06/482 6351.
Checchino dal 1887 €€
30 Via Monte Testaccio. Tel: 06/574 6318. *Roman specialities. Closed 24 Dec–3 Jan, Sun eve, Mon & Jun–Sep.*

ANAGNI
Villa la Floridiana €€
Via Casilina. Tel: 0775/769 960; fax: 0775/774 527.

SPERLONGA
La Sirenella €€
Via Cristoforo Colombo 25. Tel: 0771/549 186; fax: 0771/549 189.
La Bisaccia €€
25 Via I Romita. Tel: 0771/548 576. *Regional cooking. Closed Nov & Tue.*

CASTEL GANDOLFO
Castelvecchio €€
Viale Pio XI 23. Tel: 06/936 0308; fax: 06/936 0579.
Antico Ristorante Pagnanelli €€
4 Via Gramsci. Tel: 06/936 0004. *Local cuisine. Closed Tue.*

TOUR 17
ROMA
Clodio €€€
Via di Santa Lucia 10. Tel: 06/372 1122; fax: 06/3735 0745.

TARQUINIA
La Torraccia €€
Viale Mediterraneo 45, Lido di Tarquinia 01010. Tel: 0766/864 375; fax: 0766/864 296.
Gradinoro €
17 Lungomare dei Tirreni. Tel: 0766/869 834. *Regional food. Closed Mar–Nov.*

VITERBO
Hotel Nibbio €€
Piazzale Gramsci. Tel: 0761/326 514; fax: 0761/311 808.
Tre Re €€
40 Via Grafferro Macei. Tel: 0761/304 619. *Excellent seafood Closed Thu.*
La Zaffera €€
7 Piazza San Carluccio. Tel: 0761/344 265. *Robust regional cooking in an ancient monastery. Closed Mon.*

TOUR 18
POZZUOLI
Tiro a Volo €
Via San Gennaro 69A. Tel/fax: 081/570 4540.

POMPEII
Forum €
Via Roma 99. Tel: 081/850 1170; fax: 081/850 6132.
Maiuri €€
Via Acquasalsa 20. Tel/fax: 081/856 2716.
President €€€
12/13 Piazza Schettini. Tel: 081/850 7245. *Seafood. Closed 10–25 Aug.*

CAPRI
Florida €€
Via Fuorlovado 34, Capri Town. Tel: 081/837 0497; fax: 081/837 0042.
Villa Krupp €€€
Via Matteotti 12, Capri Town. Tel: 081/837 0362; fax: 081/837 6489.
Le Grottelle €
5 Via Arco Naturale. Tel: 081/837 5719. *Seafood, salads, pasta. Closed Thu.*
Quisi €€€
Grand Hotel Quisisana, 2 Via Camerelle. Tel: 081/837 0788. *Grand-style international cooking. Closed Sun evening.*

AMALFI
Hotel Luna Convento €€€
Via Pantaleone Comité. Tel: 089/871 002; fax: 089/871 333.
SALERNO
Fiorenza €
Via Trento 145, località. Tel: 089/338 800; fax: 089/337 772.

AGROPOLI
Serenella €
Via San Marco 150. Tel: 0974/823 333.
Carola €
1 Via Piscacane. Tel: 0974/826 422. *Speciality pasta. Closed 8 Jan–8 Feb.*

TOUR 19
NAPOLI
Mercure Angioino €€
Via Depretis 123. Tel: 081/552 9500; fax: 081/552 9509.
Nuovo Rebecchino €€
Corso Garibaldi 356. Tel: 081/553 5327; fax: 081/268 026.
San Carlo €€
17 Via Cesario Console. Tel: 081/764 9757. *Typical regional dishes. Closed Sun & 10–24 Aug.*

CASERTA
Jolly €€
Via Vittorio Veneto 9. Tel: 0823/325 222; fax: 0823/354 522.
Le Colonne €€€
7–13 Via Nazionale Appia. Tel: 0823/467 494. *Regional cooking. Closed Tue.*

BENEVENTO
Italiano €€
Viale Principe di Napoli 137. Tel: 0824/24 111; fax: 0824/24923.

AVELLINO
Hotel de la Ville €€€
Via Palatucci 20. Tel: 0825/780 911; fax: 0825/780 921.

TOUR 20
CATANZARO
Guglielmo €€
Via Tedeschi 1. Tel: 0961/741 922; fax: 0961/41900.

SIDERNO
President €€
Strada Statale 106 (2km southwest of Siderno). Tel: 0964/343 191 or 1-800/359 4827; fax: 0964/342 746.
La Vecchia Hosteria €
5 Via Matteotti. Tel: 0964/388 880. *Rustic cuisine. Closed Wed.*

REGGIO DI CALABRIA
Ascioti €€
Via San Francesco da Paola 79. Tel: 0965/897 041; fax: 0965/26063.

TROPEA
Punta Faro €
San Nicolo di Ricardi, Capo Vaticano (10km southwest). Tel: 0963/663 139; fax: 0963/663 968.

PIZZO
Marinella €
Via Riviera Prangi Nord. Tel: 0963/534 860; fax: 0963/534 884.
A Casa Janca €
Riviera Prangi Nord. Tel: 0963/264 364. *Typical regional dishes.*

TOUR 21
COSENZA
Royal €
Via Molinella 24. Tel: 0984/412 165.
L'Arco Vecchio €€
21 Piazza Archi di Ciaccio. Tel: 0984/72 564. *Local specialities. Closed Sun eve and 14–18 Aug.*
Da Giacondo €
53 Via Piave. Tel: 0984/29 810. *Regional local cuisine. Closed 7–22 Aug.*

SPEZZANO ALBANESE TERME
San Francesco Terme €
SS 19, Strada delle Terme. Tel: 0981/953 068; fax: 0981 953 251.

ROSSANO STAZIONE
Scigliano €€
Viale Margherita 257. Tel: 0983/511 846; fax: 0983/511 848.

CATANZARO
Guglielmo €€
Via Tedeschi 1. Tel: 0961/741 922; fax: 0961/722 181.

TOUR 22
MATERA
De Nicola €
Via Nazionale 158. Tel: 0835/385 111; fax: 0835/385 113.
Casino del Diavolo-da Francolino €
Via La Martella Ovest. Tel: 0835/261 986. *Country-style cuisine. Closed Mon.*
Trattoria Lucana €
48 Via Lucana. Tel: 0835/336 117. *Regional dishes Closed Sun & 10–25 Sep.*

MARATEA
La Locanda delle Donne Monache €€€
Via Carlo Mazzei 4. Tel: 0973/877 487; fax: 0973/877 687.

POTENZA
Vittoria €
Via della Tecnica. Tel: 0971/56 632; fax: 0971/56 802.
Antica Osteria Marconi €€
235 Via Marconi. Tel: 0971/56 900. *Traditional rustic cuisine. Closed Sun eve, Mon, Christmas Day, New Year, 10–25 Aug.*

TOUR 23
BARI
Boston €€
Via Piccinni 155. Tel: 080/521 6633; fax: 080/524 6802.
Costa €€
Via Crisanzio 12. Tel: 080/521 9015; fax: 080/521 0006.
La Pignata €€€
173 Corso Vittorio Emanuele. Tel: 080/523 2481. *Seafood. Closed Mon & Aug.*

BARLETTA
Del Cavalieri €€
Via Foggia 24. Tel: 0883/571 461; fax: 0883/526 640.
Antica Cucina €€
73 Via Milano. Tel: 0883/521 718. *Fresh pasta & fish. Closed Mon & 1–20 Jul.*

MONOPOLI
Vecchio Mulino €€
Viale Aldo Moro 192. Tel: 080/777 133; fax: 080/777 654.
Lido Bianco €€
3 Via Procaccia. Tel: 080/887 6737. *Seafood. Closed Nov & Mon Jun–Sep.*

TOUR 24
BRINDISI
La Rosetta €€
Via San Dionisio 2. Tel: 0831/523 423; fax: 0831/563 110.
Orientale €€
Corso Garibaldi 40. Tel: 0831/568 451; fax: 0831/568 460.
Cascipo €€
45–47 Via San Benedetto. Tel: 0831/528 348. *Pizza; fish. Closed Wed & Aug.*

GROTTAGLIE
Gill €
Via Brodolini 75. Tel: 099/563 8207; fax: 099/563 8756.

LECCE
Risorgimento €€
Via Augusto Imperatore 19. Tel: 0832/252 125; fax: 0832/245 571.
Barbablu €€–€€€
Via Umberto 17. Tel: 0832/241 183. *Regional specialities. Excellent meat and fish dishes. Closed Mon & Sun evening.*

OTRANTO
Rosa Antico €
Strada Statale 16. Tel/fax: 0836/801 563.
Acmet Pascia €€
Via Lungomare degli Eori. Tel: 0836/801 282. *Emphasis on good home-cooking. Closed Mon & 20 Oct–20 Nov.*

TOUR 25
FOGGIA
Atleti €
Via Bari. Tel: 0881/630 100; fax: 0881/630 101.
President €€
Via degli Aviatori 130. Tel: 0881/618 010; fax: 0881/617 930.
Il Ventaglio €€
6 Via Posiglione. Tel: 0881/661 500. *Seafood. Closed 1–7 Jan, 13–30 Aug, 23–31 Dec, Sat & Sun 21 Jun–27 Aug, & Sun eve rest of year.*
La Locanda di Hansel €
59 Via Ricci. Tel: 0881/773 871. *Simple, home-style cooking.*

VIESTE
Punta San Francesco €€
Via San Francesco 2. Tel: 0884/701 422; fax: 0884/701 424.
Seggio €€
Via Vieste 7. Tel: 0884/708 123; fax: 0884/708 727.
Al Dragone €€
8 Via Duomo. Tel: 0884/701 212. *Regional cuisine and fish.*

[i] Tourist Information Office
[12] Number on tour

Practical Information
The addresses, telephone numbers and opening times of attractions in the tours, including telephone numbers of the Tourist Information Offices, are listed below tour by tour.

TOUR 1

[i] Piazza Solferino, Torino. Tel: 011/535 181.

[i] Piazza Alfieri 34, Asti. Tel: 0141/530 357.

[i] Via Savona 26, Alessandria. Tel: 0131/251 021.

[i] Corso Nizza 17, Cuneo. Tel: 0171/66 615.

1 Moncalvo
Galleria Civica d'Arte Moderna
Piazza Municipio 2, Tel: 0141/917 505.

2 Asti
San Pietro in Consavia and Archaeological Museum
Corso Alfieri 2. Tel: 0141/530 072. *Open Apr–Oct Tue–Sun 10–1, 4–7; Nov–Mar Tues–Sun 10–1, 3–6.*

3 Alessandria
Museo del Capello Borsalino
Corso Cento Cannoni. Tel: 0131/202 111. *Closed for renovation.*

4 Acqui Terme
Castello dei Paleologi and Archaeological Museum
Via Morelli 2. Tel: 0144/57555. *Open May–Oct, Wed–Sat 9.30–12.30, 3.30–6.30, Sun 3.30–6.30. Closed 15 Aug.*

7 Barolo
Castello Falletti
Piazza Falletti. Tel: 0173/56 277. *Open Mar–Nov Fri–Wed 10–12.30, 3–6.30; Dec Fri–Wed 10–4.30; Feb Sat–Sun 10–4.30.*

8 La Morra
Museo Ratti
Frazzione Annunziata. Tel: 0173/50 185. *Open Mon–Fri 8.30–noon, 2–5 by reservation*

10 Cuneo
Galimberti House
Piazza Galimberti 6. Tel: 0171/693 344. *Closed for restoration till Dec 2004.*

TOUR 2

[i] Via Marconi 1, Milano. Tel: 02/7252 4301.

[i] Piazza Cavour 17, Como. Tel: 031/330 0111.

[i] Via Nazario Sauro 6, Lecco. Tel: 0341/362 360.

[i] Piazzale Marconi 106, Bergamo. Tel: 035/242 226.

[i] Piazza A Mantegna 6, Mantova. Tel: 0376/350 681.

[i] Piazza del Comune 5, Cremona. Tel: 0372/23233 or 21722.

[i] Via Fabio Filzi 2, Pavia. Tel: 0382/272 338.

2 Lago Maggiore
Borromeo Fortress and Museums
Via della Rocca, Angera. Tel: 0331/931 300. *Open mid-Mar to mid-Oct, Mon–Sat 9–5.30, Sun 9–6.*

Villa Pallavicino Gardens
Lake Front, Stresa. Tel: 0323/32 407. *Open Mar–Oct, daily 9–6.*

Palazzo Borromeo and Gardens
Isola Bella (boat from Stresa). Tel: 0323/30 556. *Open Apr–Oct, daily 9–5.30.*

Palace and Botanical Garden
Isola Madre (boat from Stresa). *Open late-Mar–Oct, daily 9–noon, 1.30–5.30.*

3 Como
Educational Museum of Silk
Via Valleggio 3. Tel: 031/303 180. *Open Tue–Fri 9–noon, 3–6, Sat on request.*

Municipal Museum of Archaeology and History
Piazza Medaglie d'Orol.
Palazzo Grovio-Olginati, Tel: 031/271 343. *Open Tue–Sat 9.30–12.30, 2–5, Sun 10–1.*

Pinacoteca Civica
Via Diaz 84. Tel: 031/269 869. *Open Tue–Sat 9.30–12.30, 2–5, Sun 10–1.*

Temple of Alessandro Volta
Viale Marconi. Tel: 031/574 705. *Open Tue–Sun, summer 10–noon, 3– 6, winter 10–noon, 2–4.*

4 Lago di Como
Villa Carlotta
Via Regina 2, Tremezzo. Tel: 0344/41011 or 40405. *Open Mar and Oct, daily 9–11.30, 2–4.30; Apr–Sep, daily 9–6.*

Villa Monastero
Varenna. Tel: 0341/295 450. *Open: garden Apr–Oct daily 9–7; villa tour by reservation.*

5 Lecco
Villa Manzoni
Via Guanella. Tel: 0341/481 247. *Open Tue–Sun 9.30–2.*

6 Bellagio
Villa Serbelloni
Behind the Church of San Giacomo. Tel: 031/950 204. *Open (grounds only) Apr–Oct, Tue–Sun, guided walks 10.30 & 4.*

Villa Melzi d'Eril
On the Loppia road. Tel: 031/950 318 or 950 132. *Open Mar–Oct daily 9–6.30.*

Malpaga Castle
South of Bergamo. Tel: 035/840 003. *Open: guided tours Sun and hols 2.30–sunset or by appointment.*

7 Bergamo
Biblioteca Civica
Piazza Vecchia 15. Tel: 035/399 430 or 399 431. *Open Mon–Sat 8.30–6.30 (closes 12.30 Wed & Sat). Closed last week Aug.*

Museo Donizettiano
Via Arena 9. Tel: 035/399 269. *Open Apr–Sep Tue–Sun 10–1, 2.30–5; Oct–Mar Tue–Fri 10–1.*

Galleria dell'Accademia Carrara
Piazza dell'Accademia. Tel: 035/399 643. *Open all year Tue–Sun 10–1, 3–7.*

8 Lago di Garda
Vittoriale degli Italiani
Via Vittoriale 12, Gardone Riviera. Tel: 0365/20 130. *Open Apr–Sep 8.30–8; Oct–Mar daily 9–5.*

Rocca and Museo Civico
Piazza C Battisti 3, Riva del Garda. Tel: 0464/573 869. *Open Tue–Sun 10.30–6.30 (daily mid-Jun to mid-Sep).*

Castello Scaligero
Malcesine. Tel: 045/740 0873. Open Apr–Nov Tue–Sun 9–7.30.

Castello Scaligero
Sirmione. Tel: 030/916 468. *Open Mar–Oct Tue–Sun, 9–2.*

9 Mantova
Palazzo Ducale and Castel di San Giorgio
Piazza Sordello. Tel: 0376/352 100. *Open Tue–Sun 8.45–7.15; Carrera degli Sposi mid-Mar to mid-Jun by appointment.*

Casetta dei Nani
Open Mon 9–2, Tue–Sat 9–2, 2.30–6 or 7.

Palazzo del Té
Viale Te. Tel: 0376/323 266. *Open Mon 1–6, Tue–Sun 9–6.*

10 Cremona
Museo Stradivariano
Via Palestro 17. Tel: 0372/461 886. *Open Tue–Sat 8.30–5.45, Sun and holidays 9.15–12.15, 2.30–6.*

Town Hall Collection of Violins
Piazza del Comune 8. Tel: 0372/22 138. *Open Tue–Sat 8.30–6, Sun 9.15–12.15, 3–6.*

Museo Civico
Palazzo Affaitati, Via Ugolani Dati 4. Tel: 0372/407 770. *Open Tue–Sat 8.30–6, Sun and holidays 10–7.*

Torrazzo (bell tower)
Piazza del Commune 5. Tel: 0372/23 233. *Open Easter–Oct, Mon–Sat 10.30–noon, 3–6, Sun till 7; Nov–Easter, Sun 10.30–noon, 3–6.*

11 Pavia
Museo Civico
Castello Visconteo, Piazza

Castello. Tel: 0332/33 853 or 304 816. *Open Tue–Fri 9–1.30, Sat and Sun 10–7 (closes 1pm at weekends Dec–Feb, Jul–Aug).*

Certosa di Pavia
Viale del Monumento, 9km north of Pavia on Milano road. Tel: 0382/925 613. *Open Tue–Sat 9–11.30, 2.30–4.30, Sun and hols 9–11.30, 12.30–5 (to 5.30 Apr, 6pm May–Sep).*

For History Buffs

Museum of Geology and Paleontology
Via Ferrata. Tel 0382/505 895. *Open Mon–Thu 9–noon, 2–5.*

Special to...

Monte Baldo Cable Car
Malcesine to Monte Baldo. Tel: 045/740 0206. *Open daily 8–7, every 30 minutes.*

TOUR 3

i Galleria d'Accursio, Piazza Maggiore 6, Bologna. Tel: 051/246 541.

i Castello Estense Largo Castello, Ferrara. Tel: 0532/209 370.

i Piazzetta dei Mercanti, Piacenza. Tel: 0523/329 324.

i Via Melloni 1, Parma. Tel: 0521/218 889.

i Piazza Prampolini 5/C, Reggio nell'Emilia. Tel: 0522/451 152.

i Piazza Grande 17, Modena. Tel: 059/206 660.

1 Ferrara

Castello Estense
Via Ercole I d'Este 16. Tel: 0532/299 233. *Open Tue–Sun 9.30–5.30.*

Museo Archeologico
Palazzo di Ludovico il Moro, Via XX Settembre 122. Tel: 0532/66 299. *Open Tue–Sun 9–2.*

Palazzo Schifanoia
Via Scandiana 23. Tel: 0532/64 178. *Open Tue–Sun 9–6.*

2 Piacenza

Museo Civico
Palazzo Farnese, Piazza Citadella 29. Tel: 0532/328 270 or 326 981. *Open Tue–Sat 8.45–1 (also 3–6 Fri–Sat), Sun 3–6.*

Teatro Municipale
Via Chiapponi. *Call at Via Verdi 41 for admission.*

Galleria d'Arte Moderna Ricci Oddi
Via San Siro 13. Tel: 0523/320 742. *Open Tue–Sun 10–noon, 3–6*

3 Parma

Pinacoteca, Teatro Farnese and Museo Archeologico Nazionale
Piazzale della Pilotta 15. Tel: 0521/233 309 or 233 718 (museum). *Open Tue–Sun 8.30–7.30 (Pinacoteca and Teatro Tue–Sun 9–1.45.*

Casa Toscanini
Via R Tanzi. Tel: 0521/391 320. *Open Tue–Sat 10–1, 3–6, Sun 10–1.*

4 Reggio nell'Emilia

Museo Civico and Museo Numismatico
Via Spallanzani. Tel: 0522/456 477. *Open Tue–Sat 9–noon (also 3–7 on Sat); longer hours in summer.*

5 Modena

Museo Lapidario del Duomo
Via Lanfranco 6. Tel: 0592/16078. *Open Tue–Sun 9.30–12.30, 3.30–7*

Ghirlandina Tower
Duomo (key from Commune). Tel: 059/216 078. *Open summer, Sun and holidays 10–1, 3–7.*

Biblioteca Estense
Palazzo dei Musei, Largo di Porta Sant'Agostino 337. Tel: 059/439 5711. *Open Mon–Sat 9–1.*

Galleria Estense
Palazzo dei Musei, Largo di Porta Sant'Agostino 337. Tel: 059/439 5711. *Open Tue–Sun 8.30–7.*

Museo d'Arte Medievale e Moderne e Etnologia
Palazzo dei Musei, Largo Porta Sant'Agostino 337. Tel: 059/200 100. *Open Wed–Sat 9–noon, 3–6, Sun 10–1, 3–7.*

For History Buffs

Castello di Sanvitale
Fontanellato. Tel 0521/822 346. *Open 9.30–12.30, 3–6 (shorter hours in winter).*

Palazzo di Soragna
Soragna. *Open Tue–Sun 9.30–11, 3–6 (shorter hours in winter).*

TOUR 4

i Piazza Fellini 3, Rimini. Tel: 0541/56 902.

i Viale Roma 112, Cesenatico. Tel: 0547/673 287.

i Via Salara 8–12, Ravenna. Tel: 0544/35 404.

i Piazzetta Novanta Pacifici, Forli. Tel 0543/712 445.

1 Cesenatico

Museum of Antiquities
Via Armellini. Tel: 0547/79264 (library) *Closed for renovation until late 2005.*

Maritime Museum
Via Armellini Tel: 0547/79264 (library) *Closed for renovation until late 2005, but boats visible in the dock.*

2 Ravenna

Museo dell'Arcivescovado
Piazza Arcivescovado. Tel: 0544/215 201. *Open daily 9–7 (chapel closed for restoration).*

Museo Dante
Via Dante Alighieri 4. Tel: 0544/30252. *Open Tue–Sun 9–noon; also 3.30–6 in summer.*

Municipal Gallery
Via di Roma 13. Tel: 0544/482 356. *Open Tue–Fri 9–1, 3–6, Sat–Sun 10–6.*

Museo Nazionale
Via Flandrini. Tel: 0544/31241. *Open Tue–Sat 8.30–7.*

4 Faenza

Museo Internazionale Delle Ceramiche
Viale Baccarin 19. Tel: 0546/697 311. *Open summer, Tue–Sat 9–7, Sun 9.30–6; winter, Wed–Fri 9–1.30, Sat–Sun 9.30–5.30. Closed 1 May, 15 Aug.*

Palazzo Milzetti
Via C Tonducci 15. Tel: 0546/26493. *Open Mon–Sat 8.45–1.30 (also 2.15–4.30 Thu).*

5 Brisighella

Rocca and Museo del Lavoro Contadino
Tel: 0546/83129. *Open mid-Apr–mid-Oct, Tue–Sun 10–noon, 3.30–7; Oct–Apr, Sat 2.30–4.30, Sun 10–noon, 2.30–4.30.*

6 Forli

Museo Archeologico
Corso della Repubblica 72. Tel: 0543/12606. *Closed for restoration.*

TOUR 5

i Piazza Trento e Trieste 9, Feltre. Tel: 0439/2540.

i Piazzetta Monte di Pietà 8, Treviso. Tel: 0422/547 632.

i Castello 4421, Venezia. Tel: 041/529 8711.

1 Possagno

Canova's House and Art Gallery
Via Canova 85. *Open Tue–Sun 9–noon, 3–6.*

2 Feltre

Museo Civico
Palazzo Villabruna, Via L Luzzo 43. Tel: 0439/885 241 or 885 242. *Open Tue–Sun 10.30–12.30, 4–7 (from 9.30 Sat & Sun).*

Museo Rizzarda
Via del Paradiso 8. Tel: 0439/234 142. *Open summer Tue–Fri 10.30–12.30, 3–8, Sat–Sun 9.30–12.30, 3–8*

3 Conegliano

Cima da Conegliano's Birthplace
Via Cima 24. Tel: 0438/411 026. *Call for opening hours.*

Sala dei Battuti
Open Sat 10–noon, Sun 3–6 and certain other times.

Castle, Museum and Art Gallery
Tel: 0438/22 871. *Open Tue–Sun 10–12.30, 3.30–7 (to 6 in winter). Closed Nov.*

4 Treviso
Diocesan Museum of Religious Art
Vicolo Duomo 1. Tel 0422/ 416 707. *Open Mon–Thu 9–noon, Sat 9–noon, 3–6.*

Museo Civico
Borgo Cavour 24. Tel: 0422/591 337. *Temporarily closed – call for information.*

5 Venezia
Galleria della Basilica di San Marco
Piazza San Marco. Tel 041/ 522 5205. *Open daily 9.30–4.30.*

Palazzo Ducale
Piazzetta San Marco. Tel: 041/271 5911. *Open daily 9–7 (5 in winter).*

Chiesa di San Giorgio Maggiore
Isola di San Georgio Maggiore. Tel: 041/522 7827. *Open Mon–Sun 9.30–1, 2.30–6.30 (lunch closure varies Sun & hols)*

Ca' d'Oro
Cannaregio. Tel: 041/523 8790. *Open daily 9–1.*

Galleria dell' Accademia
Campo della Carita. *Open Mon 8.15–2, Wed–Sun 8.15–7.15.*

Collezione Peggy Guggenheim
Palazzo Vernier dei Leoni. Tel: 041/240 5411. *Open Wed–Mon 10–6.*

6 Murano
Museo Vetrario
Palazzo Giustinian, Fondamenta Giustinian 8 and Fondamenta Man n. Tel: 041/739 586. *Open Thu–Tue 10–4.*

7 Burano
Museo dei Merletti
Piazza Galuppi. Tel: 041/730 034. *Open Apr–Oct Wed–Mon 10–5.*

San Francesco del Deserto
By boat from Burano (20 min). *Open 9–11, 3–5.*

8 Torcello
Museo dell'Estuario
Piazza del Consiglio. Tel: 041/730 761. *Open Tue–Sun 10–12.30, 2–4.*

9 Castelfranco Veneto
Casa del Giorgione
Piazzetta S Liberale. Tel: 0423/725 022. *Open Tue–Sun 9.30–1, 2.30–7.*

For History Buffs
Villa Barbaro
Via Cornuda 7, Maser. Tel: 0423/923 004. *Open Mar–Sep, Tue, Sat, Sun 3–6; Oct–Feb 2.30–5.*

Special to...
La Fenice
Isola del Tronchetto. Tel: 041/520 4010. *Open Mon–Fri 8.30–1.30 or for performances.*

TOUR 6

[i] Via degli Alpini 9, Verona. Tel: 045/806 8680.

[i] Piazza Matteotti 12, Vicenza. Tel: 0444/320 854.

[i] Riviera dei Mugnai 8, Padova. Tel: 049/876 7911.

1 Montecchio Maggiore
G Zannato Museum
Piazza G Marconi 15. Tel: 0444/698 874. *Open Mon–Fri 9–12.30, 2.30–7, Sat–Sun 9–noon.*

2 Vicenza
Museo Civico Pinacoteca Palazzo Chiericati
Piazza Matteotti 39. Tel: 0444/325 071 or 321 348. *Open Tue–Sun 9–5 (till 6pm Jul–Aug).*

Teatro Olimpico
Piazza Matteotti. Tel: 0444/ 222 800. *Open Tue–Sun 9–5 (to 7pm Jul–Aug)*

Villa Valmarana ai Nani
Via dei Nani 2–8. Tel: 0444/543 868. *Open Mar–Nov Tue–Sun afternoons (times depend on season).*

La Rotonda
Via della Rotonda 2. Tel: 0444/321 793. *Open mid-Mar–Oct, house Wed 10–noon, 3–6 (times may vary); grounds Tue–Thu.*

3 Marostica
Castello Inferiore and Museum of the Chess Game Costumes
Piazza del Castello 1. Tel: 0424/72 127 *Open: castle daily 9.30–noon, 3–6; museum on request.*

4 Padova
Palazzo del Bo' and Anatomical Theatre
Via 8 Febbraio. Tel: 049/827 3044. *Guided tours: Mon, Wed, Fri 3.15, 4.15, 5.15; Tue, Thu, Sat 9.15, 10.15, 11.15 (less often in winter).*

Cappella degli Scrovegni
Tel: 049/201 0020. *Open daily 9–7 by appointment.*

5 Arqua Petrarca
Francesco Petrarca's House and Tomb
Via Valleselle 6. Tel: 0429/ 718 294. *Open Feb–Sep Tue–Sun 9–noon, 3–6.30 (reduced hours in winter).*

6 Monselice
Ca'Marcello
Open Tue, Fri and Sat, guided tours at 9, 10, 11, 3, 4; also 3.30 and 5 on the3rd Sun of month.

Villa Duodo Gardens
Open daily, dawn–dusk.

7 Este
Museo Nazionale Atestino
Palazzo Mocenigo, via G Negri. Tel: 0429/2085. *Open daily 9–7.*

Recommended Trip
Villa Barbarigo
Valsanzibio. Tel: 0444/913 0042. *Open Mar–Nov 9–noon, 2–sunset.*

TOUR 7

[i] Largo Nuvolini 1, San Remo. Tel: 0181/59059.

[i] Via Boselli, Taggia.

5 Triora
Museo Etnografico e della Stregameroa
Corso Italia 1. Tel: 0184/ 94 477. *Open daily 2.30–6, also Sat–Sun 10–noon (longer hours in summer).*

TOUR 8

[i] Via Roma 11, Genova. Tel: 010/576 791.

[i] Via XX Settembre 33, Camogli. Tel: 0185/771 066.

[i] Via Roma 35, Portofino. Tel: 0185/269 024.

[i] Via A Diaz 9, Rapallo. Tel: 0185/230 346.

1 Camogli
Museo Archeologico and Biblioteca Civica
Via Gio Bono Ferrari 41. Tel: 0185/729 048. *Open Mon–Fri 8.45–11.45, 3–5.45, Sat 8.45–11.45.*

Museo Marinaro
Via Gio Bono Ferrari 41. Tel: 0185/729 049. *Open Wed–Mon 9–noon.*

Acquario
Castello della Dragonara, Piazza Colombo. Tel: 0185/ 773 375. *Open Tue–Sun 10–noon, 3–7 (shorter hours in winter) .*

2 Portofino
Castello di San Georgio
The Harbour. Tel: 0185/26 907. *Open Tue–Sun 10–5 (till 6pm in summer). Closed Jan.*

3 Rapallo
Museo del Merlotto
Villa Tiguillio, Parco Casale, Viale G Maggio. Tel: 0185/ 63 305. *Open Tue, Wed, Fri and Sat 3–6, Thu 10–11.30.*

Montallegro Cable Car
Tel: 0185/239 000. *Open daily 7.30–6 (5.30 in winter).*

6 Portovenere
Ruined Fortress
Above the village. *Open Sat–Sun 10–1, 2–5 (possibly also during week).*

For History Buffs
Abbey of San Fruttuoso
San Fruttuoso di Camogli, near Portofino (accessible only by boat or by 2-hours walk). Tel: 0185/772 703. *Open Jun–Sep, daily 10–6; Mar–May & Oct, Tue–Sun 10–4; Dec–Feb weekends and holidays only. Closed Nov.*

TOUR 9

[i] Piazza del Duomo, Pisa. Tel: 050/560 464.

[i] Piazza Mazzini, Viareggio. Tel: 0584/962 233.

[i] Piazzale Verdi, Lucca. Tel: 0583/583 150.

[i] Piazza Duomo 4, Pistoia. Tel: 0573/21 622.

[i] Piazza Duomo 1, San Gimignano. Tel: 0577/940 008.

[i] Piazza dei Priori 20, Volterra. Tel: 0588/87 257 or 87 580.

2 Lucca

Museo Nazionale
Palazzo Mansi, Via Galli Tassi 43. Tel: 0583/55 570. *Open Tue–Sat 9–7, Sun and public holidays 9–2.*

Museum of the 1943–1945 Liberation
Palazzo Guinigi, Via Sant'Andrea 43. *Open Wed and Sat 4–6 or on request.*

Museo della Cattedrale
Piazza del Duomo. Tel: 0583/490 530. *Open Apr–Oct, Tue–Sun 10–6; Nov–Mar, Tue–Sun 10–3, public holidays 10–6.*

3 Pistoia

Museo San Zeno
Piazza Duomo. Tel: 0573/369 272. *Open Tue, Thu and Fri 10–1, 3–5 on request for guided tours only.*

Palazzo del Comune
Piazza del Duomo. Tel: 0572/371 296. *Open Tue–Sun 10–6, hols 9.30–12.30.*

4 Prato

Castello dell'Imperatore
Piazza Santa Maria delle Carceri. *Open Apr–Oct Wed–Mon 9–1, 4–7.*

Municipal Museum and Art Gallery
Palazzo Pretorio, Piazza del Comune 2. Tel: 0574/616 385. *Closed for restoration.*

Museo dell Opera del Duomo
Piazza del Duomo 49. Tel: 0574/29 339. *Open 9.30–12.30, 3–6.30, Closed Tue and Sun mornings.*

Museo Pittura Murale
Chiesa di San Domenico, Piazza San Domenico 8. Tel: 0574/29 339. *Open 10–1, 3.30–7, Sun 10–1. Closed Tue.*

5 Poggio a Caiano

Villa and Gardens
Piazza Medici 14. Tel: 055/877 012. *Open 9–3.30 or 4.30 (later in summer).*

6 Artimino

Villa Medicea La Ferdinando
Via Papa Giovanni XXII 5. Tel: 055/871 8124 (museum). *Open – villa Tue mornings by appointment; museum 9–12.30, Sun 9–noon; by appointment Wed and Nov–Jan.*

7 Empoli

Museo Collegiata
Piazzetta della Propositura 3. Tel: 0571/76 284. *Open Tue–Sun 9–noon, 4–7.*

Ferruccio Busoni House
Piazza della Vittoria 16. Tel: 0571/711 122. *Open Mon–Fri 10–1, 3–6.*

8 Certaldo

Palazzo Pretorio
Piazza del Vicariato 4. Tel: 0571/661 219. *Open summer, daily 10–7; winter, Tue–Sun 10.30–4.30.*

Casa del Boccaccio
Via G Boccaccio. Tel: 0571/664 208. *Open Apr–Sep 10–7; Oct–Mar 10.30–4.30. Closed Tue.*

9 San Gimignano

Collegiata museums
Piazza Pecori 1. *Open Mar–Oct Mon–Fri 9.30–7.30, Sat 9.30–5, Sun 1–5; Nov–Jan Mon–Sat 9.30–5, Sun 1–5 (may close for lunch). Jan, Feb open for Mass only.*

Museo Civico and Pinacoteca
Palazzo del Popolo, Piazza del Duomo. Tel: 0577/940 340. *Open Mar–Oct daily 9.30–7; Nov–Feb 10–5.30.*

10 Volterra

Museo Etrusco Guarnacci
Via Don Minzoni 15. Tel: 0588/86 347 *Open Apr–Oct, daily 9–1, 3–6.30; Nov–Mar, daily 9–2.*

Pinacoteca Comunale and Museo Civico
Palazzo Minucci-Solaini, Via dei Sarti 1. Tel: 0588/87 580. *Open summer, daily 9–7; winter, daily 9–2.*

Special to...

Leaning Tower of Pisa
Piazza del Duomo. Tel: 0505/60 547. *Open summer, daily 8–7.20; winter, 9–5. Reservations required.*

For History Buffs

Puccini's House
Via di Poggio 9, Corte di San Lorenzo. Tel: 0583/341 445. *Open Mar–Apr Tue–Sun 10.30–12.30, 3.30–5.30; May–Oct 10.30–12.30, 3–6, Dec–Feb 10.30–12.30, 2.30–5.30.*

Castle and Leonardo da Vinci Museum
Castello dei Conti Guidi, Via della Torre 2, Vinci. Tel: 0571/56 055. *Open daily 9.30–6.*

TOUR 10

[i] Via Manzoni 16, Firenze. Tel: 055/23 320.

[i] Via Campana 18, Colle di Val d'Elsa. Tel: 0577/920 015 (summer only).

[i] Piazza del Campo 56, Siena. Tel: 0577/280 551.

[i] Costa del Municipio 8, off Piazza del Popolo, Montalcino. Tel: 0575/849 331.

[i] Via Nazionale 42, Cortona. Tel: 0575/630 352.

[i] Piazza della Repubblica 116, Arezzo. Tel: 0575/20 839.

[i] Piazza Amerighi, Poppi.

1 Colle di Val d'Elsa

Municipal and Religious Art Museum
Palazzo dei Priori, Via del Castello 32. Tel: 0577/923 888. *Open Easter–Oct Wed–Fri 11–12.30, 4.30–7.30; Nov–Easter Sat–Sun 10.30–12.30, 3.30–6.30.*

R Bianchi-Bandinelli Museum of Archaeology
Palazzo Pretoria, Piazza Duomo 42. Tel: 0577/922 954. *Open Wed–Fri 11–12.30, 4.30–7.30.*

2 Siena

Palazzo Pubblico
Piazza del Campo 1. Tel: 0557/292 263. *Open daily, summer 10–7, winter 10–5.30*

Museo dell'Opera Metropolitana
Piazza del Duomo 8. Tel: 0577/283 048. *Open mid-Mar–Oct, daily 9–7.30; Nov–mid Mar 9–1.30.*

Pinacoteca Nazionale
Palazzo Buonsignori e Brigidi, Via San Pietro 29. Tel: 0577/286 143 or 281 161. *Open Tue–Sat 9.30–4, Sun 9.30–1.*

Casa di Santa Caterina
Via Camporegio, Siena. Tel: 0577/44 177. *Open daily.*

Abbey of Monte Oliveo Maggiore
Monte Olivio Maggiore (about 27km/17 miles south of Siena on the SS2). Tel: 0577/70 716. *Open daily 9.15–noon, 3.15–5 (6 in summer).*

3 Montalcino

Rocca
Entrance through Enoteca (Wine Shop), Piazzale della Fortezza, Montalcino. Tel: 0577/849 211. *Open summer, daily 9–1, 2.30–8; winter, Tue–Sun 9–1, 2–6.*

Museo Civico and Museo Diocesano
Ricasoli 31. Tel: 0577/846 014. *Open Tue–Sun 10–3 (later in summer).*

Palazzo Piccolomini Museum
Piazza Pio II 2. Tel: 0578/48 503. *Open 10–12.30, 3–6 (later Jul–Sep).*

[i] Tourist Information Office
12 Number on tour

4 Monte San Savino
Municipal Museum
Cassero, Piazza Gamurrini. Tel: 0575/843 098 (tourist office). *Open Sat and Sun 10–noon, 3–7 or by request*

5 Cortona
Museo Diocesano
Chiesa del Gesù, Piazza del Duomo 1. Tel: 0575/62 830. *Open Tue–Sun 9–1, 3.30–7 (closes 5 Oct–Mar).*

Museo dell'Accademia Etrusca
Palazzo Casali, Piazza Signorelli 19. Tel: 0575/630 415. *Open Apr–Oct, Tue–Sun 10–7; Nov–Mar, 9–5.*

6 Arezzo
Casa del Vasari
Via XX Settembre 55. Tel: 0575/409 040. *Open 9–7, Sun 9–1 (ring for admission).*

Museo Statale d'Arte Medioevale e Moderna
Via San Lorentino 8. Tel: 0575/409 050. *Open Tue–Sun 8.30–7.30.*

Museo Archeologico
Via Margaritone 10. Tel: 0575/20 882. *Open Mon–Sat (but closed 1st and 3rd Mon of month) 9–2, Sun 9–1.30.*

8 Caprese Michelangelo
Michelangelo's Birthplace
Via Capoluogo 1. Tel: 0575/793 776. *Open Jun–Sep 9.30–6.30 (to 7.30 Aug); Apr–May & Oct 10.30–5.30; Nov–Mar 11–5.*

9 Poppi
Abbey of Camaldoli
Camaldoli (8km north). Tel: 0575/556 012. *Open daily 8.30–12.30, 2.30–6.30.*

10 Pratovecchio
Museum of Archaeology and Weapons
Castello di Romena. Tel: 0575/582 520 or 335/122 0930. *Phone for times.*

TOUR 11

[i] Piazza IV Novembre 3, Perugia. Tel: 075/572 3327.

[i] Piazza Oderisi 6, Gubbio. Tel: 075/922 0693.

[i] Piazza del Comune 27, Assisi. Tel: 075/812 534.

[i] Piazza della Libertà 7, Spoleto. Tel: 0743/49890.

[i] Piazza Umberto 1, Todi. Tel: 075/894 3395.

[i] Piazza del Duomo 24, Orvieto. Tel: 0763/341 911.

1 Gubbio
Museum and Art Gallery
Palazzo dei Consoli, Piazza della Signoria. Tel: 075/927 4298. *Open daily 10–1, 3–6 (10–1, 2–5 in winter). Closed 13–15 May.*

Palazzo Ducale
Via Federico Da Montefeltro. Tel: 075/927 5872. *Open Thu–Tue 8.30–7.30.*

2 Assisi
Basilica di San Francesco
Piazza San Francesco. Tel: 075/813 337. *Parts closed for restoration – phone for information.*

Chapter House Museum
Chiesa di San Rufino, Piazza San Rufino. Tel: 075/812 712. *Open daily 10–1, 3–6 (5.30 in winter).*

Pinacoteca Civica
Piazza del Comune. Tel: 075/812 033. *Open daily 10–1, 2–6 (5 in winter).*

Rocca Maggiore
Via della Rocca. Tel: 075/815 292. *Open daily 10–dusk.*

3 Spello
Villa Fidelia/Straka-Coppa Collection
Via Flaminia 72. Tel: 0742/301 866. *Open Apr–Jun & Sep Thu–Sun 10–1, 3.30–6; Jul–Aug 10.30–1, 4–7; Oct–Mar weekends only.*

4 Trevi
Pinacoteca Comunale
Largo Don Bosco, ex-Convento di San Francisco. Tel: 0742/3321. *Open Apr, May and Sep, Tue–Sun 10.30–1, 2.30–6; Jun and Jul, Tue–Sun 10.30–1, 3.30–7; Aug, Tue–Sun 10.30–1, 3–7.30; Oct–Mar, Fri–Sun 10.30–1, 2.30–5.*

Trevi Flash Art Museum
Palazzo Lucarini, Via Lucarini 1. Tel: 0742/381 978. *Open Tue–Sun 3–7.*

5 Montefalco
Museo Civico di San Francesco
Via Ringhiera Umbra 5. Tel: 0742/379 598. *Open Mar–May and Sep–Oct, daily 10.30–1, 2–6; Aug, 10.30–1, 3–7.30; Nov–Feb, Tue–Sun 10.30–1, 2.30–5.*

6 Spoleto
Rocca
Piazza Campello, Spoleto. Tel: 0743/43707. *Openmid-Jun to mid Sep daily 10–8; Apr–mid Jun and mid-Sep–Oct Mon–Fri 10–1, 3–7, Sat–Sun 10–7; Nov–Mar Mon–Fri 2.30–5 (also mornings from mid Mar), Sat–Sun 10–5*

Museo Archeologico and Teatro Romano
Via S Agata. Tel: 0743/223 277. *Open daily 8.30–7.30.*

7 Narni
Art Gallery
Palazzo Vescovile, Piazza Cavour. Tel: 0744/747 258. *Open Tue–Thu 11–1, 3–7, Fri–Sun 10–1, 2.30–7.*

9 Orvieto
Museo dell'Opera del Duomo
Palazzo Soliano, Piazza del Duomo. Tel: 0763/342 477. *May be closed for restoration.*

For History Buffs
Museum of Archaeology
Piazza del Duomo. Tel: 0763/341 511. *Open Apr–Sep Mon–Sat 9–6; Oct–Mar Tue–Sat 10–5.*

Pozzo di San Patrizio
Viale Sangallo. Tel: 0763/343 768. *Open Apr–Sep, daily 10–6.45; Oct–Mar, daily 10–5.45.*

TOUR 12

[i] Via Thaon de Revel 4, Ancona. Tel: 071/358 991.

[i] Via G Solari 3, Loreto. Tel: 071/970 276.

[i] Via Garibaldi 87, Macerata. Tel: 0733/231 547.

[i] Piazza del Popolo 5, Fermo. Tel: 0734/228 738.

[i] Piazza Arringo 7, Ascoli Piceno. Tel: 0736/298 204.

[i] Via Luigi Ferri 17, Cingoli. Tel: 0733/602 444.

3 Loreto
Santa Casa and Santuario della Santa Casa
Piazza della Madonna. Tel: 071/970 104. *Open Apr–Oct, Tue–Sun 9–1, 4–7; Nov–Mar 10–1, 3–6.*

4 Macerata
Museum and Art Gallery
Piazza Vittorio Veneto. Tel: 0733/256 361. *Open Tue–Sat 9–1, 4–7.30, Sun 9–1.*

5 Fermo
Municipal Gallery
Palazzo dei Priori, Piazza del Pópolo 1. Tel: 0734/217 140. *Open 10–1, 3.30–7.30; winter 9.30–1, 3.30–7.*

Teatro dell'Aquila Museum
Viale G Mazzini 4. Tel: 0734/284 349. *Phone for opening hours.*

6 Ascoli Piceno
Art Gallery
Palazzo Arringo, Piazza dell'Arringo. Tel: 0736/298 213 or 298 282. *Open summer Mon–Fri 9–1, 3–7.30, , Sat 9–1, Sun 4–8; winter Mon–Fri 9–1, Sat–Sun 9–12.30.*

7 Tolentino
Museums, Basilica di San Nicola da Tolentino
Tel: 0733/969 996. *Open daily 9.30–noon, 4–7.*

International Museum of Caricatures
Palazzo Sangallo, Piazza della Libertà. Tel: 0733/969 797. *Open Tue–Sun 10–1, 3–6 (7 in summer).*

8 Camerino
Museo Diocesano
Piazza Cavour 12. Tel: 0737/630 400. *May be closed for refurbishment.*

Soriano, to the east of Bagnaia, is dominated by Castello Orsini

Pinacoteca e Museo Civico
Piazza dei Constanti. Tel: 0737/402 309. *Open Apr–Sep, Tue–Sun 10–1, 4–7; Oct–Mar, Tue–Sun 10–1, 3–6.*

University Botanic Garden
Viale Oberdan 2 e Via Venezian. Tel: 0737/403 084. *Open Mon–Fri 9–1, 3–5.*

9 San Severino Marche

Municipal Gallery of Modern Art
Palazzo Comunale, Piazza del Popolo 45. Tel: 0733/ 6411 (town hall) or 638 414. *Open on request.*

Tacchi Venturi Municipal Gallery
Palazzo Manuzzini, via Salimbeni 39. Tel: 0733/638 095. *Open Jul–Sep, Tue–Sun 9–1, 4.30–6.30; Oct–Jun, Tue–Sat and alternate Sun 9–1.*

TOUR 13

[i] Via Puccinotti 35, Urbino. Tel: 0722/2613.

[i] Via Mazzolari 4, Pesaro. Tel: 0721/30 258.

[i] Via C Battisti 10, Fano. Tel: 0721/803 534.

[i] Piazza Manin II, Fabriano. Tel: 0732/625 067.

1 San Leo

Renaissance Fortress
Via Battaglione Cacciatori. Tel: 0541/916 231. *Open daily 9–7.*

Museum of Sacred Art
Palazzo Mediceo, Piazza Dante 14. Tel: 0541/916 306. *Open daily 9–7.*

3 Pesaro

Casa Rossini
Via Rossini 34. Tel: 0721/ 387 357. *Open Jul–Aug Tue–Sun 9.30–12.30, 5–8, (to 11pm Tue, Thu); Sep–Jun Tue–Wed 9.30–12.30, Thu–Sun 9.30–12.30, 4–7*

Tempietta
Piazza Olivieri 5. Tel: 0721/ 30 053. *Open Jul–Aug, Mon–Sat 10–noon, 5–7; Sep–Jun on request.*

Museo Archeologico Oliveriano
Via Mazza 97. Tel: 0721/33 344. *Open Mon–Sat mornings on request, also 4–7 Jul–Aug.*

Museo Civico, Museo delle Ceriche and Pinacoteca
Piazza Toschi-Mosca 29. Tel 0721/387 541. *Open Tue–Wed 9.30–12.30, Thu–Sun 9.30–12.30, 4–7 (longer hours some days in summer).*

4 Fano

Museo Civico and Pinacoteca
Palazzo Malatestiano, Piazza XX Settembre 4. Tel: 0721/887 523. *Open Tue–Sat 8.30–12.30 (also 3–6 Wed & Fri).*

6 Jesi

Museo Civico
Palazzo della Signoria, Piazza Colocci. Tel: 0731/ 538 341. *May be closed for restoration.*

Pinacoteca Civica
Palazzo Pianetti, Via XV Settembre. Tel: 073/538 342. *Open Tue–Sat 10–1, 4–7, Sun 10–1, 5–8 (10–8 mid-Jun to mid-Sep).*

7 Fabriano

Paper and Watermark Museum
Convent of San Domenico. Tel: 0732/709 297. *Open Tue–Sat 10–6, Sun and hols 10–noon, 2–5 (also Tue–Sat 9–11pm Jul–Aug).*

Grand Museum
Loggiato San Francesco 1. Tel: 0732/5726. *Open Sun 5–7.30pm, or by request.*

9 Urbania

Palazzo Ducale
Corso Vittorio Emanuele 23. Tel: 0722/313 151. *Open Tue–Sun 10–noon, 3–6.*

10 Fossombrone

Municipal Museum and Gallery
Palazzo Ducale Corte Alta, Via del Verziere. Tel: 0721/ 714 645. *Open Jul–early Nov Tue–Sun 10.30–12.30, 4–8 (closes 7 Sep–early Nov); Nov–May Sat 3.30–6.30, Sun 10–noon, 3.30–6.30.*

Cesarini Picture Gallery
Via Pergamino 23. Tel: 0721/714 650. *Open Jun–mid-Sep, Sat 3–6, Sun 10.30–12.30, 3–6.*

[i] Tourist Information Office
12 Number on tour

TOUR 14

[i] Via N Fabrizi 171, Pescara. Tel: 085/429 00212.

[i] Via del Castello 10, Teramo. Tel: 0861/244 222.

[i] Via B Spaventa 29, Chieti. Tel: 0871/63 640.

2 Teramo
Museo Archeologico
Villa Delfico 30. Tel: 0861/ 247 772 or 247 120 *Open daily 9–1, 3–7 (10–noon, 5–10 Jul–Aug).*

Picture Gallery
Viale Bovio 4. Tel: 0861/247 772. *Open daily, summer 10–noon, 5–10; winter 9–1, 3–7.*

3 Atri
Chapter House Museum
Cattedrale Santa Maria Assunta, Via Roma. Tel: 085/879 8140. *Open Jun–Sep, daily 10–noon, 4–8; Oct–May, Thu–Tue 10–noon, 3–5.*

4 Penne
Municipal and Diocesan Museum
Palazzo Vescovile, Piazza Duomo. Tel: 085/821 1727. *Open Tue–Sun 10–1, 4–7 (10–1, 3–6 in winter).*

5 Loreto Aprutino
Galleria Acerbo delle Antiche Ceramiche Abruzzesi
Palazzo Acerbo, Via del Baio. Tel: 085/829 0484. *Phone for opening hours.*

6 Ortona
M Cascella Gallery
Palazzo Farnese, Passeggiata Orientale. Tel: 085/906 6202. *Open Wed–Sat 10.30–12.30, 5.30–7.30 (6–11pm Jul–Aug).*

8 Vasto
Museo Civico
Palazza D'Avalos, Piazza Lucio Valerio Pudente. Tel: 0873/367 773. *Open summer Tue–Sun 10.30–12.30, 5–midnight; winter Wed–Sun 9.30–12.30, 4.30–7.30.*

9 Chieti
Museo Nazionale Archeologico
Villa Comunale. Tel: 0871/ 331 668. *Open daily 9–7.*

Museo d'Arte Constantino Barbella
Palazzo Martinetti Bianchi, Via Cesare de Lollis 10. Tel: 0871/330 873. *Open Tue–Thu 9–1, 4–7, Fri–Sat 9–1, Sun 9–noon.*

For Children
The Ceramics Museum
Castelli. Tel: 0861/979 398. *May be closed for refurbishment.*

Back to Nature
N De Leone Natural History Museum
Contrada Collalto 1, Penne. Tel: 0858/215 003. *Open daily 8.30–12.30, 2.30–6.30.*

For History Buffs
Cathedral Museum
Piazza Santa Maria Maggiore, Guardiagrele. Tel: 0871/82 117. *Open Aug, daily 10–noon, 4.30–7.30; other months on request.*

TOUR 15

[i] Via XX Settembre 10, L'Aquila. Tel: 0862/22 306.

[i] Via Piave 2, Pescasseroli. Tel: 0863/910 461.

[i] Vico delle Carceri 4, Pescocostanzo. Tel: 0864/691 440.

[i] Corso Ovidio 208, Sulmona. Tel: 0864/53 276.

3 Pescasseroli
Natural History Museum
Viale Cabinovia. Tel: 0863/91 998 (museum) or 910 405 (study centre). *Open daily 10–1, 3–7.*

5 Sulmona
Museo Civico
Palazzo Santa Maria dell'Annunziata, Corso Ovidio. Tel: 0864/210 216. *Open Tue–Fri 9–1, 3.30–7, Sat–Sun 10–1, 4–7.*

'In Situ' Museum
Palazzo Santa Maria dell'Annunziata, Corso Ovidio. Tel: 0864/210 216 (Museo Civico). *Open Tue–Sat 10–12.30, Sun 10–1.*

Museum of the Sugared-Almond Confectionery Art and Technology
Via Stazione Introdacqua 55. Tel: 0864/210 047 (factory). *Open Mon–Sat 9–12.30, 3.30–6.30.*

7 Celano
Marsica National Museum
Castello Piccolomini, Largo Cavalieri di Vittorio Veneto. Tel: 0863/792 922. *Open mid-Mar–mid-Sep, Mon–Fri 9–2, Sat and Sun 9–7; mid-Sep–mid-Mar, Mon–Sat 9–2, Sun 9–1.*

For History Buffs
De Nino Municipal Museum of Aufidena
Largo della Chiesa, Alfedena (due to relocate – telephone for information). Tel: 0865/87 114 (town hall). *Open summer, daily 10–1, 4–7; winter, 10–11, Wed 4–5.*

TOUR 16

[i] Via Parigi 11, Roma. Tel: 06/488 991.

[i] Largo Garibaldi, Tivoli. Tel: 0774/334 522.

[i] Piazza Traniello 19, Gaeta. Tel: 0771/462 767.

[i] Piazza Libertà 5, Castel Gandolfo. Tel: 06/932 4081.

[i] Piazza G Marconi 1, Frascati. Tel: 06/942 0331.

1 Tivoli
Villa Adriana
Via di Villa Adriana. Tel: 0774/382 733. *Open daily 9–one hour before sunset.*
Villa d'Este
Piazza Trento. Tel: 0774/312 070. *Open May–Sep, Tue–Sun 9–6.30; Oct–Mar, Tue–Sun 8.30–one hour before sunset.*

Villa Gregoriana
Largo S Angelo. Tel: 0774/ 311 249. *May be closed for restoration.*

3 Subiaco
Monastery of Santa Scolastica
3km east of Subiaco. Tel: 0774/85 525. *May be closed for restoration.*

4 Gaeta
Museum of Palazzo De Vio
Piazza Cardinale de Vio 9. Tel: 0771/464 293. *Open Mon–Sat 4.30–7.30 (mornings on request), Sun 10–12.30.*

5 Sperlonga
Zona Archeologica, including Grotta di Tiberio, Roman Villa and Museo Archeologico Nazionale di Sperlonga
Via Flacca. Tel: 0771/54 028. *Open daily from 9am. Closes between 5 and 8pm, depending on season.*

7 Frascati
Villa Aldobrandini
Tel: 06/942 0331. *Open Mon–Fri 9–1 by appointment only.*

Museum of Tuscolo
Ex-Scuderie Aldobrandini, Piazza Marconi 6. Tel: 06/941 7195/6. *Open Mon, Wed & Fri 10–1.*

8 Ostia
Ostia Antica and Museo Ostiense
Via Ostrense. Tel: 06/5635 8099. *Open daily 8.30–4 (closes at 5 or 6pm Mar–Oct). Museum has similar hours but may close for lunch.*

For History Buffs
National Museum of Archaeology
Piazza della Vittoria 1, Formia. Tel: 0771/770 382. *Open daily 9–7 (till 8pm in summer)*

Cicero's Tomb
Via Appia. Tel: 0771/177 0382. *Open Sat and Sun in summer, but by appointment only.*

TOUR 17

[i] Via Parigi 11, Roma. Tel: 06/488 991.

[i] Piazza Cavour 1, Tarquinia. Tel: 0766/849 282.

[i] Piazza San Carluccio 5, Viterbo. Tel: 0761/304 795.

1 Cerveteri
Etruscan Remains: Banditaccia Necropolis
Via delle Necropoli, 3km west of town centre. Tel: 06/994 0001. *Open Tue–Sat 9–one hour before sunset (museum 9–7, Sun 9–1)*

Museo Nazionale di Cerveteri
Piazza Santa Maria. Tel: 06/994 1354. *Open Tue–Sun 9–7.*

3 Tarquinia
Museo Nazionale Tarquiniese
Palazzo Vitelleschi, Piazza Cavour. Tel: 0766/856 036. *Open Tue–Sun 9–7.*

Necropolis
2km (1.2 miles) southeast of Tarquinia. *Open Tue–Sun 9–one hour before sunset (closes 7pm in summer).*

4 Tuscania
National Museum of Etruscan Archaeology
Via Madonna del Riposo. Tel: 0761/436 209. *Open Tue–Sun 9–7 (closes 5pm Oct–Apr).*

5 Caprarola
Villa Farnese
Piazza Farnese. Tel: 0761/646 157. *Open Tue–Sun from 9am. Closes between 3.30 and 7.30pm, depending on season.*

6 Viterbo
Palazzo dei Papi
Piazza San Lorenzo. Tel: 0761/341 124 (curia). *If not open, make enquiries at the curia.*

7 Bagnaia
Villa Lante
Tel: 0761/288 008. *Open (parkland only) 9am–one hour before sunset.*

9 Bomarzo
Parco dei Mostri
Tel: 0761/924 029. *Open daily dawn to dusk.*

TOUR 18

[i] Piazza del Gesù Nuovo, Napoli. Tel: 081/551 2701 or 552/3328.

[i] Piazza Matteotti, Pozzuoli. Tel: 081/526 5068.

[i] Via Sacra 1, Pompeii. Tel: 081/850 7255.

[i] Piazza Umberto 1, Capri. Tel: 081/837 0686.

[i] Via del Saracino 4, Positano. Tel: 089/875 067.

[i] Corso delle Repubbliche Marinare 19–21, Amalfi. Tel: 089/871 107.

[i] Piazza Duomo 10, Ravello. Tel: 089/857 096.

[i] Piazza Ferrovia, Salerno. Tel: 089/231 432.

[i] Via Magna Grecia 887, Paestum. Tel: 0828/811 016.

1 Pozzuoli
Archaeological Park, including Anfiteatro Flavio
Via Rossini. *Open daily 9–one hour before sunset.*

2 Ercolano
Herculaneum Roman Site
Corso Ercolano. Tel: 081/739 0963. *Open daily 9–one hour before sunset (from 8.30am in winter).*

3 Pompeii
Ruins
Piazza Esedra 5. Tel: 081/861 1774. *Open daily 9–one hour before sunset; last admission one hour before closing.*

Napoli Museum (for finds from Pompeii)
Piazza Museo Nazionale 19, Napoli. Tel: 081/440 166. *Open Mon and Wed–Sun 9–8.*

Vesuvian Museum
Via Colle S Bartolomeo 10. Tel: 081/850 7255. *Open Mon–Sat 9–2.*

4 Capri
Villa Jovis
Viale Amelio Maiuri. Tel: 081/837 0381. *Open daily 9–one hour before sunset.*

Villa San Michele
Anacapri. Tel: 081/837 1401. *Open May–Sep, daily 9–6; Mar, Apr and Oct 9.30–4.30 or 5; Nov–Feb 10.30–3.30.*

Monte Solaro Chair Lift
Piazza Vittoria, Anacapri. Tel: 081/837 1428. *Open daily Mar–Oct 9.30–1 hour before sunset; Nov–Feb 10.30–3.*

Grotta Azzurra
Boats from Marina Grande. *Tours from 9, unless sea is too rough.*

5 Positano
Grotta dello Smeraldo
Southeast on SS163 coast road. *Open daily 9.30–4; (shorter hours. Nov–Mar).*

6 Amalfi
Arsenale
Via Matteo Camera. No phone. *Open Easter–Sep, Mon–Sa 10–1.*

Museo Civico
Piazza Municipio. Tel: 089/873 6211. *Open Mon–Fri 8–2.*

Museo della Carta (Paper Museum)
Via delle Cartière. Tel: 089/872 615. *Open Tue–Sun 10–6.30.*

7 Ravello
Villa Cimbrone Gardens
Tel: 089/857 459. *Open daily 9–one hour before sunset.*

Villa Rufolo
Tel: 089/857 657. *Open daily Apr–Sep 9–8; Oct–Mar 9–5.*

Cathedral Museum
Piazza Duomo. Tel: 089/857 212. *Open daily 9.30–1, 3–7.*

8 Salerno
Diocesan Museum
Largo Plebiscito 12. Tel: 089/231 387 *Open daily 9–6.30.*

Provincial Museum
Via San Benedetto 28. Tel: 089/231 135. *Open Mon–Sat 9–8.*

9 Paestum
Temple Remains and Museum
Zona Archeologica, Via Aquilia. Tel: 0828/811 016. *Open daily 9am–1 hour before sunset. Museum closes 6.30pm and is closed 1st and 3rd Mon in month.*

For History Buffs
Cumae
About 5km from Pozzuoli. Tel: 081/854 3060. *Open daily 9–5 (closes earlier in winter).*

Baia
About 4km from Pozzuoli. *Glass-bottomed boat trips to submerged ruins Apr–Sep weekends.*

TOUR 19

[i] Piazza del Gesù Nuovo, Napoli. Tel: 081/551 2701.

[i] Palazzo Reale, Piazza Dante 35, Caserta. Tel: 0823/326 832.

[i] Via N Sala 31, Benevento. Tel: 0824/319 911.

[i] Via Due Principanti 5, Avellino. Tel: 0825/747 321.

2 Capua
Santa Maria di Capua Vetere Roman Remains
Piazza Adriano. Tel: 0823/798 864 or 844 206. *Open daily 9–6.*

Museo Campano
Via Roma. Tel: 0823/961 402. *Open Tue–Sun 9–1.30 (1 on Sun).*

3 Caserta
La Reggia
Viale Douhet. Tel: 0823/321 400 or 448 084. *Open Tue–Sat 8.30–7.30 (park 9–one hour before sunset).*

4 Benevento
Roman Remains
Piazza Gaio Ponzio Telesino. *Open daily 9–one hour before sunset.*

5 Avellino
Museum of Irpinia
Palazzo della Cultura, Corso Europa. Tel: 0825/782 382. *Open Mon–Fri 8.30–1.30 (also 4–7 Tue, Thu).*

Practical Information

[i] Tourist Information Office
12 Number on tour

For History Buffs
Abbey Museum of the Monte Vergine Sanctuary
Mercogliano. Tel: 0825/72 924. *Open daily, summer 8–1, 3–8; winter 9–1, 3–5.*

TOUR 20

[i] Galleria Mancuso, Via Spasari 3, Catanzaro. Tel: 0961/743 901.

[i] Via D Tripepi 72, Reggio di Calabria. Tel: 0965/21 171.

1 Stilo
La Cattolica
2km from Stilo on Via Cattolica. Tel: 0964/775 031. *Open daily.*

3 Gerace
Diocesan Museum
Via Duomo. Tel: 0964/356 323. *Open Tue–Sun, summer 9–2, 3–9; winter 9–1, 3–6.*

4 Bova
Agro-Pastoral Museum
Instituto Ellenofono, Piazza Municipio. Tel: 0965/760 810 or 761 004. *Open Mon–Sat 8.30–12.30, 3–6.*

5 Reggio di Calabria
National Museum of Archaeology
Piazza de Nava 26. Tel: 0965/812 255. *Open daily 9–7.30. Closed 1st and 3rd Mon in month.*

6 Palmi
Cassa della Cultura Museums and Art Galleries
Via F Battaglia. Tel: 0966/ 262 248 or 262 250. *Open Mon–Fri 8.30–1.30, Mon, Thu also 3.30–5.30. One of museums may be closed for restoration.*

For History Buffs
Ancient Remains and Antiquarium
Southwest of Locri. Tel: 0964/390 023. *Open daily 9–7. Closed 1st and 3rd Mon in Month.*

V Capialbi State Museum of Archaeology
Castello Normanno Svevo. Tel: 0963/43 350. *Open daily 9–7.*

For Children
Zambrone Aquapark
SS522 Tropea–Pizzo road. Tel: 0963/392 009. *Open mid-Jun to mid-Sep, daily 10–6 (9.30–7 Aug).*

TOUR 21

[i] Corso Mazzini 92, Cosenza. Tel: 0984/27 821.

1 Morano Calabro
Historical Museum of Agriculture and Sheep Breeding
Scuola Elementare, Via Municipio (due to relocate – phone for information). Tel: 0981/31 021 (town hall). *Open Mon–Fri 9–noon, 4–6.*

4 Rossano
Museo Diocesano
Palazzo Duomo 25. Tel: 0983/520 282. *Open Mon–Sat 9.30–noon, 4–6; Sun 10–noon, 4.30–6.*

5 Santa Severina Castle
Piazza V Emanuele III 1. Tel: 0962/51 062 (town hall). *Open daily 8.30–12.30, 3–6.*

Diocesan Museum of Religious Art
Piazza V Emanuelle III. Tel: 0962/51 069. *Open daily 10–1, 3–6.*

6 San Giovanni in Fiore
Sila Folk Museum
Abbazia Florense. Tel: 0984/970 059. *Open Sun 9.30–12.30, 3.30–6.30 (Sun on request only mid-Sep–mid-Jun).*

7 Tiriolo
Museum of Antiquities
Viale Pitagora 4. Tel: 0961/ 991 004. *Open Mon–Fri 8–2, Tue and Thu also 3–6.*

9 Rogliano
Museum of Religious Art
Via Noce Greca. Tel: 0984/961 001 (town hall).

The Church of San Michele, in the little town of Lucca

Open Aug Mon–Fri 9.30–noon, 4.30–7 (rest of year by appointment only).

For History Buffs
State Museum of Archaeology
Via Risorgimento 121, Crotone. Tel: 0962/20 179 or 121 23082. *Open Tue–Sun 9–7.*

For Children
For information on horse-riding. Tel: 0360/283 252 or visit www.paglialonga.it. For information on mountain-biking. Tel: 0984/578 667 (Mountain Bike Sila Club).

TOUR 22

[i] Via De Viti De Marco 9, Matera. Tel: 0835/331 983.

[i] Piazza del Gesù 40, Maratea. Tel: 0973/876 908.

1 Metaponto
Old City Ruins and Antiquarium – Museo Archeologico Nazionale
Via Aristea, Metaponto Borgo. Tel: 0835/745 327. *Open daily 9–7.*

5 Melfi
Castle and Museum of Antiquities
Via Castello. Tel: 0972/238 726. *Open daily 9–7.*

6 Venosa
Castle and Museo Archeologico Nazionale
Piazza Castello. Tel: 0972/36 095. *Open daily 9–7.*

For History Buffs
Siris-Heraclea and Museo Nazionale della Siritide
Via Colombo 8, Policoro. Tel: 0835/972 154. *Open daily 9–7.*

TOUR 23

[i] Piazzo Moro 33, Bari. Tel: 080/524 2361.

[i] Piazza Trieste 10, Trani. Tel: 0883/535 530.

[i] Corso Garibaldi 208, Barletta. Tel: 0883/331 331 or 531 555.

1 Bitonto
Rogadeo Municipal Museum
Via G D Rogadeo 52. Tel: 080/375 1877. *Open Mon–Fri 9.30–1.30, Tue and Thu also 3.30–5.30.*

2 Molfetta
Museum of Archaeology and A Salvucci Museum and Gallery
Seminario Vescovile, Piazza G Garibaldi 65. Tel: 080/397 1559. *May be closed for restoration.*

Museum of Popular Devotion
Fabbrica di San Domenico, Via San Domenico. Tel: 080/338 1102. *Open Fri–Sat 6–9pm, Sun 10–1, 6–9.*

Municipal Collection of Contemporary Art
Via Sant'Orsola. *Open Mon–Fri 6–9pm, Sat–Sun 10–12, 6–9.*

3 Trani
Castle
Via Lionelli. Tel: 0883/506 603. *Open daily.*

4 Barletta
Museo Civico
Castello Svevo. *Open Tue–Sun 9–1, 4–7.*

5 Canosa di Puglia
Roman Remains
Open all year 9.30–1.

Museo Civico
Via Varrone 45. Tel: 0883/663 685. *Open Tue–Sat 9–1, 5–7, Sun 8–2 (shorter hours in winter).*

7 Castel del Monte
Near Ruvo di Puglia. Tel: 080/521 4361. *Open daily 9–7 (to 1pm winter); may close for lunch.*

8 Ruvo di Puglia
Museo Archeologico Nazionale Jatta
Palazzo Jatta, Piazza Bovio 35. Tel: 082/812 848. *Open Mon–Thu 8.30–1.30, Fri and Sat 2.30–7.30.*

For History Buffs
Cannae Museum of Antiquities
Frazione Canne della Battaglia. Tel: 0833/331 331 *Open daily 9–1, 2–one hour before sunset.*

TOUR 24

[i] Via C Colombo 88, Brindisi. Tel: 0831/222 126.

[i] Corso Mazzini 6, Ostuni. Tel: 0831/301 268.

[i] Via Vittorio Emanuele 23, Lecce. Tel: 0832/332 463.

[i] Piazza Castello, Otranto. Tel: 0836/801 436.

1 Ostuni
Southern Murgia Museum of Pre-Classical Civilizations
Via Cattedrale 15. Tel: 0831/336 383. *Open Tue–Sat 8.30–1, Thu also 3.30–7, Sun pm only.*

3 Grottaglie
Museo della Ceramica
Largo Mario Immacolata. Tel: 099/562 0222. *Open 9.30–12.30, 4–7 (longer hours in summer).*

4 Oria
Martino Carissimo Collection
Castello Svevo, Via Castello. *Tel: 0831/845 025. May be closed for restoration.*

5 Lecce
Roman Amphitheatre
Piazza Sant'Oronzo. *Open daily 8.30–4 (closes 2 Sun).*

Museo Provinciale S Castromediano
Tel: 0832/307 415. *Open Mon–Fri 9–1.30, 2.30–7.30, Sun 9–1.30 (may close Sat).*

6 Otranto
Castle
Beside the port, Otranto. *Open daily 9–noon, 3–6.*

TOUR 25

[i] Via Senatore E Perrone 17, Foggia. Tel: 0881/723 650 or 723 141.

[i] Piazza del Popolo 1, Manfredonia. Tel: 0884/581 998.

[i] Piazza Europa 104, San Giovanni Rotondo. Tel: 0882/456 240.

[i] Piazza Kennedy, Vieste. Tel: 0884/708 806.

1 Manfredonia
Museo Archeologico del Gargano
Castello Svevo. Tel: 0884/27838 oe 530 016. *Open Tue–Sun 8.30–1.30, 3.30–7.30.*

3 Monte Sant'Angelo
Museum of St Michael's Basilica
Via Reale Basilica 127. Tel: 0884/561 150. *Open on request.*

G Tancredi Museum of Gargano's Folk Arts and Traditions
Piazza S Francesco 15. Tel: 0884/562 098. *Open Mon–Sat 8.30–1.30, 2.30–8, Sun 10–noon.*

4 Vieste
Museo Malacologico
Via Polo 8. Tel: 0884/705 464. *Open daily 9.30–noon, 5–8.30.*

Boat Tours to Caves
Enquire at the port.

6 Lucera
Castle
Open daily until dusk.

Museo Civico
Via de Nicastri 74. Tel: 0881/547 041. *Open Tue–Sat 9–1, 3.30–6.30, Sun 9–1.*

7 Troia
Cathedral Treasury
Cathedral, Via Regina Margherita. Tel: 0881/970 258. *Open Mon–Thu on request.*

Diocesan Museum
Via Ospedale 2. Tel: 0881/970 081 or 970 064. *Open on request.*

Municipal Museum
Palazzo d'Avalos, via Regina Margherita. Tel: 0881/978 245 (town hall). *Open on request.*

INDEX

The Automobile Association
wishes to thank the following libraries and photographers for their assistance in the preparation of this book.
SPECTRUM COLOUR LIBRARY 7, 20, 27, 29, 39, 51, 106a, 122, 150, 152, 153b;

The remaining photographs are held in the Association's own library (AA PHOTO LIBRARY) with contributions from:

J EDMUNSON 55, 62; J HOLMES 90, 143, 168; M JOURDAN 121; D MITIDIERI 120; R NEWTON 130; K PATERSON 43a, 56, 58/9, 60, 70, 76, 161, 172; C SAWYER 4, 6, 8, 14, 16/7, 19, 21, 22, 25, 32, 33, 34, 35, 36, 37, 38, 40, 41, 42, 50, 57, 63, 64, 67, 71, 77, 80, 83, 89, 96, 100, 101, 103, 113, 114, 115, 116/7, 117, 126, 127, 137, 144, 154, 155, 156; B SMITH 43b; A SOUTER 2, 9, 10, 11, 12/3, 15, 18, 23, 24, 26, 28, 30/1, 31, 44, 45, 46, 47, 48/9, 52, 54, 66, 68, 69, 73, 74, 75, 78/9, 81, 82, 84, 85, 86, 87, 91, 92, 93, 94, 95, 97, 98, 99, 102, 104/5, 106b, 107, 108, 109, 110, 111a, 111b, 112, 118, 119, 124, 125, 128, 131, 132/3, 133, 134, 135, 136a, 136b, 138/9, 140, 141, 142, 145, 146, 147, 148, 149, 151, 153a, 157; P WILSON 88.

Contributors
Copy editor: Audrey Horne **Indexer:** Marie Lorimer
Thanks to **Rebecca Ford** for her updating work.